A NIKKEI HARVEST

REVIEWING THE JAPANESE AMERICAN HISTORICAL EXPERIENCE AND ITS LEGACY

ARTHUR A. HANSEN

with
WAYNE H. MAEDA

Foreword by
KENJI G. TAGUMA

日米 Nichi Bei
FOUNDATION

ADVANCE PRAISE

"*A Nikkei Harvest* calls attention to the contributions of the *Nichi Bei* newspapers to Japanese American community life by giving voice to Wayne Maeda and Arthur Hansen. These two groundbreaking scholars were prodigious producers of book reviews, which they used as a form of teaching guide to help community members learn about their own history and to interpret the work of other scholars who explored it in print."
—Greg Robinson, professor of history at l'Université du Quebec À Montreal, and co-author with Jonathan von Harmelen of *The Unknown Great: Stories of Japanese Americans at the Margins of History*

"It is not easy for non-scholars to keep up with the steady stream of books on all aspects of Japanese American history. Fortunately, the *Nichi Bei News* (formerly the *Nichi Bei Weekly*) publishes semi-annual book review issues with contributions by outstanding historians like Art Hansen and Wayne Maeda. In this volume, we are introduced to publications that meet their high standards. *A Nikkei Harvest* is an invaluable compilation of their reviews. Divided by subject matter, it serves as a guide to readers interested in exploring the profusion of new writings on the Japanese American past. Particularly noteworthy for me is the portion of the book devoted to *Nikkei* resistance to oppression during World War II. Previously slighted, it is now recognized as an essential part of the historical past. We cannot understand what our ethnic community suffered through without knowing that many protested and fought for their rights."
—Chizu Omori, journalist, activist, and co-producer of the award-winning documentary film *Rabbit in the Moon*

"This book is full of wisdom and insights from a pioneer historian of Japanese America. Through his careful and conscientious reviews of scholarly and literary works, Arthur Hansen tells us a lot about the state of the field of Japanese American studies and key aspects of *Nikkei* experience. But he also successfully weaves new research findings into narratives of his own to enhance a public understanding of their complex and fascinating history. A must-read for both academics and laypersons."
—Eiichiro Azuma, the Roy F. and Jeanette P. Nichols Professor of American History at the University of Pennsylvania, and author of *In Search of Our Frontier: Japanese America and Settler Colonialism in the Construction of Japan's Borderless Empire*

"No writer/scholar/oral historian offers more insightful book reviews than a man whose life's work is sewn into the very fabric of Japanese American history. Not only does Art Hansen know his subject matter better than anyone, his personal interactions with many of its key players result in commentaries replete with intimate revelation, gentle intelligence, and rich history. I am hopelessly driven to delve deeper into the works he so adeptly encapsulates."
—Sharon Yamato, writer/filmmaker, whose many credits include her documentary film *One Fighting Irishman* on the heroic work of lawyer Wayne Collins to regain U.S. citizenship for those Tule Lake Segregation Center inmates who renounced it under governmental duress during World War II

"Readers of the many captivating book reviews in *A Nikkei Harvest* will gather not one but two bumper crops: first, the breadth of the Nikkei experience revealed in the many books reviewed, but second, the depth of penetrating insight that only Art Hansen could bring to the subject. For anyone seeking to understand Japanese American life, this marvelous book is truly one-stop shopping."
—Eric Muller, Dan K. Moore Distinguished Professor at the University of North Carolina School of Law, and author of *Lawyer, Jailer,*

Ally, Foe: Complicity and Conscience in America's World War II Concentration Camps

"A library in a book! Beloved teacher and compassionate witness, Art Hansen brings a treasure trove of his insightful and incisive reviews of *Nikkei* literature into the pages of a single book, offering readers a broad and in-depth landscape of Asian America's past, present, and future."
—Satsuki Ina, emeritus professor at Sacramento State University, psychotherapist, documentary filmmaker, poet, activist, and author of *The Poet and the Silk Girl: A Memoir of Love, Imprisonment, and Protest*

"From the leading scholar on Japanese American oral history, *A Nikkei Harvest* is a bountiful collection of lively writings on Japanese American history, society, culture, resistance, and wartime experience from his essays in the *Nichi Bei Weekly/Nichi Bei News*. More than book reviews, Art Hansen gives us a glimpse into his thinking, relationships, joys and concerns, and avid reading to spotlight books by scholars and organic intellectuals, published by mainstream and independent presses, offering an expansive view of the field, peppered by Hansen's critique and delightful, humanizing commentary."
—Diane Fujino, professor of Asian American Studies at the University of California, Santa Barbara, co-editor of the *Journal of Asian American Studies*, community organizer and activist, and author of *Nisei Radicals: The Feminist Poetics and Transformative Ministry of Mitsuye Yamada and Michael Yasutake*

Copyright © 2024 by Nichi Bei Foundation
P.O. Box 15693
San Francisco, CA 94115

All rights reserved.

No portion of this book may be reproduced in any form without written permission from the publisher, except as permitted by U.S. copyright law.

Book Cover by Patricia M. Wakida

Portions of this book first appeared in the *Nichi Bei Weekly*, 2012-2022; and *Nichi Bei News*, 2023. Used by permission.

ISBN: 979-8-9884106-0-7 (print)
ISBN: 979-8-9884106-1-4 (ebook)

*To the Memory and Legacy of Wayne Hisashi Maeda (1947-2013) and
Martha Nakagawa (1967-2023)*

Nearly every writer writes a book with a great amount of attention and intention and hopes and dreams. And it's important to take that effort seriously and to recognize that a book may have taken ten years of a writer's life, that the writer has put heart and soul into it. And it behooves us, as book-review-editors, to treat those books with the care and attention they deserve, and to give the writer that respect.
—Pamela Paul, *New York Times book review editor*

CONTENTS

Foreword	1
Preface	7
Introduction	9
Prologue	13
PART I People	25
PART II Family	49
PART III Community	71
PART IV The Arts	117
PART V World War II Japanese American Incarceration Camps	131
PART VI World War II Japanese American Resistance	165
PART VII Asian American Movement	183
PART VIII Japanese American Redress Movement	195
PART IX International Nikkei	209
Afterword	233
About the Authors	235
Acknowledgements	237
Index	239

FOREWORD

I am deeply humbled to be asked to write this foreword for Arthur A. Hansen's *A Nikkei Harvest*, dedicated to and honoring my mentor, longtime collaborator, the *Nichi Bei Times* and *Nichi Bei Weekly*'s longest contributing writer, my closest advisor, and, mostly, my dear friend, Wayne Maeda—a founding board member of the Nichi Bei Foundation.

I'm also deeply appreciative of Art Hansen, another longtime advisor and contributing writer, for allowing me to contribute to this new and insightful volume of book reviews by both Art and Wayne. Since Wayne's untimely passing on February 27, 2013, after a courageous bout with cancer, Art has capably filled in Wayne's shoes, both as a highly trusted advisor as well as a prolific and perceptive reviewer of books on the Japanese American and Asian American experience, helping the Nichi Bei Foundation and *Nichi Bei Weekly/Nichi Bei News* fulfill our mission of keeping the Japanese American community connected, informed, and empowered.

Art is clearly one of the foremost authorities on Japanese American history, and in particular Japanese American resistance studies. We are immensely proud to include his judicious reviews in the *Nichi Bei*, which collectively represent a bountiful "harvest" of historical documentation.

The *Nichi Bei Weekly/Nichi Bei News*, like its predecessor the *Nichi Bei Times*, is proud to have done our best to run reviews of books on the Japanese American experience—not only to broadcast the varied and rich stories of our community, but also to energize a community of authors whose publishers may do very little to help publicize their works. In some cases, a review in the *Nichi Bei* may be the only review a book would garner in an established publication.

Thus, we are proud of this collection, as both Wayne and Art have contributed perhaps more than a combined 150 book reviews in the *Nichi Bei* publications over the past twenty-five years. I am profoundly grateful to Art for dedicating this volume to Wayne's legacy, and to directing all of its proceeds to the Nichi Bei Foundation's Wayne Maeda Educational Fund, which allows us to present community educational programs such as Films of Remembrance (a showcase of film on the Japanese American incarceration experience during World War II), our pilgrimages to historic sites such as the former Angel Island Immigration Station and Wakamatsu Tea and Silk Farm Colony, and assorted author-based events.

I want to share a little about Wayne Maeda, excerpted from my 2013 eulogy of him.

Wayne's Story

You might be surprised to learn that Wayne wasn't all that great of a student in high school; he didn't want to study, and hated math. He initially took some business classes in college, thinking that he might help his dad's construction business, but he declared social science as his major, graduating from California State University, Sacramento (CSUS) in 1969 after spending two years at Sacramento City College.

He always called himself the "accidental professor," because that was certainly never his goal.

In the early days of Ethnic Studies, he was still a CSUS graduate student, teaching undergraduates near his own age. Back then, he ran out to other universities like the University of California, Berkeley, the University of California, Los Angeles (UCLA), and the University of California, Davis, to help get ideas to build the curriculum.

Around 1970-71, Wayne was CSUS's director of the Asian American segment of the Equal Opportunity Program (EOP). In this capacity, he was in charge of about forty to fifty peer advisors, who each were advising up to ten students.

In the mid-1970s, Wayne received his social science master's degree. As the Ethnic Studies Program pushed the CSUS Library to expand its collection, the library hired Wayne to help add relevant books. Ethnic Studies, Wayne recalled, "asserted political power to bring diversity to campus." This included taking part in hiring faculty of color.

Wayne always sought out historical accuracy, no matter who or what challenged him. He sought to inspire, educate, and make students reach their full potential. But he was not without insecurities about his teaching. "I always thought I could have done a better job," he said. "Maybe a better approach." Until the end, he said he still had some self-doubt about "not knowing enough."

Toward the end of Wayne's life, many told him how much they appreciated his countless book reviews in the *Nichi Bei Times* and the *Nichi Bei Weekly*.

"I have benefitted tremendously from the many book reviews you have had published relative to Japanese American history, society, and culture," wrote Art Hansen, Emeritus Professor of History and Asian American Studies at California State University, Fullerton. "In my opinion, you have been spot-on in all of your reviews."

UCLA Asian American Studies professor Lane Hirabayashi, the late holder of the prestigious Aratani Endowed Chair, assured Wayne that his reviews kept him "on top of current publications," commenting, "If you praised an author's work, I always made note of it."

Paul Osaki, the executive director of the Japanese Cultural and Community Center of Northern California, related to me that he remembered Wayne fondly: "Wayne was just one of those guys you could always go to when you needed help, advice, or anything," said

Paul. "Wayne was also one of those guys who could get things done, didn't bullshit, and never brought attention to himself."

Others recollected to me Wayne's generosity.

"When my brother-in-law became paralyzed from the waist down, Wayne promptly built a ramp at my mother-in-law's house," said Raymond Lee, who was an early student of Wayne's at CSUS. "Whenever I bring up Wayne in conversation, my mother-in-law always tears up."

One-time CSUS colleague, psychotherapist, filmmaker, and social activist Satsuki Ina related to me that Wayne would financially assist EOP students by buying books for them and covering other costs. "Students who had never been on a college campus—anxious, confused, fearful, and overwhelmed—not only got help from Wayne, but really knew that he cared about them."

Still another CSUS colleague, Dr. Otis Scott, called Wayne "the heart and soul of Asian American Studies," who "remained a solid and intellectual force" within the Ethnic Studies Department and one of its "most respected teacher-scholars."

Sacramento City College counselor Keith Muraki mentioned Wayne's high ratings on ratemyprofessor.com: "I hated history until I took his class," one student wrote. "He tells it how it is. I love this teacher. I recommend him to anyone, but you have to be willing to learn."

"No BS with this guy," another student wrote. "He minces no words."

Congresswoman Doris Matsui called Wayne "one of Sacramento's treasures [who was] loved by so many of us." She thanked Wayne for his role in developing the Robert T. Matsui Legacy Project Website, a collection of audio and video clips, as well as documents and photographs of the late congressman.

Lastly, I want to share an excerpt of my February 23, 2013, letter to Wayne, written four days before his passing. It's a letter I'm virtually certain he never read, as he was too far gone by that point.

Dear Wayne,

It's hard to imagine the mass transformation that I've made since wandering into your [CSUS] Asian American Studies class more than twenty years ago. I wandered in, probably on accident, still a painfully shy kid. To this day, I think I actually wanted to take an Asian Studies class, learning more about Asia. But this may have been the best "mistake" I ever made, because it led me to you, and to my destiny. And while I was "lost," through you I would find my true calling. Through you, my eyes were truly opened, as I saw a fellow *Sansei*, albeit a bit older, who cared enough to document our community's history. You were the greatest role model at the most crucial time for me. Not only did you help me understand the importance of my father's World War II draft resistance based upon constitutional principle, but you also validated his experience in the eyes of history, helping me to "connect the dots," as you would say. For years, my father had complained that "no one knows about us guys. No one knows about us resisters." Thanks to you, he started to get his ultimate vindication.

After taking your class, I went full steam ahead in changing my major to Ethnic Studies, and in becoming, what I was told, the most active student on campus. In just one and a half years, under the Ethnic Studies Student Association, this once-shy country boy would go on to help organize some two dozen events or forums. I was even able to publish three editions of an Asian American campus newspaper, the *AsiAmerican Journal*. None of this, however, would have happened if you had not touched me. You quickly taught me what my life mission was to be, to make sure that our stories were documented, in an accurate manner. You, along with my father's wartime experience, helped to give me a voice that I never knew I had.

Everything I've done, and will continue to do, is a testament to and dedication to what you taught me. I want to thank you for the incredible example and legacy that you have given to me, and for helping to vindicate my father in the eyes of history. You really saved me.

With deepest respect and gratitude,
   Kenji

Simply put, there would be no Nichi Bei Foundation without Wayne Maeda planting those seeds decades ago. Furthermore, Art Hansen has continually facilitated academic credibility to our organization with his sage advice and contributions. We are proud to offer this volume of their work, and are sure that this "harvest" will help to not only feed your mind, but also nourish your soul.

Note: The Nichi Bei Foundation launched the *Nichi Bei Weekly* on Sept. 17, 2009. The publication was renamed the *Nichi Bei News* on Jan. 1, 2023.

PREFACE

The February 27, 2013 death of celebrated historian Wayne Hisashi Maeda, at age sixty-five, represented a profound personal and professional loss for Kenji Taguma, the longtime editor of the *Nichi Bei Times* newspaper and its transformed successor, the *Nichi Bei Weekly*. During Taguma's undergraduate years at California State University, Sacramento, Professor Maeda, one of the founders and prime movers of CSUS's Asian American Studies Program, had catalyzed Taguma's passion for Japanese American history, society, and culture. Later on, from 1995 until his untimely 2013 death, Maeda progressively assumed the role of lead book reviewer for the two Taguma-edited newspapers.

While I was not privy to Maeda's *Nichi Bei Times* reviews, upon my 2009 appointment to the Nichi Bei Foundation advisory board, I read every one of the many stunning reviews he produced for the *Nichi Bei Weekly*'s special semi-annual book review issues. In doing so, I became enthralled not only by the extraordinary breadth and depth of his knowledge about the Japanese American experience, but also his capacity for penetrating to the core contribution of each work he assayed, his facility for rendering his critical assessment in exquisite prose, and his penchant for treating the authors of the books under review by him with empathetic respect.

In the wake of Maeda's passing, Taguma asked me if I would be interested in multiplying the scanty number of my contributions to the *Nichi Bei Weekly*'s special review issues to take up the slack created by his mentor's gaping loss. I found this request daunting, for I was certain I could never replace Wayne Maeda, but merely succeed him. However, I ultimately reasoned that my standing, however precariously, upon the shoulders of this fallen giant might possibly afford me the necessary perspective to put my own shoulder to the wheel and undertake the formidable task confronting me.

Although this volume, which is dedicated to the memory and legacy of Wayne Maeda (and Martha Nakagawa), consists largely of the sixty-eight book reviews that I have written for the *Nichi Bei Weekly* between 2010 and 2023 relative to the Japanese American historical experience, its opening chapter showcases a sampling of Maeda's reviews that appeared in the July 26, 2012 issue of the *Nichi Bei Weekly*. These "past" reviews by Maeda will serve in *A Nikkei Harvest* as a "prologue" to those I have written up to the "present." My own reviews are organized not by chronology but rather grouped within nine thematic chapters encompassing the Japanese American past and present. All of these chapters are prefaced by extensive headnotes that provide a means of contextualizing their respective subject area. The reviews themselves, taken collectively, are designed to simultaneously illuminate and interrogate the Japanese American historical experience and legacy. What makes it significant is not merely that so much continues to be written about it, but rather because the story of Japanese Americans, most especially their unjust World War II exclusion, incarceration, and attendant loss of human, civil, and constitutional rights, demands the rapt attention of all Americans in our democracy's perilously unfolding socio-political climate.

INTRODUCTION

On June 3, 2010, a thought-provoking article by John Palattella appeared in *The Nation* entitled "The Death and Life of the Book Review." In it he bemoaned the "steep erosion" in book coverage by newspapers over the past few years. In support of this decline, he adduced the depressing fact that, among many other papers, such notable ones as the *Los Angeles Times*, the *Washington Post*, the *Chicago Tribune*, *Newsday*, the *Minneapolis Star Tribune*, the *Boston Globe*, the *Atlanta Journal-Constitution*, and the Cleveland *Plain Dealer* had "killed or drastically reduced" their coverage of books.

That this situation had not been sudden but went back at least to the 1990s, claimed Palattella, was epitomized by the progressive shrinkage in the size of the *New York Times Book Review*, the nation's most visible newspaper book section. During its "golden age" in the 1970s, this section consisted of a minimum of eighty pages. By 1985, it averaged forty-four pages. Two decades later the average fell to between thirty-two and thirty-six pages. In 2010, it had plummeted to between twenty-four and twenty-eight pages. Although still the bellwether of U.S. book sections, rued Palattella, "there is not much to read in it."

When the internet increasingly undermined the economic base of newspapers, their owners responded by cutting back both the size of the paper (print and online) and the staff of the newsroom. Some sections, particularly those dealing with a public agenda and aimed at the general reader, naturally still commanded considerable resources. As summarized by Palattella, "Such journalism is essential —and expensive, [but] paying for it means deciding not to pay for something else, and at many papers that something else is books coverage."

On the other hand, Palattella felt it disingenuous for newspaper executives to base their slashing or downsizing of the book section on the grounds that it fails to turn a profit. While conceding that the book section does indeed lose money, he argued that the same situation prevails for other sections of the newspaper, like the sports section and the metro section. "Yet," he complained, "of all the sections that fail to turn a profit on their own, it's the books section that is most often killed or pinched." To his mind, although it is indisputable that newspapers had been hindered by difficult times and a major technological transformation in the dissemination of the news, it did not follow that coverage of books by newspapers had suffered for the same reasons. Rather than economic forces, he maintained, the book section had been eviscerated primarily by cultural forces, with the most hard-headed of those lying within, not outside, the newsroom. Concluded Palattella: "It is not iPads or the internet but the anti-intellectual ethos of newspapers themselves. ... In a news context, 'anti-intellectual' does not necessarily mean an antipathy to ideas, though it can be that too. I use ... 'anti-intellectual' to describe a suspicion of ideas not gleaned from reporting and a lack of interest in ideas that are not utterly topical."

Fortunately, Kenji Taguma, the editor of the *Nichi Bei Weekly/Nichi Bei News*, has been neither antipathetic to ideas per se nor to those transcending outright topicality. Instead, because he takes editorial pride in "helping to develop and empower a community of writers," the *Nichi Bei* has included an average of between four and six pages of book reviews in his modest-sized winter/summer special review issues. Penned by a strategic mix of seasoned and neophyte reviewers, these typically 500-word reviews encompass subjects of notable interest to *Nichi Bei's* largely, though certainly not exclusively, Japanese American and Asian American readership. Although reviewers traditionally were uncompensated for their contributions, beginning in 2018 they have been equitably remunerated.

In the case of my own reviewing for the *Nichi Bei Weekly/Nichi Bei News*, I was saddled with no guidelines apart from length, which I frequently violated when I believed that the subject matter of a given volume demanded a more detailed appraisal. I have greatly appreciated Kenji Taguma's editorial indulgence of my abuse in this regard, especially since he had become inured over the years with Wayne Maeda's extraordinary capacity for distilling his assessment of any book he reviewed, irrespective of length and complexity of subject matter, into 500 words or less.

Prior to having my services enlisted for book reviewing in the *Nichi Bei Weekly/Nichi Bei News*, my only experience in reviewing books was for academic journals, mostly in the field of history, and overwhelmingly in relation to the subject of the World War II Japanese American Incarceration. To be honest, I never fully enjoyed writing these reviews. I say this for several reasons: first, because such reviews were primarily aimed at other scholarly researchers who shared my sub-disciplinary fields of expertise; second, due to the expectation that my reviews would privilege commentary on a book's theoretical, methodological, and bibliographical aspects; third, owing to the unspoken assumption that the hallmark of writing a truly worthwhile review was the obligation to point up the comparative limitations of a given volume's topical or thematic treatment; and fourth, since it was considered basically inappropriate to insinuate one's personal background and experience into reviews.

In contrast to this situation, I have found reviewing books for the *Nichi Bei Weekly/Nichi Bei News* an altogether satisfying undertaking. The newspaper's readership, while chiefly constituted of Japanese Americans, is a very diversified and cosmopolitan one in all other significant respects. This permits me through my reviews to be engaged in stimulating conversation with readers about a wide variety of subjects and concerns falling within the general province of the Japanese American historical experience. While I do not hesitate in my reviews to refer to matters touching on theory, method, and bibliography, I place the main emphasis upon such criteria as subject content, writing style, organization of material, nature of evidence, and quality of analysis. At the same time, I am far less concerned as a reviewer in drawing invidious distinctions between how authors transact their themes and topics as against other writers than in clarifying and celebrating what they have accomplished in their own books. Finally, because I have been engaged for a half-century in Japanese American studies as a classroom teacher, a fieldworker, an archival researcher, and an oral, public, and community historian, I feel very comfortable infusing my reviews with personal commentary when deemed especially relevant and useful.

It is my hope that the harvest of *Nikkei* books that I have been permitted to reap in my assorted *Nichi Bei Weekly/Nichi Bei News* reviews will simultaneously honor the memory of Wayne Maeda and provide readers of this volume a worthwhile immersion within the experiential world of Japanese America.

PROLOGUE

This section of A Nikkei Harvest *features seven of the reviews that Wayne Maeda had published in the* Nichi Bei Weekly *during the year prior to his 2013 passing. Taken together they illustrate his perspicacious capacity for assaying books treating Japanese American studies in an abundant variety of subject fields and topics.*

Two of the reviewed books, Amy Sueyoshi's Queer Compulsions *(2012) and Diane C. Fujino's* Samurai Panthers *(2012), are primarily biographical in nature, but the first explores sexuality relative to its subject,* Issei poet *Yone Noguchi, while the second examines the radical politics embraced by the* Sansei Richard Aoki as a Black Panthers member. Two other volumes, Isami (Mike) Tsuji's *Go for Broke (2011) and Greg Robinson's edited work* Pacific Citizens *(2012), share a biographical dimension, but the former emphasizes the author's military experience during World War II, and the latter spotlights the 1942-1952 journalistic writings of Larry and Guyo Tajiri in the Japanese American Citizens League-sponsored* Pacific Citizen *newspaper. The remaining three reviewed books are nonbiographical. One of them, Sayuri Guthrie-Shimizu's* Transpacific Field of Dreams *(2012), scrutinizes baseball in the United States and Japan as a species of transnational global history. A second review, the Gail Honda-edited study* Family Torn Apart *(2012), surveys the World War II odyssey of a Hawai`i Japanese* Issei, Otokichi Muin Ozaki, *and his family in main-*

land U.S. internment and concentration camps. As for the third review, Greg Robinson's After Camp (2012), it investigates, via social and political history, the heretofore largely understudied topic of Japanese American post-World War II resettlement.

AFTER CAMP: Portraits in Midcentury Japanese American Life and Politics
By Greg Robinson (Berkeley, CA: University of California Press, 2012, 328 pp., $27.95, paperback)

PACIFIC CITIZENS: Larry and Guyo Tajiri and Japanese American Journalism in the World War II Era
Edited by Greg Robinson (Champaign, IL: University of Illinois Press, 2012, 344 pp., $60, hardcover)

Published in the July 26, 2012 edition of the *Nichi Bei Weekly*.

Readers of the *Nichi Bei Weekly* will no doubt be familiar with Greg Robinson and his regular column "The Great Unknown and the Unknown Great," or his book *By Order of the President: FDR and the Internment of Japanese Americans* and his magnum opus *A Tragedy of Democracy: Japanese Confinement in North America*.

Robinson has done it again in these two publications of uncovering our "buried past" in a way that is refreshing, accessible, smart, and above all free of useless trendy theories and jargon meant to impress fellow academicians. He follows in the footsteps of pre-eminent historians like Roger Daniels and Yuji Ichioka, doing difficult and time-consuming primary source research and analysis "connecting the dots."

In *After Camp*, Robinson explores the little known and researched area of *Nisei* life after the incarceration period in a comparative approach. He breaks new ground as he tries to answer the question of "what happened afterward?"

This volume consists of essays and articles organized around five major topics. Part I, "Resettlement and New Lives," contains three articles; perhaps the most interesting is "Political Science? FDR, Japanese Americans, and the Postwar Dispersion of Minorities," in which Robinson connects the dots from FDR to other officials, and their views on resettlement of European refugees and Japanese Americans to race and eugenic ideas. This should provide a different lens to view the "scattering" as merely a neutral administrative policy and a wonderful adventure that was good for Japanese Americans.

Part II covers assimilation, with Part III, IV, and V breaking new ground by placing the *Nisei* within the matrix of the interethnic political world of Mexican and African American organizations. The *Sansei* generation may think that they were the first to take part in "Third World" coalitions, but once again Robinson sheds light on *Nisei* activists on both coasts and connects the dots from Korematsu to the landmark Brown case. This volume should be required reading for all those who are serious about recovering our "buried past."

Pacific Citizens: Larry and Guyo Tajiri and Japanese American Journalism in the World War II Era is another example of Robinson's wide-ranging scholarship and ability "to connect the dots" by researching the lives, activities, and writings of the Tajiris, both in ethnic and non-ethnic presses, before, during, and after World War II. He deftly combines all these sources to develop a complex and nuanced portrait of Larry and Guyo Tajiri, the Japanese American Citizens League (JACL) newspaper, *Pacific Citizen,* and the National JACL.

There have been celebratory accounts of the JACL's accomplishments in past publications; however, Robinson's vast research using correspondence, published articles, and editorials—from many ethnic as well as non-ethnic sources—help create biographies of Larry and his wife Guyo that bring them out of obscurity into sharp relief, adding to our collective historical memories.

Equally valuable is that Robinson provides each of the seven chapters with the all-important historical context that frames Larry Tajiri the man, along with his imprint on the *Pacific Citizen* and many other topics. His wide-ranging work will no doubt force many in the Japanese American community to re-examine the simplistic view of the postwar JACL and its leaders as conservative accommodationists or worse, "sell-outs."

Both these publications by Robinson break new ground and should act to broaden our understanding of the past.

FAMILY TORN APART: The Internment Story of the Otokichi Muin Ozaki Family
Edited by Gail Honda (Honolulu: Japanese Cultural Center of Hawai`i, 2012, 312 pp., $26, paperback)

GO FOR BROKE! Me and the War
By Isami (Mike) Tsuji (Fullerton, CA: Nikkei Writers Guild, A Division of Japanese American Living Legacy, 2011, 160 pp., $14, paperback)

Published in the July 26, 2012 edition of the *Nichi Bei Weekly*.

These two stories of two Japanese Americans in Hawai`i—one a composite of an *Issei* and the other an autobiography of a *Nisei*—both make for an interesting read. After December 7, 1941, they both travel to the mainland at the United States government's expense. While the trajectories of these two men seem to parallel each other, their reasons for being in America, their experiences, and their destinations could not be more different.

Family Torn Apart is a reconstructed story of Otokichi Muin Ozaki and his family's odyssey after December 7, 1941. Ozaki's confinement in six different internment camps and two American concentration camps and his family's journey to try to reunite is chronicled through extensive use of letters, poetry, radio scripts (Ozaki's remembrances after the war), archival and FBI files, and other sources.

The reader is treated to a complex portrait of an educated, philosophical father and husband who during peacetime was a highly respected community leader in Hilo, Hawai`i. He greeted Japanese naval ships that visited Hawai`i, received many awards from the Japanese government for his community service, and had pieced together a shortwave radio that provided him with news from Domei News that he would transcribe for the Hilo station.

Ozaki naturally was on the FBI radar screen from the late '30s for activities that under ordinary circumstances would be part of his job, but when Japan bombed Pearl Harbor, times changed and he along with many other *Issei* community leaders began their journey to internment facilities.

However, his story is unique not just because he was incarcerated in six different centers and two concentration camps, but because his story is of a family torn apart trying desperately to reunite on the mainland and a testament of the human spirit to survive. Through meticulous research and skillful editing, we are treated to an "insider's" view of an entire family and their experiences during those very difficult times.

Go for Broke is an interesting short autobiography of Isami (Mike) Tsuji, the other Japanese American from Hawai`i. His voice comes out loud and clear in a very straightforward account of why he volunteered for the 442$^{nd}$ Regimental Combat Team, his experiences as he traveled from Hawai`i to mainland boot camps in the heart of the Jim Crow South, of visiting one of the concentration camps in Arkansas, his first day of combat in Italy, and being wounded in France that ended his war days of World War II.

His story, as he tells it, is not a story of medals or the extraordinary exploits of the 100th/442nd across Europe, but rather a "soldier's story." In fact, his saga, precisely because of his understated style, allows the reader to explore not only what was said but what was left unsaid.

No doubt Tsuji faced many situations where he had to deal with feelings of loss of close buddies, anger, self-doubt, sheer terror of combat, and looking into the face of death itself. He, nevertheless, avoids the temptation of glorifying his own deeds of bravery, courage, and valor on the battlefields to just telling an ordinary story.

SAMURAI AMONG PANTHERS: Richard Aoki on Race, Resistance, and a Paradoxical Life
By Diane C. Fujino (Minneapolis: University of Minnesota Press, 2012, 496 pp., $24.95, paperback)

Published in the July 26, 2012 edition of the *Nichi Bei Weekly*.

It has been more than 70 years since that fateful day that forever changed the lives of Japanese Americans, and it has been more than forty years since Richard Aoki became a member of the Black Panthers. Aoki played key roles in the group's formation and served as a field marshal, and at the same time became one of the leaders in the Asian American Movement.

Reading this biography put together by Fujino reminded me of the last time I saw Richard Aoki, at the fortieth anniversary of the Third World Liberation Strike (I really did not know him except meeting him a few times at the University of California, Berkeley, back in the day and at various conferences and other events). To many, Richard was an enigmatic character who wore a beret, leather jacket (or field jacket), and sunglasses even on foggy days, someone who never stopped talking and—he had guns.

This publication contains something for everyone. For the average reader interested in biography, his story begins with his happy childhood that he doesn't remember, to the trauma of incarceration, to his gung ho desire to join the U.S. Army, to his political awakening and journey of self-education on a wide range of radical political ideas and theories, his joining the Black Panthers and taking part in the Asian American Movement at Berkeley and eventually becoming a counselor, teacher, and administrator. With each of these segments Fujino allows Aoki's words, syntax, and rhythms to ring clear (for those who have heard him speak it will be like sitting in the same room listening to him talk).

Fujino does a masterful job in researching and in interviewing Aoki and others to produce a highly readable and enlightening narrative by allowing him to tell his story.

For the academic audience there are the commentaries and interpretations (I find these disruptive) one can negotiate through, an eclectic maze of historical, psychological, and other theories from across disciplines at the end of each chapter and in the epilogue. To the author's credit, she wrestles with how to present and assess Aoki's legacy in the introduction. Of the various strategies of how to present his story, Fujino decides the best is to put her "views and research" and her interpretation at the end of each chapter. The author's rationale is that these "commentaries would serve to complicate ... [and] contextualize his life within historic social forces and political economies, and to raise alternative perspectives on Aoki and ultimately on the meaning of political agency." Furthermore, writes Fujino, her commentaries "allow for a conversation to occur between the historical actor and his biographer."

However, the problem with this "conversation" between Fujino and the historic actor, Aoki, is that he is no longer with us. He cannot agree, contest, or modify these interpretations and so one wonders what exactly does political agency mean and who is being given "voice," and why is there a need to further complicate and contextualize his life more than how he presented his story? Nevertheless, the author combines a wonderful, sensitive, flowing, and spellbinding narrative to allow Richard Aoki to tell his story—that itself is worth the read.

QUEER COMPULSIONS: Race, Nations, and Sexuality in the Affairs of Yone Noguchi
By Amy Sueyoshi (Honolulu: University of Hawai`i Press, 2012, 248 pp., $40, hardcover)

Published in the July 26, 2012 edition of the *Nichi Bei Weekly*.

Amy Sueyoshi, an associate professor of ethnic studies at San Francisco State University, has produced an important and timely study of racial, class, sexual, and gender hierarchies at the turn of the twentieth century in America through illuminating the life of Yone Noguchi (the father of the more famous sculptor, Isamu Noguchi). As the courts, nation, and no doubt Asian American communities are deeply embroiled over the issue of same-sex marriage, history might be useful in providing the all-important context for this conversation to take place.

For Asian Americans, it might be useful to recall a time when they were denied the "right to life, liberty, and the pursuit of happiness," in California (until 1948) and nationally (until 1967) through various anti-miscegenation laws; just as odious was the Cable Act (which stripped citizenship from any woman marrying an "alien ineligible" to citizenship—a code for male Asian immigrant).

Beyond the legal barriers, *Queer Compulsions* begins to shed light and uncover another aspect of the "buried past." Sueyoshi uses both English and Japanese sources, and more than 800 correspondences between Yone Noguchi and Charles Stoddard (poet, novelist, and co-editor of the *Overland Monthly*, among other things). Their correspondences go beyond conjecture and innuendos about the romantic and erotic nature of their relationship. Moreover, what makes Noguchi's sexuality even more complicated is that during this time of legal barriers and social taboos concerning crossing the "color line," he manages to impregnate Leonie Gilmour and proposes marriage to journalist Ethel Armes, and ultimately returns to Japan to marry and live a "normal and respectable life."

Sueyoshi is not so much interested in "outing" or labeling Noguchi's sexual orientation, but rather in demonstrating the intricacies of racial, sexual, and gender hierarchies in American society as they play out in his life. Noguchi realizes early on that his racial and cultural differences will relegate him, even among the elite "bohemian" society of San Francisco, as a perpetual foreigner—the "other."

Noguchi realizes that he cannot escape being an object of entertainment and viewed through the gaze of orientalism at the turn of the twentieth century. More importantly, Sueyoshi, in recovering the "buried past" of one *Issei* man, explores the distinct possibility that other "penniless bachelor" *Issei* may have found alternative ways to navigate their sexual orientation and desires in America.

TRANSPACIFIC FIELD OF DREAMS: How Baseball Linked the United States and Japan in Peace and War
By Sayuri Guthrie-Shimizu (Chapel Hill, NC: University of North Carolina Press, 2012, 344 pp., $39.95, hardcover)

Published in the July 26, 2012 edition of the *Nichi Bei Weekly*.

How many times have we heard the adage, "You can't judge a book by its cover?" *Transpacific Field of Dreams* is one of those books that should not be judged by its cover. What seems like a lazy summer read about the game of baseball between the United States and Japan turns out to be anything but a lazy summer read.

The author has written a wide-ranging, extremely detailed, and meticulously researched (secondary sources are in both English and Japanese) account of the "transnationalization" and "globalization" of baseball from America to Asia, Hawai`i, and the Caribbean. The author begins with an ambitious attempt to "integrate various nationally segmented historiographies and disciplinary subfields." By combining "vantage points and thematic concerns derived from U.S. and Japanese histories while weaving together U.S. ethnic history (Japanese American history) and Asian (Japanese) history," the author hopes to "make sports [serve as] a useful platform of international history."

Guthrie-Shimizu begins with tracing the diffusion of baseball in Japan during the Meiji period and then moves to how baseball spread to Japan (Korea, Taiwan, etc.), as well as to American imperial colonial adventures (Hawai`i, the Philippines, and Cuba, etc.). However, she tries to cover so much ground that the book descends into details of who, when, and where baseball was introduced, and the origins of numerous amateur, semi-pro, and professional teams/leagues in numerous territories and counties.

This book will be a delight for baseball aficionadas, those aspiring to be one, and/or those spellbound with reading encyclopedic-like chronicling of baseball. The author tries to cover too much ground by providing so much fact and detail that many parts of the book border on minutia filled with arcane facts. These include the invention of a uniquely Japanese rubber baseball, *nanshiki*, made by a Kobe company; "The Philadelphia Bobbies 1925-26," a mostly female baseball team that traveled to Japan; and John Fisher, a founding member of the San Francisco Eagles, the first known organized baseball club in California in the 1850s.

This shotgun approach has several weaknesses, including a lack of real focus and analysis. The author never clearly addresses her own question, "Why and how did baseball manage to become a transnational pastime in certain parts of the world (but not others)?" And by using trendy terms like "transnational" and "globalization," she adds little in the way of analysis. Moreover, by trying to cover so much ground, there are bound to be editorial oversights ("Marco Paulo [sic] Bridge Incident") and glaring factual errors, like listing "South Dakota" as one of the ten concentration camps for Japanese Americans during World War II or by placing Manzanar in the "Mojave Desert."

Having said that, for aficionadas or those seeking to become one, this is a singular source for details on debunking myths of the origins of baseball at multiple sites, while providing information on agents, players, the role of expatriates, corporations, leagues (amateur, college, semipro, and pro), and much more.

PART I

PEOPLE

According to the late Hawai`i-born Nisei *anthropologist Toshio Yatsushiro (1917-2015), six basic cultural themes defined the pre-World War II Japanese American community. Arguably the most important of these themes was the one maintaining that "the welfare of the group is far more important than that of any single individual." While the force of this theme has lessened progressively over time due to "Americanization," it remains salient. It follows, then, that in all eight of the reviews constituting this first part of* A Nikkei Harvest *the theme of suppressed self-focus is evident in one or another form.*

In Gene Oishi's 2014 autobiographical novel, Fox Drum Bebop, *he explicitly tried to overcome the constraints of subjective personal truth-telling that plagued him in his 1987 memoir,* In Search of Hiroshi, *by using imagination and embroidered fact to supplant his stylized self-identity with an authentic one. Matthew M. Briones, in his biographically-oriented cultural history book,* Jim and Jap Crow, *informs readers that his study's main figure, the diarist and social worker Charles Kikuchi (1916-1988), "never explicitly sought the spotlight." Regarding Hank Umemoto's 2013 memoir,* Manzanar to Mount Whitney, *when I first met him in 2011, he told me about his family and noted that we shared a best* Nisei *friend, but he neglected to mention that he had written an important soon-to-be published book rooted in his three World War years as an adolescent inmate at the Manzanar War Relocation Center in eastern California. As for Sandra Vea's 2016 oral history biography* Masao, *centered on the secret and heroic World War II role of* Kibei-Nisei *Masao Abe (1916-2013), she allows that it took her three years of a close friendship with him to coax out of him his life experiences and, most especially, his courageous wartime exploits as an interpreter/translator infantry-attached soldier in fiercely waged South Pacific campaigns. In respect to* Nisei *Sam Mihara's* Blindsided *volume, he relates his mission of spreading far and wide the World War II Japanese American story with inordinate modesty and self-restraint. As for psychotherapist Judy Kawamoto's* Forced Out, *it depicts how, ironically, she and her family's life apart from other* Nikkei *deepened their orientation toward community as against singularity. Lastly, in the case of Greg Robinson's 2016 and 2020 volumes sketching the activities and/or achievements of selected noteworthy Japanese Americans, its bottom-line message of* Nikkei *self-effacement is encapsulated in the titles of the two works,* The Great Unknown *and* The Unsung Great.

FOX DRUM BEBOP
By Gene Oishi (Los Angeles: Kaya Press, 2014, 276 pp., $16.95, paperback)

Published in the July 24, 2014 edition of the *Nichi Bei Weekly*.

I knew of Gene Oishi (b. 1933), the *Nisei* author of *Fox Drum Bebop*, well before I actually met him. This was because in 1968 he became implicated in a national (even international) cause célèbre for his victimization in a high-profile racist episode. Then a *Baltimore Sun* reporter, Oishi was slumbering in his seat on a political campaign plane flying from Las Vegas to Los Angeles when a fellow passenger, Republican vice-presidential candidate Spiro Agnew, gestured toward him and inquired, "What's the matter with the fat Jap?"

Charged with insensitivity, Agnew responded that he had long known Oishi and was merely "jesting." Deferring to Oishi's desire to keep the episode private, the *Washington Post* initially hesitated to go public with it. When it did, Agnew first proffered lame excuses and only later reluctantly expressed remorse. But precisely because "words do matter"—a point academic and community historians of the Japanese American World War II eviction and incarceration experience have driven home in recent years—Agnew's insult retained a long shelf life.

Some five years after the Agnew flap, I encountered Oishi when he made a research visit to the Japanese American Oral History Project at California State University, Fullerton. Then on leave from the *Sun* to write a book about his life in relation to his wartime incarceration, he wondered what stories our project's interviews might contain to facilitate his undertaking. Previously, I had read a piece by him in *West Magazine*, a *Los Angeles Times* supplement, decrying the racist treatment grade school administrators and teachers in the north Santa Barbara County farm hamlet of Guadalupe were then imposing upon their largely Mexican American students. Having attended, in the early 1950s, a grammar school in south Santa Barbara County's agricultural village of Goleta with a quite similar demographic profile, and having also read in Oishi's article that prewar Guadalupe, in concert with its substantially larger neighboring agrarian town of Santa Maria, had constituted a major *Nikkei* center within California's central coast region, I longed to talk with him at great length about these topics. However, because I had classes to teach, Oishi spent most of that day with a close *Nisei* colleague and friend of mine at a Japanese restaurant in Los Angeles's Little Tokyo, ostensibly eating *sushi*, drinking beer and *sake*, and very likely conversing about their common youth in "camp" and abiding passion for jazz.

Fortuitously, in the late 1980s, I stumbled upon Oishi's 1987 memoir, *In Search of Hiroshi*. What prompted me to read it was something I recalled him writing two years earlier in a *New York Times Magazine* article provocatively titled "The Anxiety of Being a Japanese

American." After recollecting his near breakdown in 1981 when speaking before the Commission on Wartime Relocation and Internment of Civilians, Oishi confessed that not until his subsequent return to the scene of his wartime imprisonment at the Gila River Concentration Camp in Arizona did he first sense that perhaps the discomfort he and other *Nisei* felt about stereotypes (whether negative or positive) was rooted in fear, and that it was very likely fear that ruled much of his life and theirs. Thus, the "search" embodied in his memoir represented an earnest quest to exorcise his fear and, in the process, to divest himself of a contrived standard-issue identity and to supplant it with an authentic one.

As good a book as *In Search of Hiroshi* is, *Fox Drum Bebop* is still better. Both are memoirs and they cover much of the same ground, though strictly speaking the latter is a novel since, as Oishi allows in his editorial note, it is "based on memories that have been reimagined and embroidered in the story making." This difference makes all the difference, however, in that Oishi, being freed from the bonds of strict factuality, is released to plumb the depths of subjective truth. Temporally, the book encompasses the author's life from 1940 through 1982; structurally, it artfully orchestrates a medley of chronologically ordered short stories into a unified narrative; and topically, it presents the "coming of age" of a younger *Nisei* in a manner that illuminates the historical contours of that generational cohort group without sacrificing the nuances and complexities of one of its talented, idiosyncratic members. Before reading this book, I had been told by fellow historian Greg Robinson that, in his opinion, it ranks near the top of fictional works produced by *Nisei* writers. I now agree wholeheartedly with this assessment.

JIM AND JAP CROW: A Cultural History of 1940s Interracial America
By Matthew M. Briones (Princeton, NJ: Princeton University Press, 2012, 288 pp., $39.50, hardcover)

Published in the July 24, 2014 edition of the *Nichi Bei Weekly*.

It is rare that I find myself reviewing a book on a friend of mine authored by still another friend, but that is the case with Matt Briones's Charles Kikuchi-centered cultural history *Jim and Jap Crow*. My friendship with Kikuchi revolved around two events: our participation on a controversial panel at a September 1987 conference held at UC Berkeley to reassess the World War II work of the [Japanese American] Evacuation and Resettlement Study (JERS), and the oral history interview I transacted with Kikuchi in Rhode Island at his family's Block Island vacation home in August 1988, a month prior to his death. As for my friendship with Briones, it began in Boston at the 2004 Association of Asian American Studies (AAAS) annual meeting, and it was nurtured by a series of informal meetings held in Southern California over the next several years in which we discussed our common interest in Charles Kikuchi.

During my interactions with Kikuchi and Briones, I was enlightened by their capacious intellects and warmed by their infectious personalities. But what most affected me about these two Asian American men—one nearing the end of his life, the other embarking on his scholarly career—was the depth of their humanity and the tenacity of their commitment to America's promise as a multicultural, democratic nation. It is the combination of these two qualities that provide the mainspring for elevating *Jim and Jap Crow* from the status of an important book to one of seminal significance.

I will admit to being disappointed that this volume did not include the name of Charles Kikuchi in either its title or subtitle. Publication by Princeton University Press probably led to the book being marketed under a designation that would privilege its cultural historical mission vis-à-vis the role played by 1940s progressive intellectuals championing an authentically interethnic, interracial democracy for the United States as against its biographical purpose to probingly explore one unique yet representative American of Japanese ancestry whose life and work quintessentially embodied what those liberal democratic thinkers boldly espoused.

Books, of course, should not be judged by their titles alone, and the one utilized for the book under review is both appropriate and defensible. However, had the publisher asked me to provide a promotional blurb for *Jim and Jap Crow*, I would either have prioritized it as a biography over a cultural history or granted these two genres equal billing.

In fact, the dustcover recommendation by Lane Hirabayashi, a UCLA professor of Asian American Studies, nicely encapsulates what I would have written: "Briones's masterful biography of Charles Kikuchi gives us an intimate portrait of how one Japanese American's firsthand encounters with discrimination during and after World War II transformed him into an enlightened citizen who envisioned a nation and world unbound by racial prejudice. *Jim and Jap Crow* is a profound meditation on race in American society."

My rationale for regretting that Briones's book title did not showcase Charles Kikuchi is grounded in my awareness of his having been similarly "marginalized" throughout his seventy-two-year life (1916-1988), even though quite often at his own behest. At age eight, after being repeatedly brutalized by his father, Kikuchi (the oldest male sibling) was banished from his Vallejo, California, home and remanded to a multicultural Salvation Army-run orphanage in the northern California community of Healdsburg, where he remained (as the only resident of Japanese ancestry) until his 1934 high school graduation.

Thereafter, Kikuchi matriculated at San Francisco State, a college with a distinctly working-class and multiethnic/multiracial student body which few other *Nisei* attended, as opposed to the less diverse and more elite institution across the bay of the University of California, Berkeley. Shortly after graduating in 1939, Kikuchi was invited by the writer Louis Adamic, a Slovenian immigrant and proponent of American ethnic diversity, to contribute an autobiographical essay to his forthcoming *From Many Lands* anthology. When Kikuchi's life story, substantially edited by Adamic, was published in 1940, it was titled "A Young American with a Japanese Face." Appearing under anonymous authorship, it represented its protagonist as a prototypical "marginal man" (living on the margins of two cultures and societies, as well as his own *Nisei* generation).

In 1940, when Kikuchi landed a celery-pulling summer job in the San Joaquin Valley, he confronted racial differences pitting Filipino and Japanese workforces against each other. Because of his efforts to model interracial friendship with the Filipinos for his Japanese workmates, they demonized him as a discredit to his race and forced him to quit their bunkhouse for the Filipino one and to thereafter work within the Filipino crew.

Then, after his 1941 UC Berkeley enrollment as a graduate student to become a social worker, he distanced himself from most *Nisei* students, and instead befriended a circle of politically progressive social science undergraduates (Warren Tsuneishi, Kenji Murase, James Sakoda, Tamotsu "Tom" Shibutani, and Lillian Oda). But Kikuchi was even marginal to this group. According to Briones, Shibutani and others warned him: "Well, you don't want to go into social work. Social work is sissy work. Men go into sociology and then women go into social work."

Moreover, although affiliating himself, like his Cal comrades, with far-left international causes and organizations, Kikuchi also got involved in the multiethnic San Francisco-based Yamato Garage Gang, "a group of young men who were unemployed, unmarried, and unfazed by outside attempts to corral them into organized activity," and who, in the words of another Kikuchi biographer, John Modell, were "devoted mainly to gambling, mischief, whoring, and especially to talking about these exploits."

In Pearl Harbor's wake, Shibutani and Sakoda introduced Kikuchi to Cal sociologist Dorothy Thomas, who having already hired these budding social scientists as researchers on the UC Berkeley-connected JERS project that she led, persuaded Kikuchi to join them. But even during the 1942-45 interval in which Kikuchi participated in JERS's interdisciplinary undertaking to analyze and document the causes and effects of the forced mass migration of *Nikkei* into concentration camps plus their subsequent resettlement into so-called "free zone" U.S. settlement areas (Chicago being the most notable), both what Kikuchi did and where he did it were marginal to that of the mainstream JERS researchers of Japanese ancestry. Whereas the War Relocation Authority (WRA)-administered detainment center of Tule Lake in northern California became JERS's principal study site and the place where Thomas dispatched Shibutani and Sakoda (among others) to enact participant-observation fieldwork and write diverse research reports based upon it, she assigned Kikuchi to the study's secondary check site of Gila River detention camp in southcentral Arizona with the primary duty of maintaining a diary concentrated on his observations and his and his family members' experiences.

Following the infamous "loyalty oath" administered by the WRA and the U.S. Army to the imprisoned *Nikkei* in the detention camps and the ensuing conversion of Tule Lake from a "relocation center" to a "segregation center" for incarcerating those deemed "disloyal," the core of JERS's Japanese American staff, including Kikuchi, was transferred to the University of Chicago to record and interpret the life and work experiences of the twenty to thirty thousand *Nikkei* who had resettled in the Windy City.

However, while most staffers were preoccupied with preparing research reports in the JERS office, Kikuchi largely spent his time away from the office collecting life histories from Chicago resettlers. Moreover, notwithstanding that most of the flagship JERS publication devoted to resettlement, *The Salvage* (1952), consisted of fifteen of Kikuchi's total sixty-four life histories, instead of him being listed as a coeditor for this volume with Dorothy Thomas, he was relegated to sharing marginalized subsidiary credit with James Sakoda.

After leaving JERS and spending more than a year in the U.S. Army as a psychiatric social trainee at military hospitals, followed by completing his master's degree in social work at New York's Columbia University, he embarked on a twenty-four-year career in New York as a psychiatric social worker in Veterans Administration (VA) hospitals in Brooklyn and the Bronx, where mainly he counseled Vietnam War veterans. Disenchanted by the doctrinaire VA emphasis on Freudian social-work theory and the virtual absence of "minority" social workers, a disgruntled Kikuchi was shunted to the sidelines and denied promotions. In addition, he was the only VA social worker to picket against the Vietnam War, right outside the VA hospital, and was threatened with arrest for violating federal property.

Not surprisingly, Kikuchi quit the VA in 1973. That same year saw the publication by the University of Illinois Press of *The Kikuchi Diary*, a compilation of selected diary entries Kikuchi logged for JERS during his four-month incarceration in 1942 at the Tanforan Assembly Center near San Francisco. Although his name was highlighted in the book's title, what perhaps most people, and particularly scholars, remember about that volume was the magnificent editing of and introduction to Kikuchi's diary by historian John Modell. As for Charles Kikuchi, he spent the final fifteen years of his life serving as the behind-the-scenes manager for the internationally renowned dancing troupe of his world-famous wife, Yuriko Amemiya Kikuchi, the onetime star performer for the Martha Graham Company.

So, it might be asked, what justification, however implicit, did Matthew Briones offer for ostensibly marginalizing Charles Kikuchi by excluding his name from the title of the book under review? Assuredly, Briones provides one overarching reason for this absence by telling readers that "Kikuchi never explicitly sought the spotlight," a statement that certainly squares with historical reality. But Briones also informs readers that from the time of Pearl Harbor in 1941 to Kikuchi's death in 1988, he maintained a daily diary that added up to more than 100,000 pages, and that in these pages, covering the World War II period, he commented on "nearly every significant moment" of it. More to the point, Briones goes on to discuss Kikuchi's voluminous diaries as providing "a narrative through-line for the 1940s within the broader cultural history of home-front America" and what he, Briones, considers "its unprecedented level of interracial interactions." Furthermore, observes Briones, "Kikuchi not only discussed the various possibilities of a multiracial American democracy with a number of intellectual players, but also invariably recorded these in his trusted diary day after day, providing a road map through the winding and uncharted topography of the era." In a stroke of genius, Briones concludes his assessment of the importance of Kikuchi and his diaries and the relationship of both to the 1940s and what has come to be called the staging ground for "the long Civil Rights Movement" by contemporary U.S. historians.

His, then, is not the role of a downstage actor… nor the bit part of a minor player who appears only sparingly; rather, Kikuchi and his diaries inhabit the traditional Greek chorus in an all-too-real staging of democratic America in flux during the 1940s; he touches upon almost every major historical event, records it in his diary, and ultimately fades ever so subtly into the background.

MANZANAR TO MOUNT WHITNEY: The Life and Times of a Lost Hiker
By Hank Umemoto (Berkeley, CA: Heyday, 2013, 224 pp., $16.95, paperback)

Published in the July 25, 2013 edition of the *Nichi Bei Weekly*.

My first trip of many to the World War II Manzanar concentration camp site occurred in spring 1972. On that occasion I accompanied my California State University, Fullerton, *Nisei* colleague, Kinji Yada, on his personal pilgrimage to the place in eastern California's Owens Valley where, as a young teenager in 1942, the U.S. government had imprisoned him and his family "for the duration" and to which he had not returned since his 1945 departure.

Four decades later, in May 2011, I found myself again in the Manzanar vicinity to attend a Manzanar National Historic Site ranger's retirement party held in a nearby Independence park. There I met Hank Umemoto, the author of the volume under review. When he disclosed that he had entered Manzanar at thirteen, I asked if perhaps he had known Kinji Yada, whom I regarded as "my best friend." Startled, Hank sputtered, "At Manzanar Kinji was *my* best friend. Moreover, we were in the army together in post-Occupied Japan, and later I was his best man at his wedding to a Japanese woman." I discovered, too, that Hank's *Sansei* daughter was Karen Umemoto, an urban and regional planning professor at the University of Hawai`i with a UCLA background in Asian American Studies, and that her *Sansei* husband was Brian Niiya, a scholar-journalist then preparing to edit an online Japanese American history encyclopedia for the Seattle-based DENSHO organization.

What Umemoto did not reveal was that he was finishing a book rooted in his three Manzanar years. This I found out somewhat later when Niiya informed me that Heyday was publishing his father-in-law's book. Maintaining that Umemoto is a great storyteller, he extolled his autobiographical manuscript as manifest evidence. "But Hank," cautioned Niiya, "is among those *Nisei* who has little to say bad about his wartime camp experiences." Hearing Niiya's appraisal of Umemoto's narrative, and later reflecting upon how his caveat about his outlook on camp seemingly applied as well to Yada and many others of my acquaintance in their common *Nisei* age group, I eagerly anticipated reading *Manzanar to Mount Whitney*.

Having now read the book, let me emphatically affirm Umemoto's extraordinary flair for relating true-life stories. His typically unflinching and often quite witty accounts cover the full extent of the author's taxing and intriguing lifetime, from his pre-World War II childhood in the Sacramento-area California farm community of Florin, through his present-day retirement in suburban Los Angeles County. Along the way, he recounts his late wartime short-term leave from Manzanar (with several sixteen-year-old *Nisei* buddies) to secure remunerative agricultural labor (and taste personal liberation) close by the Central California inland port city of Stockton, his immediate postwar resettlement experience in Los Angeles's transitional *nihonmachi*, his Korean War-era Military Intelligence Service duty in Tokyo, and his Cold War and beyond Southern California pursuit of gainful employment, advanced education, and individual and family enhancement.

What strikes me as the most significant of Umemoto's several story strands for fashioning a new and richer narrative for Japanese American history is his palpable representation of the precarious existence undergone by *Nikkei* resettlers during the still greatly understudied "after camp" period. Less satisfying in this same regard is Umemoto's strand treating his Tokyo army experience. Since he was stationed in this metropolitan nerve center right after Japan regained its national sovereignty, it is unfortunate that Umemoto not only neglects a fortuitous opportunity to paint a miniature portrait of that nation's affairs of state at this critical juncture, but also ignores a chance to offer readers a personal perspective on the transnational role Japanese Americans played in relation to this situation.

Mostly, though, Umemoto's memoir consists of an artistic interweaving of his adolescent Manzanar stories and his senior hiking narratives, culminating in his graphic and gripping depiction of his multiple septuagenarian ascents of Mount Whitney—the contiguous United States' highest peak in the towering Sierra Nevada mountain range above Manzanar. Contained within this exemplary rendering is a Horatio Alger rags-to-riches, onward and upward motif, but it varies significantly from the standard-issue model. Those readers who interpret Umemoto's *Manzanar to Mount Whitney* title too literally will likely expect his book to convey them on a journey from the lowly abyss of American civil rights, race relations, and social justice symbolized by Manzanar to the lofty physical, psychological, aesthetic, and spiritual Shangri-La epitomized by Mount Whitney. This would be a mistaken expectation, however, since life at Manzanar for Umemoto was apparently itself something of a "peak experience," leastwise as compared to both the dark months he, his family, and their *Nikkei* neighbors had endured in the aftermath of Pearl Harbor "as anti-Japanese sentiment became stronger with each passing day" and during the unsettling years of so-called "resettlement" following the closing of Manzanar and the other War Relocation Authority camps when "the future appeared bleak, unpredictable, and uncertain," and when Japanese Americans were "starting a life from square one, with a twenty-five dollar stipend" as "the hardships and challenges had just begun."

Perhaps this representation of his own experience by Umemoto accounts for the rose-colored impression of Manzanar that he purportedly felt at his final departure: "I came to realize that my warm, friendly, sheltered, and carefree life would soon be over, and Manzanar would be but a memory." After all, whereas Umemoto titles his camp chapter gently as "Hello Manzanar," the title choices for both his post-Pearl Harbor chapter, "'Because We're Japs, That's How Come,'" and his resettlement chapter, "A Life in Skid Row," are contrastingly harsh. It may also explain why Umemoto in his "Closure" chapter stresses how upon arriving at Manzanar in 1942 as an "angry and frustrated teenager ... full of aggression and rage," these initial feelings soon "began to wane, in part because there were plenty of upsides to being a young person in camp." It may well be the underlying reason, too, why he so honors his parental *Issei* generation for living by the Japanese phrase of "*Shigata-ga-nai*, which means 'Whatever will be, will be'," and why, in spite of having "great respect and admiration" for those *Nikkei* who fought to achieve redress and reparations from the U.S. government for their community's mistreatment, he chose to decline his $20,000 redress payment on the grounds that he would prefer that Japanese Americans "go down in history as a patient, proud and courageous group" who endured their wartime exclusion and detention "with pride, courage and determination," rather than as victims of injustice.

One could plausibly argue that if Umemoto, as well as others in his peer group at Manzanar and the other WRA lockups, can look back positively on their camp time because there were "plenty of upsides to being a young person in camp," it was also the case that their very status as young teenagers in camp shielded them from many of the "slings and arrows" that even their slightly older *Nisei* and *Kibei-Nisei* siblings and neighbors had to confront and withstand. These included, most notably, the loyalty registration and military draft, since the response to one or the other could lead to being remanded to a high-security segregation center and/or an alien enemy internment camp, consigned to the perilous war fronts of Europe and Asia or a federal prison, or plagued by the loss of U.S.

citizenship and postwar life in war-devastated Japan. Hank Umemoto makes abundantly clear in his stirring memoir that he is aware of these downsides of camp life, but mostly from the perspective of an intimate observer than of an engaged participant. When he turns his attention from Manzanar to Mount Whitney, his perspective is dramatically and, for me, mercifully reversed.

MASAO: A Nisei Soldier's Secret and Heroic Role in World War II
By Sandra Vea (New York: DMA Books, 2016, 343 pp., $18.99, paperback)

Published in the July 19, 2018 edition of the *Nichi Bei Weekly*.

As a visit to almost any American new or used bookstore will quickly confirm, military history is an exceedingly popular genre of literature. This is particularly the case as involves World War II, including that of the heroic role played by Japanese American troops. For the most part, the special role that has commanded primary attention in this connection has been the exploits of the segregated 100th Infantry Battalion, the 442nd Regimental Combat Team, and the 552nd Field Artillery Battalion in the European Theater. More recently, however, long overdue notice is increasingly being accorded the valorous efforts of *Nikkei* in the U.S. Army Military Intelligence Service (MIS) forces in the Pacific Theater. It is this topic that occupies center stage in native Seattleite Sandra Vea's extraordinarily fine biographically-themed book on *Kibei-Nisei* Masao Abe (1916-2013). It revolves around, but is certainly not limited to, his front-lines service as an interpreter/translator soldier attached to the 81st Infantry Division during some of its most ferociously fought South Pacific campaigns.

Skillfully crafted in the fashion of a non-fiction novel, Vea explains that she has "reimagined portions of Masao's story, rendering those in fictionalized form, although ... carefully attending to the 'facts' of those stories as he told them." The book is divided into two main parts. The first of these focuses on Abe's life up to 1925 as an English-speaking youth within San Bernardino, California, where in its small and tight-knit Japantown his father and uncle owned and operated a grocery store. It then shifts to his 1925-36 years living with his paternal grandparents in an increasingly militant Japan and being educated in the Japanese language and culture while being prepped to become a Japanese Army officer. It then turns to his pre-World War II return to San Bernardino, as mandated by his father, and his having to endure his *Kibei* status among *Nisei* while working in the family grocery store, before being drafted into the U.S. Army.

Part II first covers Abe's training at Camp Robinson in Little Rock, Arkansas, to become a medic, followed by his submission of a successful application for entrance into the fourth class of the Military Intelligence Service Language School at Minnesota's Camp Savage. After due attention to his vigorous MIS schooling, it proceeds to Abe being ordered to the South Pacific in 1944, where he and other MIS soldiers did intelligence duty in a regular army regiment and thus required two body guards to protect them from being shot by Japanese soldiers and American G.I.s alike. It culminates with Abe being shot in the leg by a Japanese sniper while trying to flush Japanese soldiers out of a cave on the island of Peleliu, thereby receiving a combat wound that earned him a Purple Heart. This part closes with the end of the Pacific War in August 1945 and Abe's transfer, with fellow MIS interpreters, for extended duty in Occupied Japan under the command of General Douglas MacArthur.

Throughout *Masao*, Vea interweaves two elements. On the one hand, she narrates the ordeal suffered by the immediate and extended Abe family, both on the West Coast at the time after Japan's attack on Pearl Harbor and during the war in both Department of Justice internment and War Relocation Authority concentration camps. More impressively, she shares with readers her close three-year relationship with Masao Abe, and how she simultaneously developed a loving relationship with him and periodically coaxed out of him on tape the fascinating details of his life experience, his family relations, and, most especially, his courageous wartime exploits.

This is an exceptionally well-researched and composed book, replete with an excellent complement of photographs, and lacking only an index. To learn more about this exemplary book before reading it, you would be well advised to read what the author herself has expressed so movingly in an online posting about its content and character: http://www.discovernikkei.org/en/journal/2017/9/26/we-should-lisren/

BLINDSIDED: The Life and Times of Sam Mihara
By Sam Mihara, as told to Alexander Villarreal (Self-published, 2019, 2nd ed., 121 pp., $20.00, paperback)

Published in the July 16, 2020 edition of the *Nichi Bei Weekly*.

In 2019, Paramount released the biopic feature film on British rock singer Elton John entitled *Rocket Man*. Sam Mihara's slender and well-written autobiographical book *Blindsided* also showcases the life of a rocket man. It, too, could have been titled *Rocket Man*. After all, upon completing his undergraduate and graduate engineering degrees at UC Berkeley and UCLA, Mihara enjoyed a distinguished forty-two-year career at Boeing as a rocket scientist. Then, fourteen years after his 1997 retirement, he forged a new career, one which saw him rocketing around the entire country giving talks about mass incarceration in the U.S. to audiences totaling over 60,000 and reaching students, teachers, lawyers, libraries, museums, and other institutions.

Mihara's presentations are rooted in his three-year World War II incarceration experience as a San Francisco born-and-bred, pre-teen *Nisei* inmate within the Pomona Assembly Center in Los Angeles County and the Heart Mountain Relocation Center in northwest Wyoming. In the opening three-fourths of his book, Mihara first provides a riveting account of his pre-WWII life in San Francisco's Japantown, where his father was a writer on the bilingual *New World Sun* newspaper and his family lived in an upscale Victorian home. He then bitingly depicts the Mihara family's incarceration at Pomona ("A purgatory that looked more like hell than heaven ... a world where we were animals with perhaps less respect than the prize mares that came before us at this racetrack") and Heart Mountain ("We were prisoners. Tucked away in Wyoming's expanse, we were forgotten by the outside world. No one cared what happened to us, and no one fought for justice.").

In the remainder of his book, Mihara concisely covers his family's resettlement experience in a low-income neighborhood of Salt Lake City, Utah, in which diverse ethnic communities clashed and the Miharas found "racial slurs or worse graffitied on our rental house." He next relates his postwar education upon the family's return to San Francisco and his education at Lick-Wilmerding High School and UC Berkeley (a fallback choice because his family could not fund his matriculation at the Massachusetts Institute of Technology), and his courtship and marriage to Helene Hideno Nakamoto. He then turns his resolute attention to his second career as arguably "the only survivor of the camps touring the United States to talk about what we lived and witnessed." But, notes the self-effacing Mihara, in his down-to-earth talks he also unfailingly addresses the pernicious detention of non-Japanese American groups in contemporary America, particularly refugees entering our southern border seeking asylum. Although he has long ago forgiven America for what it did to him and his family, Mihara refuses to let Americans forget it. For if we should do so, he cautions, future generations will judge us harshly.

Blindsided deserves to be adopted by school systems nationwide for consumption by adolescent students. It also merits the rapt attention of general readers of every age who are unfamiliar with the Japanese American World War II story and the related stories of other unjustly oppressed communities within our country.

**FORCED OUT: A Nikkei Woman's Search for a Home in America
By Judy Y. Kawamoto (Louisville: University Press of Colorado,
2020, 189 pp., $29.95, hardcover)**

Published in the July 22, 2021 edition of the *Nichi Bei Weekly*.

I immensely enjoyed and was greatly enlightened by *Sansei* psychotherapist Judy Kawamoto's singular book. I would classify its genre as a meditative memoir. As she succinctly notes at one point, "psychotherapy is dubbed 'the talking cure'." It typically involves a therapist asking patients probing, in-depth questions about every aspect of their lives so as to assist them with addressing and redressing their problems. In the case of *Forced Out*, Kawamoto enacts the twin role of therapist and patient. All of her questions, therefore, are rhetorical ones posed to herself for contemplation, understanding, and healing.

Kawamoto's central problem is intergenerational trauma resulting from the World War II uprooting of her parents and older sister Lillian from their prewar Seattle, Washington, home in the wake of Japan's December 7, 1941 attack on Pearl Harbor and U.S. President Franklin D. Roosevelt's subsequent issuance of Executive Order 9066 on February 19, 1942. Whereas the overwhelming majority of more than 110,000 West Coast Japanese Americans were evicted from their homes and communities and, eventually, incarcerated in American-style concentration camps in remote sites within California, Arizona, Idaho, Colorado, Utah, Wyoming, and Arkansas, the Kawamotos were among the some 5,000 "forced out" *Nikkei* who gained governmental permission to resettle independently in assorted inland areas of the country outside of the military security zones.

As for the Kawamoto family, they moved first to Sheridan, Wyoming, where Judy Kawamoto was born and her *Nisei* father had graduated from high school. There they lived for a short while on the vegetable farm belonging to Judy's paternal *Issei* grandparents. When an opportunity presented itself to raise food, quite ironically, for the U.S. government that had dispossessed them, all of the Kawamotos moved to Indian country in southeastern Montana's Bighorn River Valley, close to the small town of Hardin. There her parents farmed mainly sugar beets and wheat, aided by German prisoners of war, while her grandparents were growing vegetables for local sale and consumption. After the war, when Judy Kawamoto was entering junior high school, she and her three siblings, along with her parents, moved once again, this time to Denver, Colorado, to be near her maternal grandparents and other family members. In all of these places, the Kawamotos were virtually on their own. Unlike those *Nikkei* imprisoned en masse in camps during the war who in large part afterwards returned to live in their familiar prewar racial-ethnic neighborhoods, the Kawamotos were cut off from the Japanese American community, people who "looked like them, shared a language that wasn't English, ate the same food, automatically held similar beliefs about how to treat and interact with each other, [and gave] them a sense of belonging and a shared understanding that they were all in this together and together they would make it through."

Moreover, Judy Kawamoto's parents, like many other *Nisei* who experienced the cultural shame, dishonor, and psychic humiliation of being treated as potentially dangerous pariahs during the Pacific war, suffered "pure trauma." As a survival mechanism, they sought to put the trauma behind them—which meant not talking about it, even to their children—and to get on with their "normal" lives. This process led to gaps in the family story that the next generation had to deal with in the best way they could. Fortunately, once Judy Kawamoto became a psychotherapist, she not only acquired an understanding of the workings of trauma, but also hit upon how best to "mind" and "mine" the gaps in her family's story so as to achieve psychological well-being. Readers of her remarkably well-written book, especially Japanese Americans of the post-*Nisei* generations, will benefit greatly from heeding her therapeutic words and deeds of wisdom. They more than likely will not be bothered by her book's repetitious passages and lack of an index.

THE GREAT UNKNOWN: Japanese American Sketches
By Greg Robinson (Boulder: University Press of Colorado, 2016, 345 pp., $45.00, hardcover)

Published in the January 1, 2017 edition of the *Nichi Bei Weekly*.

In Kenji Taguma's resplendent foreword to this latest of historian Greg Robinson's cavalcade of exemplary volumes devoted to illuminating the Japanese American experience, he rightly observes that *The Great Unknown* is a work that "epitomizes the importance of the community press in preserving history." Of course, had Taguma and his allied supporters within the Nichi Bei Foundation not labored so mightily and resourcefully to keep alive the most venerable of the Japanese American community newspapers, the columns underpinning Robinson's book likely would never have been written. Now then, with this backdrop in place, let me pose the following query: Had Greg Robinson's "The Great Unknown and the Unknown Great" 2007-2012 columns in the *Nichi Bei Times* and the *Nichi Bei Weekly* not appeared in print, what difference, if any, would this hypothetical situation have made to our understanding and appreciation of Japanese American history? Naturally, those of you who elect to become readers of *The Great Unknown* will respond to this question in your own special ways, but please indulge me while I share with you my considered response.

In her immensely significant 2016 Verso book *Serve the People: Making Asian America in the Long Sixties*, Karen Ishizuka advances an astute observation that provides me with a point of departure for formulating a reply to my rhetorical question. In a section of her study titled "Recovering the Past," Ishizuka describes historical recovery as a "major theme" of the 1960s-1970s Asian American movement, one that has left a "tangible legacy." Elaborating on this contention, she writes: "Recovering history was not just an intellectual pursuit, it was critical for political longevity. Without an historical understanding, every generation of activists thinks it is the first. We did. We had no idea of the legacy and long history of Asian American resistance [to racism and imperialism]." I certainly agree with Ishizuka that the tradition of resistance to oppression by Asian Americans is both deeply rooted and substantial, and in my own work on Japanese American resistance I have labored to document its historically robust quality.

I would argue, however, that the brand of historical recovery undertaken by Greg Robinson within the pages of *The Great Unknown* relative to the Japanese America past, while assuredly akin to that articulated so consummately by Ishizuka, is both dissimilar to and more comprehensive in character than it. Clearly, Robinson's historical recovery process applies primarily not to particularly striking "unknown" group actions or social movements of consequence, but rather to the "unknown" activities and/or achievements of selected noteworthy individuals. Thus, the book's ten chapters exhibit such component units as "The Hidden Contributions of Guyo Tajiri," "Masuji Miyakawa: First Issei Attorney," "Yasuo Sasaki: Poet, Physician, and Abortion Rights Pioneer," "Arthur Matsu: First Japanese American in the National Football League," "Shinkichi Tajiri: Sculptor," "Kiyoshi Kuromiya: A Queer Activist for Civil Rights," and "Gordon Hirabayashi's Surprising Postwar Career."

In addition, Robinson's species of historical recovery, while it entails a distinct concern for exhuming a usable Japanese American lineage to fortify ongoing community resistance to domination and persecution, greatly transcends this bounded instrumental objective. Instead, his apparent goal is to remind his *Nikkei* and non-*Nikkei* readers alike that the Japanese American backstory was far more colorful, complex, and cosmopolitan than it has been typically chronicled to be through history and memory, and that in fact the community's past was populated by a variety of "great" people (mostly but not exclusively *Nikkei*) whose thoughts and deeds can be resourcefully exploited by subsequent generations to inspire and enrich their personal and collective pursuits. To facilitate his ostensible aim, Robinson organizes his volume into subject chapters designed to vividly elucidate it: *Issei* women, mixed-race Japanese Americans, literature and journalism, wartime confinement, sports, arts, and Japanese Americans' queer heritage.

Having read most of the selections in *The Great Unknown* when they originally appeared as newspaper columns, I was nonetheless overwhelmed during my reading them anew within a published book. Each of them attests to Robinson's insatiable curiosity about and unquenchable passion for virtually every aspect of Japanese American history, society, and culture; his extraordinary expenditure of time and energy in unearthing previously unmined source material and extracting rich and engaging information and perspectives from it; and his enthralled devotion to converting his findings into fluid narrative prose pieces that are lively, thought-provoking, and far-reaching.

I wholeheartedly agree with the trenchant conclusion of Kenji Taguma's foreword wherein he asserts that, while many of the individuals sketched by Greg Robinson in *The Great Unknown* may be unsung heroes, his book has ensured that they are no longer unknown. This is truly a first-rate book, and the University Press of Colorado is to be applauded for making its contents available to a wide audience (which, hopefully, will become still wider if it is made available in a paperback edition).

THE UNSUNG GREAT: Stories of Extraordinary Japanese Americans
By Greg Robinson (Seattle: University of Washington Press, 2020, 294 pp., $29.95, paperback)

Published in the July 22, 2021 edition of the *Nichi Bei Weekly*.

This is the second of two outstanding books by eminent historian and journalist Greg Robinson consisting primarily of his "The Great Unknown and the Unknown Great" columns in the San Francisco-based *Nichi Bei Weekly*. In reviewing for the *NBW* the first book, *The Great Unknown: Japanese American Sketches*, published by the University Press of Colorado in 2016, I explained that its ten chapters encompassed the "'unknown' activities and/or achievements of selected noteworthy individuals." As for the University of Washington Press volume here under review—which also includes postings on *Discover Nikkei*, the blog of the Los Angeles-based Japanese American National Museum, among several other venues—its eight thematic chapters are devoted to the same general objective as its predecessor.

As Robinson sets forth in his masterful introduction, the themes of his chapters (a half-dozen of which are co-authored) are not only diverse in content but also consistently treat understudied aspects of the Japanese American past: mixed-race Japanese American families; Japanese American literature; political activism of the *Nisei* and their quest for civil rights and social justice; *Nikkei* creative artists and their respective productions; Japanese American queer history; and non-West Coast Japanese American populations. Even Robinson's two chapters focused on the much-studied World War II era are given over to atypical *Nikkei* happenings, on the one hand, and, on the other hand, to the stories of those humane non-*Nikkei* who provided support for Japanese Americans during their incarceration in American-style concentration camps.

In the nearly quarter of a century that I have been in contact with Greg Robinson, he continues to amaze me anew. A professor of history at the University of Quebec, Montreal, where he teaches courses in the French language, he is a prolific writer of books, all of them relating to some dimension or other of the Japanese American historical experience. While these works are very well-researched and deeply rooted in a wide variety of primary and secondary sources, they are expressed in terms that are comprehensible by a general readership as against one comprised exclusively by other academicians. Even though Robinson is attuned to new theoretical and methodological breakthroughs in the discipline of history, he opts, consistent with his background in journalism, to seamlessly incorporate them into an eloquent narrative style that places a premium on powerful and consequential storytelling.

Since *The Unsung Great* covers so much territory in its pages, which readers of the volume need to ponder in their own way, I will restrict myself here to highlighting what grabbed my attention when consuming its abundant contents. First, Robinson leaves very few informational stones unturned when zealously developing his biographical portraits. Second, his graphic descriptions of neglected individuals frequently get converted into life histories of similarly overlooked family members. Third, Robinson's profiles are often complexified and humanized by his penchant for including, in his depiction, both pro and con character traits and behavior. Fourth, when sketching not such unsung great Japanese Americans, like civil rights activist Clifford Uyeda and war hero Ben Kuroki, Robinson supplies readers with unconventional and inconvenient information not heretofore given public (or even private) attention. Although having conducted in-depth oral histories in the past with both of these *Nisei* men, upon perusing Robinson's representations of them, I realized that I had barely scratched the surface of their multiplex lives.

Japanese Americans and non-Japanese Americans alike will benefit tremendously, as I certainly did, from Greg Robinson's inspired sleuthing and artful renderings of his findings in *The Unsung Great*. The *Nichi Bei Weekly*'s formative role in facilitating this bountiful book's very existence is deserving of communal applause.

PART II
FAMILY

In her 1990 Asia Society *article titled "The Japanese Family," Anne E. Imamura makes the following pertinent observation: "Knowledge of a society's family system is essential to understanding that society. In the case of Japan, it is especially important because the family rather than the individual is considered to be the basic unit of society."* Notwithstanding Japan always having a variety of family forms, the model that was upheld as the ideal during the late nineteenth and early twentieth centuries when the first-generation of Japanese Americans, the Issei, migrated to and settled in Hawai`i and the United States mainland was the agricultural household, wherein the family was organized as a productive unit. This model entailed a strict gender-based role division featuring a patriarchal head, filial piety, hierarchy by birth, a "stem" family system in which one child (typically the eldest son) remained in the household to oversee the family business and care for the aged parents, and where the marriage of the progeny, irrespective of gender, was regarded as a relationship between households and thus subject to being arranged.

This traditional family model, though challenged by the dynamics of "Americanization," continued to prevail with the coming of age of the Nisei, U.S.-born, second-generation Japanese Americans. However, its force waned *considerably during World War II and increasingly so in the postwar years extending to the present day, as altered conditions led to new configurations of family interaction. The wartime incarceration of Japanese Americans hastened the transformation from an Issei to a Nisei-oriented family structure, with individual concerns replacing family ones and the Issei-dominated family economy being supplanted by a War Relocation Authority-controlled one.*

Postwar developments, such as the resettlement of Japanese Americans into non-West Coast areas of the U.S. mainland and the concomitant dissolution of prewar Nikkei communities *and the dispersal of their populations into non-segregated suburbs, the replacement of the family and ethnic economy with a wage economy, the steep rise in out-marriages, heightened educational and professional opportunities for the post-*Nisei *generations (*Sansei, Yonsei, Gosei*), the sharp reduction in family size and increase in family income, and the enhancement of women's rights, status, and power —all these, and still other factors, have eroded the traditional Japanese American family.*

At the same time, though, recent comparative clinical studies have disclosed that Japanese Americans' opinion of family values and roles were more likely than those of European Americans to suggest a higher family status with greater role differentiation and the male role as central. Additionally, these studies have revealed that Japanese Americans stressed collective harmony, cooperation, interpersonal concurrence, and clear-cut mutual social interactions. Apart from such formal studies, it is generally believed that Japanese Americans are even today expected to honor their family's interest before their own and to demonstrate preferential treatment to family members.

The persisting tight-knitted and collective nature of the Japanese American family is variably expressed within all eight book reviews comprising this section of A Nikkei Harvest. *Neil Nakadate, a comparatively young Nisei born in 1943, dramatizes this fact by his very decision to transact his 2013 autobiographical book,* **Looking After Minidoka,** *as a family memoir. As for the 2016 transnational historical account of the Sakamoto family experiences before, during, and after World War II,* **Midnight in Broad Daylight,** *by Jewish American writer Pamela Rotner Sakamoto, its* content highlights the distinctive character of the Japanese American family. So, too, does Matthew Elms' 2015 book, When the Akimotos Went to War, *a World War II-centered depiction of the embattled lives (and, in two cases, deaths) of the three* Nisei *sons of their devastated* Issei *parents, Masanori and Mary Akimoto. With respect to* Sansei *Naomi Shibata's 2014 biographical tribute to her* Nisei *mother, Grace Eto Shibata,* Bend with the Wind, *it is approached from a decidedly family perspective and enacted as a richly documented inter-generational representation of the significance of* Nikkei *family values. Similarly,* Sansei *Karen Tei Yamashita's 2017 hybridized volume,* Letters to Memory, *is an exceedingly deep dive into her interconnected family's history that results not only in a work of imaginative splendor and importance, but also one that generates a capacious Yamashita family archive that is posted for public access and use on a University of California campus website. As for Tom Coffman's intertwined history of a Hawai`i* Nikkei *family,* Tadaima, *it explores its subject from a multicultural, transnational outlook. In the case of Janice Munemitsu's* The Kindness of Color, *it places a premium on the exemplary and consequential World War II and postwar cooperation between two families of color, one Japanese American and the other Mexican American. Lastly, and quintessentially,* Sansei *David Mas Masumoto–aided by his mixed race* Yonsei *daughter, Nikiko Masumoto–in the aptly titled 2016 meditation about farming and family,* Changing Season, *has crafted a book which, according to one reviewer, is at bottom, "a love story of duty and honor to both the family and the land."*

LOOKING AFTER MINIDOKA: An American Memoir
By Neil Nakadate (Bloomington, IN: Indiana University Press, 2013, 236 pp., $20.00, paperback)

Published in the January 1, 2014 edition of the *Nichi Bei Weekly*.

Although its publisher markets *Looking After Minidoka* as a "memoir," this volume can lay equal claim as a "history." It is, in fact, the superlative fusion of these two genres that accounts for the most fundamental value and utility of this richly documented, exquisitely composed, and diversely illustrated work. Rather than a personal memoir, Neil Nakadate (an emeritus professor of English at Iowa State University) has fashioned a family memoir that conveys to readers the historical experience of his immigrant *Issei* grandparents, his U.S.-born *Nisei* parents, and his own *Sansei* generation of American citizens. Moreover, he has resourcefully and strategically situated this family memoir into the context of the larger Japanese American story.

Whereas three of Nakadate's five chapters are designated generationally as "Issei," "Nisei," and "Sansei," the longest of his chapters, by a wide margin, is titled "Minidoka, 1942-1945." He constructs this chapter on the unstated premise that the social disaster inflicted upon people of Japanese ancestry by the U.S. government during World War II was the defining moment for both his *Nikkei* family and Japanese America generally. (Notwithstanding that Neil Nakadate was born in 1943 in East Chicago, Indiana—where his father Katsumi had been undertaking his medical residency before assignment to the segregated 442nd Regimental Combat Team—the Minidoka concentration camp in Idaho functions as his foremost life history "search engine" owing to his six-month confinement there in 1944 with his mother Mary and her Marumoto family.) A final short chapter, "Unfinished," focuses upon the post-WWII redress and reparations movement. Therein he not only explores what this intergenerational and interracial movement signified for different people within both his ethno-racial family/community and mainstream America, but also ruminates as to what it might possibly come to mean "going forward, to the vast majority of [all] Americans."

Looking After Minidoka breaks little in the way of new ground for those who have extensively researched the Japanese American experience and/or lived through a protracted stretch of it. However, in the process of making better sense for himself of this experience, Nakadate has consulted, comprehended, and conveyed the essential core of secondary literature bearing upon it. Moreover, he has illuminated his research findings in so strikingly engaging a manner as to render his book both an ideal informational platform relative to Japanese American history, society, and culture and a powerful springboard for further inquiry into this noteworthy sphere of knowledge. This remarkable book is highly recommended reading for (younger) *Sansei, Yonsei, Gosei,* and members of the burgeoning Hapa population, as well as those of whatever background, in and out of educational institutions, who seek enrichment as individuals and communal beings within a multicultural nation via greater awareness of the *Nikkei* experience in the United States.

My only reservation about *Looking After Minidoka* is the very modest one that it lacks an index, which unfortunately seems to be standard practice these days for published memoirs.

MIDNIGHT IN BROAD DAYLIGHT: A Japanese American Family Caught Between Two Worlds
By Pamela Rotner Sakamoto (New York: Harper, 2016, 464 pp., $29.99, hardcover)

Published in the July 21, 2016 edition of the *Nichi Bei Weekly.*

At our vacation residence in the small San Luis Obispo County community of Los Osos, California, my wife and I have a delightful neighbor who is genuinely a "voracious reader." By far this woman's favorite genre of literature is historical fiction. While customarily she shuns non-fiction books, she is open to perusing such works with one proviso: they must read like captivating novels. It is for this reason I have previously recommended to her a trio of exemplary 2015 *Nikkei* history books that nicely conforms to her exacting taste: Jan Jarboe Russell's *The Train to Crystal City*, Julia Checkoway's *The Three-Year Swim Club*, and Janice P. Nimura's *Daughters of the Samurai*. I am now prepared to promote to her attention still another non-fiction book, the one under review here (likewise by a female author): Pamela

Rotner Sakamoto's new narrative masterwork, *Midnight in Broad Daylight: A Japanese American Family Caught Between Two Worlds*.

Although the novelistic elements of Sakamoto's book—graceful prose, solid plot line, dexterous character development, and philosophical heft—enthralled me, what also drew me powerfully into *Midnight in Broad Daylight* was its transpacific subject matter and the resourceful and consequential way in which Sakamoto has exploited it. As denoted by its subtitle, the book revolves around the fortunes and (chiefly) misfortunes of one Japanese American family (the Fukuharas, consisting of two immigrant *Issei* parents, Katsuji and Kinu, and their five U.S.-born *Nisei* offspring, Victor, Mary, Harry, Pierce, and Frank).

Not coincidentally, the Fukuhara story, which Sakamoto lavishly and imaginatively documents with diverse evidence, is broadly representative of the entire Japanese American community's historical experience before, during, and after World War II. The *Issei* parents both immigrate to the United States from Hiroshima, the home prefecture for the largest number of first-generation *Nikkei*. The male head of the family, Katsuji, sails to the West Coast of the U.S. mainland in 1900, and in 1911 is joined in the Pacific Northwest by Kinu, his picture bride. In the ensuing years, all five of the Fukuhara children are born and then raised in the town of Auburn, Washington. However, after the 1933 death of Katsuji places the family in dire financial straits, Kinu decides to return to her ancestral home in Japan, accompanied by her reluctant *Nisei* brood.

In the waning 1930s, Mary and Harry return to America, but after the U.S. entry into World War II against Japan, they are caught up in the mass exclusion and incarceration of the West Coast Japanese American population.

Meanwhile, Victor is conscripted into the Japanese Imperial Army, as in due time are his younger brothers Pierce and Frank. In the U.S. Harry leaves the Gila River concentration camp in Arizona to enter Japanese language school in Minnesota and become affiliated with the Allied Translator and Interpreter Section (ATIS). This action plunges him into the vortex of the Pacific war, which Sakamoto strategically treats from alternating Japanese and American perspectives. Readers of her book likely will anticipate that at some point the conflicting wartime paths of the Fukuhara brothers will cross, so I will not here compromise Sakamoto's suspenseful scenario by spilling the historical beans in relation to this real if seemingly remote contingency.

Two items bearing directly and indirectly on Sakamoto's book especially spoke to me. Using Harry Fukuhara's immediate postwar visit to his family's home site in Hiroshima permits Sakamoto to offer a rare personal account of not only the context of that city's controversial atomic bombing by the U.S. military, but also the consequences suffered by its tragically downsized population of survivors. Having only recently listened to the 2014 audiobook of Dr. Michihiko Hachiya's classic 1955 work, *Hiroshima Diary: The Journal of a Japanese Physician, August 6-September 30, 1945*, I found myself humbled by being privy to a pair of such complementary, compelling, and compassionate narratives on so pivotal (and horrendous) a moment in modern world history.

The second item about *Midnight in Broad Daylight* that particularly resonated with me derived from a December 28, 2015, videotaped ThinkTech Hawai`i interview I accessed via the internet between Jay Bidell and Pamela Rotner Sakamoto, which I strongly recommend to *Nichi Bei Weekly* readers, among others: https://www.youtube.com/watch?v=tijFvY6Fr8U

From this interview I learned that Sakamoto, a U.S. citizen of Jewish heritage, had lived in Japan for 17 years and there became conversant in Japanese language, culture, and history while concurrently serving as a historical consultant for Japan-related projects for the Holocaust Memorial Museum in Washington, D.C. I found out too that she had devoted over fifteen years in researching and writing her present book, after finishing her first and strictly academic book, *Japanese Diplomats and Jewish Refugees: A World War II Dilemma* (1998). Reflecting on this revealing information about Sakamoto reminded me anew how exceedingly important and far-reaching has been the contribution of Jewish American scholars to Japanese and Japanese American studies.

WHEN THE AKIMOTOS WENT TO WAR: An Untold Story of Family, Patriotism, and Sacrifice During World War II
By Matthew Elms (Arlington, VA: American Battle Monuments Commission, 2015, 146 pp., $15.00, paperback)

Published in the January 1, 2019 edition of the *Nichi Bei Weekly*.

This book by Matthew Elms is a heart-rending Japanese American family-themed inquiry into the dismaying "wages of war." It is published by the American Battle Monuments Commission, a national government agency charged with the maintenance of twenty-seven cemeteries worldwide that honor more than 200,000 Americans who lost their lives in the military service of their country during World War I and World War II. Consistent with the ABMC's mission, Elms wrote *When the Akimotos Went to War* "to highlight the true story of one Japanese American family for young adults."

As a teacher in ABMC's "Understanding Sacrifice" program, Elms was acutely cognizant that every person interred in the sponsoring agency's cemeteries not only played a contributing role in the defense of U.S. freedoms and liberties, but also embodied a story of selfless actions and sacrifices that, if passed along to classrooms and living rooms, could simultaneously impart meaning to their respective lives and inspiration to its readership. Moreover, Elms was mindful that the deaths of *Nisei* soldiers Johnny and Victor Akimoto, among the 405,300 Americans who died in World War II, were embedded within a larger story that rendered it especially profound and poignant. After all, both of them, as well as their brother Ted, enlisted in the army (along with over 33,000 other Japanese Americans) and served in segregated units notwithstanding that 120,000 members of their racial-ethnic community, two-thirds of whom were U.S. citizens, were unjustly uprooted from their homes, by the U.S. government and, without due process, were incarcerated in American-style concentration camps.

In his very thoughtful postscript, Elms takes pains to register for readers a critical problem that besets popular accounts of war: that too often the media, governments, and even historians "celebrate the gallantry, glamour, and courage that wars occasion," while "failing to acknowledge the savagery of war." He reminds us that such glorification of war masks the reality that war is always ugly, marked by "cruel, vicious, and dehumanizing behaviors," grisly details (such as soldiers' bodies burned by jellied gasoline), and widespread suffering experienced on the battlefield and the home front by individuals, families, communities, and entire nations.

Elms' postscript also demythologizes the notion that "everyone in the military perishes from a single shot through the heart while undertaking a courageous deed." The World War II deaths of Victor Akimoto and his youngest brother Johnny are prime cases in point. Assigned to different infantry companies in the mostly Hawaiian 100th Infantry Battalion, they maintained contact with one another during combat against German forces in the Battle of Anzio (January-June 1944). But on July 30, 1944, Johnny checked into a military field hospital in Italy and was diagnosed with acute hepatitis from an unknown source. Two days later, he slipped into a coma, and the following day, he died.

As for Victor, after the liberation of Rome via the Battle of Anzio, he was assigned (along with the rest of the 100th Infantry Battalion) to the 442nd Regimental Combat Team and fought in a series of other battles in Italy. By October 1944, the 442nd troops were deployed in France in the Vosges Mountains region and ordered to rescue the 141st Infantry Regiment, comprised mostly of Texans—the so-called Lost Battalion. It required by October 30, 1944 a combined total of 800 casualties, deaths, and injuries of the 442nd to save the 141st soldiers. But during this sacrificial mission of mercy, the German Army captured many Japanese American combatants, including Victor Akimoto, who had suffered a shattered thigh bone from enemy fire.

Transported by truck to a prisoner of war camp in Germany, his condition worsened due to a lack of antibiotics and proper sterilization procedures, his infected wound turned to gangrene, and this development led to his leg being amputated. He then refused to eat, and thus he died on December 14, 1944.

Both Johnny and Victor Akimoto were eventually buried at France's Lorraine American Cemetery. Their *Issei* father, Masanori Akimoto, died in 1951, having never visited their graveyard, but fortunately, their *Issei* mother, Mary Akimoto, accompanied by her *Nisei* son, Ted Akimoto, was able in 1960 to travel to that distant burial site and gain a measure of closure for her grieving heart.

Although *When the Akimotos Went to War* is beautifully written, well researched, adorned with a variety of illustrations and maps, and includes a useful bibliography, the book suffers from an awkward, if artful, organization, that makes it somewhat challenging to traverse.

BEND WITH THE WIND: The Life, Family, and Writings of Grace Eto Shibata
Edited by Naomi Shibata (San José, CA: Shibata Family Limited Partnership, 2014, 242 pp., $19.95, paperback)

Published in the July 20, 2017 edition of the *Nichi Bei Weekly*.

One of my favorite songs by country singer Hank Williams, Jr.—whose political and social philosophy I revile—is "Family Tradition." The book under review here falls into the same category as that record's title, and it does so in a very profound way. Indeed, it was precisely owing to family tradition that Naomi Shibata felt stirred to write *Bend with the Wind* in the first place, and which by her then doing so resulted in that tradition being significantly expanded and enriched.

In the spring of 1980, when I was a visiting professor of history at the San Luis Obispo branch of California Polytechnic State University, I taught a class that was consistent with that institution's "learn by doing" philosophy. I tasked each student to transact a tape-recorded interview with a longtime member of the San Luis Obispo County Japanese American community. To assist the students in their fieldwork, I sought out someone in that community to serve as a "key informant" and all-purpose guide. The multiple recommendations I received for someone to discharge this important role all pointed to the same person: Masaji Eto (1916-1999).

Not only was he someone with personal connections to the Cal Poly campus, but he was also the only son of the man, Tameji Eto (1883-1958), who was arguably the first person of Japanese ancestry to settle in the central California coastal county of San Luis Obispo (SLO). In addition, Masaji Eto was then president of the SLO Japanese American Citizens League chapter. As it turned out, he provided my entire class with useful background information and lined up interviews for each of the students. I was fortunate at this crucial juncture to befriend this congenial and enlightened man, to whom I was now deeply indebted, and to become acquainted at the historic Eto home site in the SLO town of Los Osos with his mother Take Yanahara Eto (1889-1985) and his wife Margaret Hisayasu Eto (1920-2001).

Then in 2005, a year after my wife and I established a vacation residence proximate to the Eto ranch, I was contacted by one of Masaji Eto's nephews, Samuel Nakamura (b. 1947). A retired executive of a major commercial airline, Nakamura sought my counsel about publishing a discovered 1948 unpublished manuscript written by his deceased mother, Toshiko Eto Nakamura (1910-1994), relative to her World War II experience as a nurse at the Manzanar detention camp in eastern California. Four years later, this manuscript, edited and annotated by Samuel Nakamura (with a foreword by me), became a sterling publication entitled *Nurse of Manzanar: A Japanese American's World War II Journey*.

To my great surprise, Samuel Nakamura again contacted me in late 2012, this time to see if I might assist his cousin Naomi Shibata (b. 1950) with the manuscript she was writing about her mother, Grace

Eto Shibata (b. 1925), the youngest of Masaji Eto's seven sisters. In conversing with Naomi Shibata about her work-in-progress, I discovered that her father, Yoshimi Shibata (1916-2016), was the author of the 2006 book *Across Two Worlds: Memoirs of a Nisei Flower Grower* and that the WWII resettlement struggles of one of her aunts, Alice Eto Sumida (b. 1914), and her husband Masuo "Mark" Sumida (1904-1981) were spotlighted in Allen Say's 2004 children's book *Music for Alice*. By this point in time I became acutely aware that books had played an important part in Naomi Shibata's "family tradition."

As to her contribution to that dimension of her family's tradition, *Bend with the Wind*, it is a stunning success, notwithstanding that it is a self-published work and does not bear the imprimatur of a prominent commercial or academic press. This is because Naomi Shibata, whose background is not in the humanities but in the high-tech world of business, is a very intelligent woman with an extraordinarily steep learning curve, someone who in her very first book has achieved estimable proficiency in the entwined crafts of historical editing, historical biography, and family history. By merely thumbing through the pages of *Bend with the Wind* a reader can grasp an appreciation for the research scholarship that its editor (and, I would argue, author) invested in her family project: the proliferation of well-selected and captioned photographs; the assortment of useful illustrations, including maps and documents; the profusion and penetration of her chapter endnotes; the array of diverse and revealing appendices; the carefully constructed and helpful timeline; and the serviceable index.

Upon reading the book, one will readily appreciate the quality of Naomi Shibata's narrative skills and the fastidious care she has taken to organize her discrete and appropriately titled chapters into an order that facilitates meaningful consumption of their separate and combined content. One comes away from reading *Bend with the Wind* with much more than an appreciation for the challenging and rewarding life history and the noteworthy literary achievements of Grace Eto Shibata (whose writings command one section of the book). Rather, via an extended family perspective, readers are given a resourcefully grounded rendering of what thousands of other Americans of Japanese ancestry confronted as pioneering immigrants, wartime victims, and postwar survivors.

While I was privileged to write the preface to *Bend with the Wind*, the best depiction of its value was supplied by Dan Krieger, a professor emeritus of history from Cal Poly, San Luis Obispo, and the foremost historian of San Luis Obispo County and its Japanese American community. In his foreword, he writes: "Naomi Shibata's historical portrait of her mother fulfills what to my mind is the most important function of teaching and learning history: to communicate the sense that we who live in the present aren't the first to encounter difficulties and crises. Others have traveled troubled paths before us and survived with dignity and grace."

LETTERS TO MEMORY
By Karen Tei Yamashita (Minneapolis: Coffee House Press, 2017, 176 pp., $19.95, paperback)

Published in the July 19, 2018 edition of the *Nichi Bei Weekly*.

In her insightful September 13, 2017 *Christian Science Monitor* review of Karen Tei Yamashita's *Letters to Memory*, Terry Hong concluded with this appraisal: "Allusive, quirky, questioning, *Letters* is a challenging text ... dense with assumptions of cultural literacy, community insight, historical background. ... [However] don't be deterred [as] *Letters* awaits your inquisitive participation and rewarding collaboration." My own initial reading of this brilliant book, whose form and content reached well beyond my grasp, inclined me toward affirming Hong's assessment. Before reading it a second time, though, I decided to listen to an engaging and illuminating interview with Yamashita about her book. Because this experience was so helpful for me, I would suggest to prospective readers of *Letters to Memory* that prior to even tackling it the first time they might want to consider listening to this interview: https://lareviewofbooks.org/av/larb-radio-hour-karen-tei-yamashitas-letters-memory-plus-sylvia-leonard-michaels

This volume, which is a hybrid of a documentary, a memoir, and an epistolary novel, had its genesis in 1995 when one of the author's four aunts from the Yamashita side of her family, Kay, passed away and left behind two folders of letters. One of these, consisting of personal correspondence, Karen Yamashita covertly appropriated, but did not seriously read, no less exploit, until the last of Kay's six siblings had died in 2004. In time this led to the assembly of a sizeable Yamashita family archive of "hundreds of photographs and documents, pamphlets and paintings, homemade films and audiotapes and gramophone records, and diaries." Upon publication of *Letters to Memory*, this archive, housed in the Special Collections at McHenry Library of the University of California, Santa Cruz, was posted online for access and use: http://yamashitaarchives.ucsc.edu. Visiting this site will supply added value to your comprehension and appreciation of the book under review.

The heart of *Letters to Memory* is Yamashita's profound journey of exploration into her family archive to discover the significance of the Japanese American World War II social disaster—not merely in relationship to herself, her family, and her ethnic-racial community, but also as a template for fathoming still more imponderable and overarching matters such as the lessons and limits of history, the character of charity, the challenge of forgiveness, the trauma of war, the quality of love, the power of death, the pain of poverty, the poignancy of memory, and the problem of evil.

The portion of this book that I found most daunting and (to be honest) somewhat off-putting was Yamashita's series of epistolary conversations with assorted "muses" and their arcane texts to investigate the Japanese American Incarceration and to greatly expand its meaning. However, I am painfully aware that this very dimension helps qualify *Letters to Memory* as a work of literary genius. The aspect of the book that most depressed me was the realization, shared by the author, that our country is now on the verge of reprising many of the "slings and arrows of outrageous fortune" that befell *Nikkei* during World War II onto different groups of demonized Americans. On the other hand, I am uplifted by the fact that Yamashita's leitmotif in *Letters to Memory* is the necessity for us to resist oppression by committing ourselves to civil and human rights, democracy, and social justice.

TADAIMA! I AM HOME: A Transitional Family History
By Tom Coffman (Honolulu: University of Hawai`i Press, 2018, 176 pp., $17.95, paperback)

Published in the July 18, 2019 edition of the *Nichi Bei Weekly*.

The volume under review, the most recent of many documentary books by award-winning veteran independent researcher, writer, and producer Tom Coffman, characteristically incorporates historical themes pertaining to Hawai`i. What makes *Tadaima! I Am Home* different, however, is that its focus is upon a Hawai`i *Nikkei* family history as viewed from a multigenerational, transnational perspective. Within its short compass, readers are provided with a fascinating five-generation exploration by Coffman of male Miwa family members extending from its fallen *samurai* progenitor in Meiji Era Japan, Marujiro Miwa (1850-1919), down through four sons of successive generations—all of whom are bound together by having their lives similarly played out in both Japan (mostly Hiroshima) and America (Hawai`i and the US mainland).

The book's origin story features the Miya family's most recent descendant, Stephen H. Miya (b. 1963), and his quest to excavate his family's roots, with particular attention to why his late mother had ominously apprised him that, owing to the family being deemed "unlucky," he might well not want to unearth its lineage. Undaunted by this forewarning, Stephen then sought and gained useful oral and written information from his father, Lawrence Fumio Miwa (b. 1931) to facilitate his quest, and thereafter commissioned Coffman to flesh out the Miwa family story. Aided by two researchers from Japan affiliated with the Hawai`i State Archives who were not only interested in transnational migration, but also able to instruct him in how to access archives in Japan and utilize other invaluable resources, Coffman was empowered to produce a book that represents a quintessential model of the new and enriched family history.

Although the stories of the five Miya generations are intermingled throughout Coffman's book, the basic organization is the sequential exposition of each generational representative's transnational experience contextualized by salient information relevant to his respective time period. While the experiences of all five generations are noteworthy, the one I found most captivating was that of Lawrence Fumio Miwa.

Born in Honolulu as a U.S. citizen, when he was two years old, in 1933, his father moved him to Japan to be rejoined with his mother and two older siblings. There he afterwards attended a series of schools. Then called by his Japanese name of Fumio, he was indoctrinated with military propaganda and became an unquestioning captive and chauvinistic proponent of it. Just prior to his fourteenth birthday, on July 3, 1945, school officials told him and his classmates that they were being relocated to the countryside, to a village located about twenty-five miles east of downtown Hiroshima, "to serve the emperor by growing vegetables." On that same date, he and his fellow students were instructed to begin maintaining a "self-reflection diary." The very next month Fumio's diary would record a catastrophic historical event. Because of a disciplinary action, Fumio and two other boys, who were scheduled on August 6 to visit their parents in Hiroshima, were substituted for by three different and tragically unlucky boys. Although Fumio did not witness or experience the atomic bombing of his hometown, nine days later, on August 15, he and his classmates were permitted to travel to Hiroshima to take a still-operating train into the city to assay the extent of its destruction and the highly possible loss of life of their family members. While some quarter of a million homes had been devastated, at the flattened Miwa house, Fumio miraculously discovered a written message affixed to the concrete wall of the well that read, in his father's hand, "Parents safe," along with an address where he could locate his family.

My recommendation of this book is that consumers of this review should either buy it or borrow it and by all means read it and reflect upon its abundant contents. The sole reservation I have about this book is one I found in an anonymous assessment that appeared in *Publishers Weekly*, and which I here somewhat reluctantly second: "Unfortunately, he [Tom Coffman] focuses exclusively on the Miwa men, obscuring women's contributions to their transnational life and limiting the book's impact."

THE KINDNESS OF COLOR: The Story of Two Families and *Mendez, et al. v. Westminster,* the 1947 Desegregation of California Public Schools
By Janice Munemitsu (Self-published, 2021, 211 pp., $14.99, paperback)

Published in the January 1, 2022 edition of the *Nichi Bei Weekly*.

In 1949, when I was ten years old, my family moved from New Jersey to Goleta, California, where I enrolled as a sixth grader in Goleta Union School. It historically had always been an integrated school, as were the schools in the neighboring county seat of Santa Barbara. However, another Santa Barbara County town, Carpinteria, for some twenty-seven years prior to 1947, had consigned its Mexican American students, mostly children of lemon workers, to the segregated classrooms of Aliso School. There, according to John McCaffery, a former Aliso School student and author of the 2003 book *For the Mexican Children,* those attending the institution were given an inferior education and were smacked with a ruler by ill-prepared and racist Caucasian teachers for speaking Spanish, even on the playground, while the school itself was regarded as basically a feeder establishment for lemon industry laborers. This deplorable situation only came to an end in 1947 after the California Supreme Court prohibited public school segregation.

In *The Kindness of Color*, Sansei Janice Munemitsu provides readers with a poignant in-depth depiction of the *Mendez, et al. v. Westminster* class action suit in 1947 by five Mexican American families in then largely agricultural Orange County, California. Speaking up on behalf of some 5,000 people of Mexican ancestry in the four school districts of Westminster, Santa Ana, Garden Grove, and El Modena, it was not only responsible for the ban on public school segregation in California but also established a precedent for the same ban to be enacted on the national level in the landmark 1954 U.S. Supreme Court case of *Brown v. Board of Education*.

However, at the heart of Munemitsu's book—which she very timely has issued to commemorate the upcoming 75th anniversary in 2022 of the *Mendez v. Westminster* triumph—is the intertwined World War II and immediate postwar connection of the author's Japanese American family and the Mendez family. Although I long ago knew about the importance of this far-reaching class-action suit, it was not until I viewed the 2003 public premiere of Sandra Robbie's film *Mendez vs. Westminster: For All the Children/Para Todos los Niños* that I became aware of this familial connection. Far more surprisingly, it was not until the previous year that Janice Munemitsu, who was born after World War II and came of age in the 1960s and 1970s, got wind of it in a surprise phone call from Robbie.

In brief, what Janice Munemitsu, in her exceedingly well-written, exquisitely organized, and richly documented narrative relates so movingly is how her youthful father, Tad, through the intervention of an honest Garden Grove banker, entered into an arrangement whereby upon the 1942 U.S. government eviction of the Munemitsu family and its subsequent wartime incarceration in Arizona's Poston Relocation Center, their forty-acre Westminster farm, replete with a farmhouse, four workers' cottages, a packing house, and a barn, was leased to the Mendez family. This arrangement led to a close wartime and postwar relationship between the Mendez and Munemitsu families. Moreover, the financial benefits accruing to the Mendez family from the lucrative harvest of its crops on the rented Munemitsu property both aided them to be the principal funding source in the costly *Mendez vs. Westminster* suit and permitted them to purchase a new café in the nearby city of Santa Ana.

What makes *The Kindness of Color* an especially timely book at this juncture when transformational ethnic studies courses are being mandated and debated in California and many other states is that while it embodies the essence of so-called critical race theory, it does so in a way that is altogether constructive, inoffensive, and promotional of the American democratic and multicultural promise.

I regret that this superb book by Janice Munemitsu lacks an index, but likely that is due to her ardent desire to have it published in time to commemorate the fortieth anniversary of *Mendez vs. Westminster* in 2022. Hopefully, future editions of *The Kindness of Color* will rectify this particular deficiency.

CHANGING SEASON: A Father, A Daughter, A Family Farm
By David Mas Masumoto with Nikiko Masumoto (Berkeley: Heyday, 2016, 192 pp., $16.00, paperback)

Published in the January 1, 2017 edition of the *Nichi Bei Weekly.*

In the mid-1980s, while researching the World War II incarceration experience of Americans of Japanese ancestry at the Gila River Relocation Center in south central Arizona, I discovered a brief yet very enlightening 1982 autobiographical volume on this subject by David Mas Masumoto. Entitled *Distant Voices: A Sansei's Journey to Gila River*, it was self-published by the twenty-eight-year-old author-agriculturalist under the aegis of the Inaka Countryside Press in Del Rey, California (20 miles south of Fresno). Five years later another book by Masumoto, bearing the same imprint, commanded my rapt attention:

Country Voices: The Oral History of a Japanese American Family Farm Community. The earlier work represented for Masumoto a means to reflect on his personal pilgrimage to the desolate site on Native American land where his youthful U.S.-born *Nisei* parents—confined with their respective immigrant *Issei* parents—first met; this book also afforded him an opportunity to meditate upon both his Japanese heritage and the impact of mass wartime imprisonment upon the *Nikkei* community. *Country Voices*, on the other hand, served Masumoto as a vehicle, via the village of Del Rey and the interpretive power of oral history, for transporting its readers into a vital ethnographic encounter with the historical development and sociocultural character of a "typical" multi-generational Japanese American family-farm community.

Upon reading *Country Voices*, I grasped instinctively what the legendary oral historian Studs Terkel had meant when he characterized it as "a gem" and "an anthem to the human spirit"—a heretofore untold story of the Japanese American farmers: "their dreams, their hopes, their ordeal, their resilience."

I was sufficiently moved to assign this book to the required "American Character" class I then taught through the American Studies Department at Cal State Fullerton, and I invited Masumoto to visit the class and engage the students in a discussion of his new masterpiece. I can no longer recall the details of his presentation, but I do recollect that central to it was an artifact, a chunk of hardpan, which he offered up for contemplation by the students, none of whom were of Japanese ancestry and very few of whom even associated Japanese Americans with farming. Although Masumoto never said so directly, he strongly implied that, in order to fathom the essence of Japanese Del Rey as a farm community, to savor the sweetness of its harvests and the soundness of the residents' down-to-earth truths, it was necessary to factor in the daily struggle its denizens waged, actually and metaphorically, against the dense layer of soil found below the uppermost topsoil of their land—that is, the intractable hardpan, which impedes drainage of water and restricts the growth of plant roots.

Even though I have not personally been in touch with Masumoto since 1988, in the intervening years between then and now, I have read several of his many poignant and timeless books, as well as a spate of his correlated *Fresno Bee* columns. There is absolutely nothing flashy about his writing and he never uses it to flaunt his celebrity or to display his erudition. He "travels" a great deal, but mostly, or so it seems, within either the confines of his 80-acre organic farm in Del Rey or in the crevices of his fertile imagination. A career family farmer, the two dominant topics in his writing are, not surprisingly, "family" and "farming," though as a core memoirist he often ruminates about such diverse things as feelings of the heart, matters of the spirit, questions of vocation, the concerns of life and death, and what has been termed "intergenerational transmission of knowledge."

All these subjects are infused into *Changing Season*, the writing of which was done primarily by David Mas Masumoto, but strategically and artfully supplemented by his daughter Nikiko in what she cannily refers to as her "field notes." Not only does the book's title and subtitle underscore its preoccupation with family, farming, and strongly imply intergenerational transmission, but so also do the dedications by the two Matsumoto authors. David writes: "To my mom, who worries every season. You will always be part of this farm." Nikiko states: "To my *jiichan* [grandfather]; I miss you every day."

As for the text of *Changing Season*, in the words of one of its reviewers, Naomi Starkman, it is about, "above all, the passing on of experience and the farm itself to the next generation, specifically, to Mas Masumoto's daughter Nikiko." The book, states Starkman, "is at its heart a love story of duty and honor to both the family and the land." It is a book written by Mas upon entering his sixties and while still in recovery from a 2014 triple-bypass heart surgery. Feeling—but not bemoaning—his mortality, he reflects backward on some lessons that his late father taught him about farming ("The fruit that gets the most sunlight will taste the best. Peaches worship the sun, and so should you.") and also about life ("Fate was built on everyday, seemingly simple, deeds. Tend to your work. Trust your acts. Believe in yourself.")

Mas also contemplates some overarching paternal lessons that he should transmit to Nikiko: "What is allowed to grow in our lives when we pare down? What are we missing when we look at what is lost instead of what remains? What is the bigger picture?"

Keeping things very much down to earth, Mas recollects at one point how after his father's stroke he had to compromise his dignity by assisting him with his toilet duties, and then shares something with readers that he half-seriously joked about with his two kids: "Someday one of you might have to wipe my ass. That may be the ultimate act of sacrifice, when you learn to lean on someone."

Reading this passage, my mind was brought back to that hunk of hardpan he had shown to my students over three decades ago, his way of communicating how pivotal the role of struggle of one sort or another is in endowing us with the truths we need to face the challenges both of living and dying with equanimity and grace.

PART III
COMMUNITY

In her 2018 Claremont Graduate University philosophy of education dissertation, "Fourth & Fifth Generation Japanese American Adults," Lorine Erika Saito perceptively observes: "The Japanese American community historically and even present day is a tight-knit community where a member's actions not only represent the family but the entire community." Still, as Cheryl Lynn Sullivan earlier cautioned in her 1993 University of California, Irvine, social science dissertation on the Japanese American community of Fresno, California, "Imagining Communities, Imagining Selves," when we speak of any Nikkei community, it is imperative to know what "community" means—whether a geographic location, a group of people, or both of these together—and to be conscious of how it has "changed dramatically over time."

In the present context, it is only possible to provide a schematic historical evolution of the so-called Japanese American "community" from its modern origins during the Meiji era of Japan, in which the first-generation Japanese American Issei were born and raised, up to the current day. The overwhelming majority of immigrants to Hawai`i and the U.S. mainland came from agricultural rice-growing villages located in a cluster of prefectures in southwestern Japan. Each village, the nation's smallest political unit, was typically comprised of fifteen to twenty hamlets, local groups that encompassed about twenty households, the social unit for most village activities. Each patriarchal household embraced three or four generations and almost every family also had relatives in their village and in nearby villages. The two most prominent features of the hamlet's civic, economic, and social life were cooperation and exchange.

The migration to Hawai`i began in 1868, when labor contractors, working for the owners of Hawai`i sugar plantations, came to Japan to recruit workers. Large-scale emigration, however, was delayed until the 1880s. Then tens of thousands of workers descended upon the plantations, where they were poorly paid, lived in humble company-owned housing, and constituted between one-half to three-fourths of the multiracial work force. Workers were segregated into competing ethnic-based plantation camps (rigidly stratified by national origin, differential pay rates, and employment status) consisting mostly of men but also having a sizeable number of women residents. This situation allowed those of Japanese ancestry to speak Japanese, eat Japanese food, and commingle with people from their homeland. It also nurtured a sense of Japanese community. So, too, did their common participation in strikes seeking better wages and working conditions. In the words of Dennis M. Ogawa and Glen Grant, "[although] their lives were contained within the boundaries of their plantation camps, yet even in the midst of poverty, a sense of community, a sense of pride and permanency began to be articulated."

What the Issei immigrants brought to America, argues Saito persuasively, was the deeply embedded bond between family and community within Japan's nationalistic culture. They also conveyed with them "traditional Japanese values such as haji, or shame, which places the family's reputation on the line within the Japanese community and society at large," as well as the traditional Japanese cultural emphasis "on the needs of the group, filial piety, and sustaining the social relations among its members."

In the case of Hawai`i, which was annexed by the U.S. in 1898, the end of contract labor freed the Japanese (who represented roughly 70 percent of the nearly 40,000 plantation workers) from their obligations and precipitated their movement elsewhere to gain better opportunities. Many left Hawai`i for Seattle and San Francisco. Others returned to Japan. However, the majority of the Japanese population remained in the Hawaiian Islands and moved to Honolulu and other developing urban centers. Barred from owning land, the immigrant Issei became independent wage earners, merchants, shopkeepers, and tradesmen, and sought improvements in their working and living conditions, and promoted educational achievement for their Nisei children. Instead of forming "Japantowns," the Japanese dispersed themselves geographically within the general population, intermarried with people of other ethnic groups, overwhelmingly of Asian ancestry, and forged interracial communities—in which they increasingly played a majority role—bound together linguistically by the use of the pidgin language. At the same time, the creation and development of Japanese newspapers, schools, stores, temples, churches, and athletic teams, along with other institutions and practices, invested the Japanese with an enduring community legacy that was passed along to succeeding generations down to today.

On the mainland U.S., the community scenario played out quite differently. The first wave of migration to the mainland, which occurred in the 1880s and 1890s, landed primarily on the Pacific Coast, though by 1900 the Japanese population was less than 25,000. The overwhelming majority consisted of single males or men who had left their wives back in Japan. A small number of them were students, some of whom were also laborers, who worked as domestic servants or were employed in various industries, including farming and fishing. The greater number of the Japanese immigrants, however, were initially employed as migratory farm labor, but they could also be found working for railroads and in lumber mills, mining camps, and canneries.

The turn of the century ushered in a twenty-five-year surge of immigration, during which over 100,000 Japanese nationals arrived in the U.S. It was in this interval that the foundation institutions and social customs of the Japanese American community were established up and down the Pacific Coast, not only in large cities like Seattle, San Francisco, and Los Angeles, but also within very small towns like Marysville and Nevada City in California and settlements like Bainbridge Island in Washington and Hood River, Oregon. Soon these Japantowns witnessed the development of businesses that served the needs of their own community: restaurants, *boarding houses, and shops selling food and supplies that could not be had elsewhere. Then, after 1908, in response to the demand by U.S. legislators for protection from "the brown toilers of the Mikado's realm," an agreement was reached between Japan and the U.S. to a so-called "Gentlemen's Agreement," whereby Japan agreed to limit emigration of laborers to the U.S., while the U.S. granted admission to the wives, children, and other relatives of those Japanese immigrants already resident. This action led to Japanese immigration becoming disproportionally female, as more women left Japan as "picture brides," betrothed to immigrant men in the U.S. who, for the most part, they had never met.*

Thereafter, until the passage in the U.S. of the Immigration Act of 1924, which effectively ended Japanese immigration, the nature of the Japanese American community was rapidly transformed into being a family-based entity. This took the shape of family farms in rural areas, largely on leased land, or family businesses within burgeoning West Coast Japantowns or Little Tokyos—places where formal and informal rules prevented them from living elsewhere. With the birth of second-generation Nisei *citizen children, the Japanese American population in California, which was just over 10,000 in 1900, swelled to almost 94,000 in 1940, a nine-fold increase. Roughly two-thirds of this population were* Nisei, *whose median age was under twenty-four. Although most* Issei *had initially come to the United States to save money and return to Japan, the birth of their children persuaded many* Issei *to remain in their adopted country and strengthen their communities. Accordingly, on the eve of World War II, "community" for Japanese Americans generally represented both a group of people and a geographic area.*

Wartime for most Japanese Americans (aside from those residing in Hawai`i and the non-West Coast mainland) meant mass removal from their homes and communities and incarceration in federal-administered concentration camps in the U.S. interior. While providing a temporary context for the survival of vestiges of the prewar meaning of a Japanese American community as something conjoining people and place, these involuntary sites of imprisonment were largely bereft of the sense of pride, purpose, and palpability that had characterized their peacetime racial-ethnic enclaves. In addition, the government's wartime policy of resettling portions of the camps' population throughout the Midwest, East, and South of the country while concurrently enjoining resettlers to avoid congregating with one another undermined the notion of a Japanese American community as either a group of people or a shared geographical area.

Once the West Coast was opened up again in 1945 to Japanese Americans, and notwithstanding legal and extralegal barriers, a substantial number both from the incarceration camps and their resettled free-zone communities sought to return to their prewar settlement places. However, the urban Japantowns were for the most part occupied by wartime workers —particularly African Americans—pressed for housing, while the leased prewar Nikkei farm acreage had been largely taken over and was now worked by non-Japanese American farm families. Living to a great degree in makeshift housing such as hostels, trailer parks, and even much less habitable facilities such as garages, cellars, and animal pens, Americans of Japanese ancestry lacked the amenities and the comforts they had once taken for granted when they had been part of an embodied Japanese American community.

This situation was less the case for those Nikkei resettlers who elected to remain at war's end in western cities such as Denver and Salt Lake City that boasted small prewar/wartime Japantowns, or in selected Midwest metropolitan centers like Chicago, St. Louis, Minneapolis, Cleveland, and Cincinnati that developed quasi-Japantowns during the war. Still, all of these ethnic settlements were loose-knit in nature and within a decade or so had their community status unraveled when the resident Nikkei either returned to the West Coast or moved to surrounding suburban areas.

Simultaneous with this development, Japanese Americans steadily repopulated, reclaimed, and reanimated the historic West Coast Japantowns of Seattle, San Francisco, San Jose, and Los Angeles, although some prewar cities with vibrant Japantowns—such as Tacoma in Washington and Stockton, Sacramento, Fresno, and San Diego in California, to name only a few—became victims to the twin forces of urban redevelopment and suburbanization and thereafter ceased to function as Japanese American community sites.

What occurred for a growing number of Nikkei on the West Coast in the 1950s, 1960s, and 1970s—at a time when the Sansei (third-generation

Japanese Americans) were coming of age and when the financial fortunes of their families were on the rise and impediments to employment, educational, housing, and intermarriage were being dismantled—was their accelerated participation in the postwar boom of suburbanization. Leaving behind their ethnic enclaves, they moved first to areas of multicultural diversity for people of color, and later sought to assimilate into places that were chiefly populated by Caucasians. In the Los Angeles region, for example, this meant movement initially to suburbs like Crenshaw, Torrance, and Gardena, followed by settlement in ones like those rapidly mushrooming in the former agricultural areas of the San Fernando Valley and Orange County.

This transformation was accompanied by a steady rise in out-marriages of Sansei, *especially* Sansei *women, not only to whites, but also in some cases to those both of other races and different Asian ethnic groups. With the subsequent emergence of the* Yonsei *and* Gosei *(fourth- and fifth-generation Japanese Americans) from the 1980s to the present day, the consequences of out-marriage—coupled with a diminution of shared geographic space for co-ethnics, a shrinkage in the size of the group's population, and reduced numbers of offspring—gave rise to speculation by many older* Nikkei, *and even a few social scientists, that the very existence of the so-called Japanese American community was threatened with extinction.*

However, to counteract this understandable misperception, it is well to reflect upon Cheryl Lynn Sullivan's aforementioned astute admonition that in speaking about any Nikkei *community, we need to comprehend the meaning of "community," whether a group of people, a geographic location, or both of these together, and to be acutely aware of how this entity has "changed dramatically over time."*

Whereas prior to World War II the "Japanese American community" was primarily a group of people of the same ancestry living within bounded geographical locations, since the end of that international war the "Japanese American community," while still connected to some definable historic spatial sites, has been altered into a group of mainstream people of increasingly mixed ancestry, different ages, social classes, and political orientation whom are tied together far less by geography than by fleeting and intermit-

tent participation in a network of organizations (e.g., churches, the Japanese American Citizens League, sports leagues), cultural practices (e.g., martial arts like judo and kendo, taiko drumming, and odori dancing), celebratory events and holidays (e.g., Nisei Week and New Year's), traditional culinary dishes (e.g., sushi, udon, miso, and mochi), and civil liberty and social justice activities (e.g., WWII camp pilgrimages, supporting senior citizen housing and services, and donating time, money, or both to humanitarian and anti-racist causes). It is this configuration then which represents the Japanese American community of today. What this entity will become in the future remains to be seen in its day and on its own terms.

In the twelve books reviewed within this section of A Nikkei Harvest the historical transformation of the Japanese American community is strikingly illuminated. In Shelley Sang-Hee Lee's Claiming the Oriental Gateway what is spotlighted is the transpacific and multiethnic character of Seattle's pre-World War II Japanese American community. As for Kenichi Sato's A Rebel's Cry, the focus is on one particularly influential member of the prewar Los Angeles Little Tokyo community, Issei journalist and civil rights lawyer Sei Fujii and his efforts on behalf of improved health care and the abolition of pernicious anti-alien land laws. What assumes center stage in Naomi Hirahara and Geraldine Knatz's Terminal Island is the historical and socio-economic nature of the fishing village-cum-Japanese American community that emerged in the first decade of the twentieth century and suffered complete erasure as a consequence of the World War II removal and imprisonment of its entire Nikkei population. Garden of the World, written by Cecilia M. Tsu, explores the Northern California region of the Santa Clara Valley in its pre-Silicon Valley period between 1880 and 1940 when it was a predominately orchard fruits and berry farming community of Asian Americans, chiefly of Japanese ancestry. Another Santa Clara Valley-based book, Curt Fukuda and Ralph M. Pearce's San Jose Japantown, is a community collaboration that examines the history, society, and culture of the full sweep of San Jose's Japanese American community experience from 1890 to 2010. Linda L. Ivey and Kevin W. Kaatz's Citizen Internees looks at the San Mateo County Japanese American community of Redwood City, depicting how a trusted Caucasian banker, Elmer Moorish, protected the properties of Nikkei flower growers in *the so-called "Chrysanthemum Center of the World" during their WWII incarceration. In* Historic Wintersburg in Huntington Beach, *Mary F. Urashima, a historic preservationist, details the ambitious community effort she spearheaded in Southern California's Orange County to preserve for posterity the Japanese American agricultural village of Wintersburg from its origination in 1887 to its 1957 annexation by Huntington Beach. Turning their concern away from the West Coast to the American heartland region, Sook Wilkinson and Victor Jew's edited anthology,* Asian Americans in Michigan, *tackles the topic of Asian American community-building in the Wolverine State, particularly Detroit's Tri-County Area, with due attention paid to the special experience of Japanese Americans (among many other Asian-ancestry populations). Ellen D. Woo's* The Color of Success *and Kristin Ann Hass's* Sacrificing Soldiers on the National Mall *are both critical with respect to the role played by the Japanese American Citizens League in branding the Japanese American community's public image, historically and in the present, with that of being the model minority, on the one hand, and enshrining martial patriotism, on the other hand. As for Yasuko Takezawa and Gary Y. Okihiro's edited compendium of essays* Trans-Pacific Japanese American Studies, *it embraces selections by Japanese Americanists in both the U.S. and Japan that, variously, complicate and complexify the standard representation of the Japanese American community by riveting not upon the experience of* Issei *and* Nisei *men, but instead upon that of post-WWII immigrants* (Shin Issei), *Americans of Japanese ancestry dwelling in areas of the U.S. other than Hawai`i and the Pacific Coast states,* Sansei *women, Korean women in San Francisco's Japantown, and Okinawan immigrant women in the San Francisco Bay Area. Similarly, Lane Ryo Hirabayashi's edited special issue of the journal* PAN-JAPAN, *released under the title of* Conjecturing Communities, *includes six pieces that, in the words of Hirabayashi, focus "on groups that may, or may very well not, become part of the larger Japanese American community in the twenty-first century":* Okinawan Americans; Shin Issei; *overseas Koreans born/raised in Japan and now living in the U.S.; Peruvian Japanese residing in California; Japanese American members of LGBTQ populations; and post-WWII mixed race individuals who came to the U.S. as adoptees.*

CLAIMING THE ORIENTAL GATEWAY: Prewar Seattle and Japanese America
By Shelley Sang-Hee Lee (Philadelphia: Temple University Press, 2012, 272 pp., $29.95, paperback)

Published in the January 1, 2014 edition of the *Nichi Bei Weekly*.

During the first two decades of the twentieth century, Seattle was the West Coast's most populated Japanese American city. However, in the subsequent years prior to World War II, both Japanese San Francisco and Japanese Los Angeles not only surpassed the then-nicknamed Queen City in numbers, but also overshadowed it in geographical, commercial, and cultural importance. This situation remains intact today. Still, it could plausibly be argued that in terms of the historical representation in published books of these three urbanized racial-ethnic communities, Japanese Seattle has fared better or at least comparably with its San Francisco and Los Angeles counterparts.

In support of this contention, I would cite such older Seattle-based classics as S. Frank Miyamoto's sociological community study, *Social Solidarity among the Japanese in Seattle* (1939); Monica Sone's autobiographical memoir, *Nisei Daughter* (1953); John Okada's novel, *No-No Boy* (1957)—works which the University of Washington Press reprised, respectively, in 1984, 1979, and 1979—and Kazuo Ito's compendium of Pacific Northwest personal narratives, *Issei: A History of Japanese Immigrants in North America* (1973).

Of more recent studies of note I would offer the following: Sylvia Yanagisako's cultural history, *Transforming the Past: Tradition and Kinship among Japanese Americans* (1985); Yasuko Takezawa's ethnographic history, *Breaking the Silence: Redress and Japanese American Ethnicity* (1995); Quintard Taylor's interracial community exploration, *The Forging of a Black Community: Seattle's Central District from 1870 through the Civil Rights Era* (1994); David Takami's historical portrait, *Divided Destiny: A History of Japanese Americans in Seattle* (1999); Robert

Shimabukuro's social movement appraisal, *Born in Seattle: The Campaign for Japanese American Redress* (2001); Gail Dubrow and Donna Graves's heritage-preservation survey, *Sento at Sixth and Main: Preserving Landmarks of Japanese Heritage* (2002); Stephen Fugita and Marilyn Fernandez's community impact analysis, *Altered Lives, Enduring Community: Japanese Americans Remember Their World War II Incarceration* (2004); Louis Fiset's camp-and-community-based inquiry, *Camp Harmony: Japanese American Internment and the Puyallup Assembly Center* (2009), and Jamie Ford's interethnic novel, *Hotel on the Corner of Bitter and Sweet* (2009).

The remarkably well researched, intelligently conceptualized, masterfully organized, and beautifully written book under review by Shelley Sang-Hee Lee, *Claiming the Oriental Gateway: Prewar Seattle and Japanese America*, considerably enriches and enlarges this laudable intellectual legacy pertaining to the Japanese Seattle experience. It does so primarily as a result of the author viewing that geographic and demographic local phenomenon through the dual lenses of cosmopolitanism and globalism. Thus, while the temporal focus of Lee's tome is the pre-World War II *Nikkei* past of Seattle, that period is interpreted by her through two tightly interwoven analytical concepts now favored by many present-day historians. That such is the case can be readily appreciated by reference to the content and contentions of the book's five core chapters.

In "Multiethnic Seattle," Lee employs a "Pacific world" perspective to showcase how Seattle, like some other West Coast cities "located within global networks of people and capital contributed ... [both] to ... the growth of a diverse population ... [and] the ideological and imaginative meanings applied to urban space and the people making claims to it." Accordingly, Lee first establishes that between the 1870s and the 1930s, there emerged a metropolitan pocket centered on Jackson Street (the part of the city south of the downtown district) that became home to most of the city's nonwhite residents and other ethnic minorities, including a burgeoning Japantown. She then argues that although this area was regarded as a skid row "ghetto" by most white Seattleites, who made it the butt of jokes, this settlement space's population, albeit increasingly dominated by *Nikkei*, was in fact radically heterogeneous. Moreover, its international medley of residents—Asians, Hispanics, Blacks—countered the denigration of outsiders by emphasizing the neighborhood's attractions and strengths (most notably its easygoing social interactions and cosmopolitanism) and muting its alleged problems and shortcomings.

In the following four core chapters, Lee builds upon how Japan and, more specifically, Japanese Seattleites (the city's largest nonwhite group) were "crucial in Seattle's bid for urban distinction as a cosmopolitan location and the nation's 'gateway to the Orient'." Consonant with this objective, in the core chapter titled "Making Seattle 'Cosmopolitan," Lee highlights two Seattle-based events, the 1909 Alaska-Yukon-Pacific Exposition and the 1934-1942 International Potlatch festivals. These commemorations simultaneously dramatized the shared interests of Japan and the United States in a coalescing Pacific world and spotlighted the vital role that Japanese Americans in Seattle could play in coming years through brokering the cosmopolitan international and intercultural relationship between these two steeply ascending national powers.

As for the succeeding core chapter, "Making Local Images for International Eyes," it focuses upon the 1924-29 historical experience of the renowned Seattle Camera Club. The cosmopolitan achievement of this nearly exclusive Japanese immigrant organization of pictorialists, or art photographers, was to foster its twenty-five to fifty locally anchored members crossing over geographical and social boundaries to exhibit their artistic images of Seattle as a developing world city at national and international exhibitions. This activity, in turn, permitted these creative artists to transcend constraints circumscribing the otherwise rather parochial lives of Seattle's *Nikkei* community.

In the final two core chapters ("'Problems of the Pacific' in 'the Great Crucible of America'" and "'That Splendid Medium of Free Play'") Lee rivets her attention on how, respectively, Seattle's public schools and organized sports acted as catalysts of cosmopolitanism and internationalism for the city's Japanese Americans. The former did this through attendance at integrated schools (particularly secondary ones) with diverse multiethnic and multiracial student bodies, a curriculum that promoted better understanding of Pacific Rim concerns, and at least some administrators and teachers who devoted their time and energy to advance a brand of Americanism that bridged the East-West span confronting their pupils. As for sports, they not only strengthened ties among Japanese Americans in Seattle, but also "linked Japanese communities throughout the Northwest, along the West Coast, and on both sides of the Pacific." In addition, athletic competition in a great variety of sports also provided ample occasions for social interaction across ethnic lines, and sometimes led to a constructive reconceptualization of the boundaries between ethnic communities.

Of course, it must be noted that Lee is acutely aware that there were definite limits to and severe constraints upon the tenuous globalism and cosmopolitanism allowing those within the pre-World War II Seattle Japanese American community to stand out among and even somewhat apart from their West Coast and Hawai`i counterparts. She makes this point abundantly clear in her pervasive reminders to readers that Japanese Seattleites, like *Nikkei* elsewhere, not only experienced discrimination through civil rights, property, political, and economic restrictions, but also were victimized by chauvinistic harassment and suffered social marginalization as racialized "others." Moreover, as Lee perceptively and eloquently and sadly reflects at the opening of her final chapter titled "The Eve of War," the Pacific Rim internationalism that combined Americanism and cosmopolitanism was no longer tenable as soon as the United States declared war on Japan. And as the Pacific world to which Seattle had long hitched its future was ripped asunder, the exigencies of wartime patriotism also swept away the conception of the city as a "gateway to the Orient."

A REBEL'S OUTCRY: Biography of Issei Civil Rights Leader Sei Fujii (1882-1954)
By Kenichi Sato (Los Angeles: Little Tokyo Historical Society, 2021, 231 pp., $60, hardcover)

Published in the July 21, 2022 edition of the *Nichi Bei Weekly.*

Prior to reading this book, my knowledge about prominent *Issei* lawyer/journalist Sei Fujii derived from two starkly contrasting experiences. The first of these was co-authoring with Ronald Larson a forthcoming published essay entitled "DOHO: The Japanese American 'Communist' Press, 1937-1942." The second was my viewing of the 30-minute award-winning 2012 film *Lil Tokyo Reporter* directed by Jeffrey Chin (the co-producer with Fumiko Carole Fujita of *A Rebel's Outcry*) at the 2016 Nichi Bei Film Showcase. Whereas *Doho* roundly denounced Fujii for packing the pages of his *Kashu Mainichi* (Japan-California Daily News) newspaper with pro-Japan, anti-democratic "propaganda" glorifying Japanese military victories in the Sino-Japanese War and suppressing Japanese atrocity stories like the Rape of Nanking, Chin's film depicts Sei Fujii as a courageous and tireless reformer of the quality of community life in Los Angeles's Little Tokyo who, in addition, greatly expanded the civil rights of all Americans of Japanese ancestry.

A Rebel's Outcry is silent on the chauvinistic charges leveled by *Doho* against Sei Fujii. Instead, in this book he is depicted as someone who characteristically assessed matters from an even-handed rational perspective and as an influential person who was simultaneously proud of being both Japanese and American. In this latter vein, he urged American-born generations of Japanese descent to wholeheartedly honor their ancestry as well as their nationality.

The centerpiece of *A Rebel's Outcry* is the comparatively short but invaluable biography of Sei Fujii written in Japanese by onetime *Kashu Mainichi* journalist Kenichi Sato. It was originally published in 1983 under a Japanese title that, as rendered in English, is *Los Angeles Rebellious Dance*. However, for present purposes in *A Rebel's Outcry*, this entire manuscript has been painstakingly translated into English by Saeko Higa Dickinson. Sato devotes his major attention to several of the many signal accomplishments of Sei Fujii. The first was Fujii's pivotal role in the 1929 construction in Los Angeles of the Japanese Hospital, which made possible quality health care for the city's *Nikkei* population. The second was his 1931 founding of the *Kashu Mainichi* newspaper, which ostensibly furnished its readers with "a truly conscientious newspaper ... concerned with ethics and morals." The third was his two-tiered campaign against the California Alien Land Law, initially through the publication of a brief 1924 book in Japanese that provided pre-World War II *Issei* farmers with loopholes that would allow them to operate an agricultural business, and later through his resourceful legal efforts to have that shameful law overturned in 1952 for having "violated the US Constitution and the Equal Protection Clause of the California Constitution."

Elegantly designed by Amy Inouye, attractively illustrated by Takashi Uchida, and expertly edited by Naomi Hirahara, the oversized volume under review is further enriched by a plenitude of well-chosen historical photographs and edifying documentary items. The quality of the writing throughout the book is exceptional. Readers are also treated to eight highly useful appendixes, most of which relate to aspects of the different iterations of alien land laws, along with richly developed endnotes, a section on relevant resources categorized by genres, and a comprehensive index.

Far more than the rather melodramatic *Lil Tokyo Reporter* film that preceded its creation, *A Rebel's Outcry* is deserving of accolades. The result of ten years of research by the Little Tokyo Historical Society, its publication is still another feather in the cap of this resplendent grassroots organization.

TERMINAL ISLAND: Lost Communities of Los Angeles Harbor
By Naomi Hirahara and Geraldine Knatz (Santa Monica, CA: Angel City Press, 2014, 288 pp., $35.00, paperback)

Published in the January 1, 2017 edition of the *Nichi Bei Weekly*.

As an oral historian I have always been addicted to reading obituaries, especially those relating to the World War II Japanese American experience. For example, a recent transfixing obituary for me was that devoted to ninety-seven-year-old Kazuko Kuwabara (1918-2016) in the *Los Angeles Times* of December 7, 2016.

There were two reasons for my interest in this particular death notice. First, it directly pertained to the book under review here, since Kuwabara was a *Kibei-Nisei* born in Los Angeles, who after being schooled in Wakayama, Japan, returned to Southern California to live out the pre-WWII years with her *Kibei-Nisei* husband Masaaki Kuwabara (1913-1993) and their children on Terminal Island, located off the Pacific Coast from the metropolitan area of Long Beach. Secondly, this obituary touched upon my primary historical research interest, *Nikkei* resistance to oppression during their community's WWII social disaster: Masaaki Kuwabara was the lead defendant among 26 draft resisters at the Tule Lake Segregation Center who, in the July 1944 *United States v. Masaaki Kuwabara* case, challenged their incarceration and loss of rights as U.S. citizens and, in so doing, laid the groundwork for the sole WWII-era Japanese American draft resistance case to be dismissed out of court based on a due process violation of the U.S. Constitution. Although none of the Kuwabara family figure directly as personalities in *Terminal Island*, the book's main story, as David Ulin accurately noted in his April 22, 2015, *Los Angeles Times* review, "has to do with the Japanese fishing village that took root in the wake of the development of 'Fish Harbor' in the 1910s." Given the primary *Nikkei* readership of the *Nichi Bei Weekly*, it is this story that will command my attention in the commentary that follows.

Because of internal evidence in the volume, I suspect that of the two co-authors, Geraldine Knatz and Naomi Hirahara, it was Hirahara who assumed primary responsibility for that portion of the book, chapters four to seven, relating the pre-World War II Japanese American experience on Terminal Island. After all, in addition to being a prize-winning author of popular fictional works, Hirahara is also a former editor of the Los Angeles-based *Rafu Shimpo* (the largest extant Japanese American daily newspaper) and a celebrated social historian responsible for a succession of *Nikkei*-themed works. Moreover, having parents raised in Japan, possessing fluency in English and Japanese, and benefitting from an education in international relations, she is ideally suited to understanding and interpreting the history and socio-culture of a transnational Japanese American fishing community like that of Terminal Island, whose 2,000-3,000 inhabitants derived from Japan's southern coastal prefecture of Wakayama (including many hailing from a network of its villages with a fishing tradition).

To her credit Hirahara steers her absorbing historical narrative of Japanese Terminal Island away from two stereotypical representations, which she tersely summarizes for reader consumption. On the one hand, as characterized by short-term mainland visitors, it was "a ghetto," an ethnic enclave consisting of "lines of nondescript housing with negligible yards and a pungent scent of fish and salt." On the other hand, as depicted from a long-time resident's perspective, it was "a fascinating, fantastic dreamland," a veritable "Enchanted Island."

What Hirahara alternatively does—via a judicious combination of sparkling prose, remarkable photographs, and exacting maps—is to immerse readers within the daily lives of the island's *Nikkei* villagers. We vicariously experience living in the leased tight quarters of some 330 nearly identical cannery-owned two-bedroom wood-framed houses, with minute yards, crowded together in a five-square-block area and divided by fish- and place-named streets; conducting business and socializing on the single commercial artery of Tuna Street; men fishing for sardines and albacore on small jig boats and large purse seiners on the open and often dangerous sea, and women, working diligently on demand in the canneries, along with white and Mexican women and Filipino men; celebrating New Year's Day, *mochitsuki*, by pounding rice for rice cakes and taking part in a rotating neighborhood party; being a participant and/or spectator in a variety of Japanese and American sports; worshipping in the *Shinto*,

Baptist, and Buddhist faiths; attending (if younger children) the island's grammar school, and (if older) sailing on ferryboats across the channel to attend mainland junior and senior high schools; and interacting, whether as youth or adults, with those of the island's non-Japanese ethnic groups.

After settling readers into the rhythm of "normal" Terminal Island life for two chapters, in her final chapter and epilogue, Hirahara plunges us into the tragic and traumatic vortex of events that followed Japan's December 7, 1941, bombing of the Pearl Harbor naval base in Hawai`i. Accordingly, we now experience the FBI raids into *Nikkei* homes; the arrest of the community's *Issei* leadership; the shuttering and padlocking of the Tuna Street stores and cafes; the descending of the armed military onto the island; the imposition of an enforced blackout; the barring of Japanese aliens from going out to sea "under any conditions"; the conversion of the island into an interrogation center; the removal of selected alien men to the Tuna Canyon Detention Center in Los Angeles, and thereafter to internment centers at Missoula, Montana, and Bismarck, North Dakota; the involuntary mass eviction of the entire Japanese American population from the island and, later, their confinement into a gulag of government concentration camps, but mostly in three inmate blocks at the Manzanar detention center in eastern California; the U.S. Navy's takeover of much of the island; and the bulldozing of the villagers' houses and grammar school, "as if they had never existed."

Although the pernicious operation of racism brought a close to the history of Terminal Island's Japanese American community, rendering it literally "terminal," it continues to exist palpably in the memories of those families who once regarded it as their hometown. It also functions as an instructive symbolic monument to the high price too often exacted from Americans when their government permits its preoccupation with security to overwhelm its concern for human and civil rights. Certainly one former Terminal Island *Nikkei*, Masaaki Kuwabara, was prompted by both his experience at Terminal Island and Tule Lake when he utilized his courageous draft resistance action in July 1944 to challenge unbridled security, an action which led presiding U.S. District Court Judge Louis Goodman to declare, "It is shocking to the conscience that an American citizen be confined on the ground of disloyalty, and then, while so under duress and restraint, be compelled to serve in the armed forces, or be prosecuted for not yielding to such a compulsion."

GARDEN OF THE WORLD: Asian Immigrants and the Making of Agriculture in California's Santa Clara Valley
By Cecilia M. Tsu (New York: Oxford University Press, 2013, 300 pp., $29.95, paperback)

Published in the July 24, 2014 edition of the *Nichi Bei Weekly*.

As Cecilia Tsu tells readers in her cogent introduction, its underlying purpose is "recovering the intertwined history of the Santa Clara Valley [in California] when it was known as the Garden of the World [1880-1940] along with the history of the Asian immigrants [Chinese, Japanese, Filipino] who farmed its famed crops [primarily orchard fruits and berries]." Clearly, and thankfully, Tsu's scholarship for her first book did not materialize within a socio-cultural vacuum; rather, it was deeply rooted in and nurtured by her personal, family, and community experience.

When in the 1980s Tsu and her Asian American family moved to the Santa Clara Valley, there existed only vestiges of the Valley's fabled agricultural past. What drew her family to this then-suburbanizing area, along with many others of Asian ancestry, was the mushrooming of the Santa Clara Valley into a high-tech mecca that became styled as Silicon Valley and rapidly gained international acclaim. As a child, Tsu assumed the area's Asians to be newcomers, with no former ties either to the region or to agriculture, who typically found employment with firms like Hewlett-Packard, Intel, and IBM. Thus, confesses Tsu, "I was surprised to discover that ... another group of Asian Americans had laid claim to the region as farmers and farm laborers long before the arrival of Asian computer engineers and dot-com entrepreneurs."

About when Cecilia Tsu was making her "discovery," a then upcoming historian, Gary Okihiro, was on the Santa Clara University faculty. Four years after co-authoring the 1985 book *Japanese Legacy: Farming and Community Life in California's Santa Clara Valley*, Okihiro built upon this achievement with the article "Fallow Field: The Rural Dimension of Asian American Studies." In it he argued that in its preoccupation with transnational, urban, and theoretical pursuits, Asian American Studies scholars had left virtually uncultivated the rural Asian American experience.

Responding to Okihiro's challenge, Tsu goes beyond previous Asian American rural historians by not making her study an ethnic-specific one. While most of her book necessarily focuses on Japanese Americans (the Santa Clara Valley's dominant Asian group), she both links and compares their variegated agricultural experiences with those of the Chinese American farmers who largely preceded them and the Filipino American farmers who mostly followed in their wake. In the process, she assesses the respective agricultural role of these groups against their stereotypical representation, the white family farm ideal, and white racism, while paying close attention to the inter-ethnic and intra-ethnic divisions instigated by race, gender, and national identity dynamics.

Tsu's epilogue carries the Asian American story in the Valley from 1940 to the present. Capitalizing on an earlier observation—that while the farms and orchards have long since disappeared from the Valley, "the complex of race relations remains rooted in its soil"—Tsu closes her study by asserting that both the rise of Silicon Valley and its fruit capital predecessor "depended largely on racial segmentation in the labor force and racial and gender ideology that established hierarchies and barriers to the advancement of nonwhites." I hope that she is here floating a promissory note that a future book of hers will explore the Silicon Valley iteration of the Santa Clara Valley via its Asian American workforce. If it is as well conceived, researched, and written as *Garden of the World*, its readers will be richly rewarded.

SAN JOSE JAPANTOWN: A Journey
By Curt Fukuda and Ralph M. Pearce (San Jose, CA: Japanese
American Museum of San Jose, 2014, 470 pp., $65.25, hardcover)

Published in the July 23, 2015 edition of the *Nichi Bei Weekly*.

While perusing this beautiful and bountiful 470-page tome affording its very lucky readers a temporal, spatial, and sociocultural journey of discovery relative to San Jose's Japantown, I reflected back upon my personal journey regarding this historic place. It was secured by my reading of editor Stephen Misawa's *Beginnings: Japanese Americans in San Jose* (1981) and Timothy J. Lukes and Gary Y. Okihiro's *Japanese Legacy: Farming and Community Life in California's Santa Clara Valley* (1985). It was then humanized by my oral history fieldwork with (1) *Kibei* Harry Ueno, a major dissenter in the Manzanar Revolt of December 5-6, 1942; (2) *Kibei* Yuriko Amemiya Kikuchi, celebrated dancer and choreographer with the Martha Graham Dance Company; (3) *Nisei* Eiichi Sakauye, visionary community leader and founding member of the Loyalty League of San Jose, a precursor to the Japanese American Citizens League; (4) the eleven mostly *Nisei* interviewees and eight primarily *Sansei* interviewees for the San Jose study site in the *REgenerations Oral History Project: Rebuilding Japanese American Families, Communities, and Civil Rights in the Resettlement Era* (1997-2000); and (5) Roy and PJ Hirabayashi, the *Sansei* moving spirits of San Jose Taiko, for the Japanese American National Museum-sponsored *Big Drum: Taiko in the United States* project (2005-2006). Finally, my journey was made palpable by my periodic visits to San Jose Japantown and participant-observation in its vibrant civic, commercial, cultural, and religious life.

An altogether striking achievement of community collaboration, the book under review is co-authored by Curt Fukuda and Ralph M. Pearce, with a huge helping hand from the other three members of its cohesive production team (Jim Nagareda, project lead; Janice Oda, designer; and June Hayashi, editor). How this stalwart team congealed and the book assumed its ultimate form represent extraordinary journeys of their own sort, and both of these are admirably detailed in *San Jose Japantown*. Further information on these journeys is available via the excellent YouTube video *MEET the AUTHORS: San Jose Japantown: A Journey* (https://www.youtube.com/watch?v=9DDbzjGbnfc).

As for the overarching journey of San Jose's Japantown, it is organized into fourteen chapters, eight of which are appropriately themed and chronologically sliced to encompass the full sweep of the district's growth and development from 1890 to 2010, with the remaining six given over to depicting Japantown's pre-history, its pre–World War II pioneers, its postwar movers and shakers, its sports scene, its religious institutions, and its foodways. All of these elegantly composed and precisely edited chapters are infused with well-chosen stories that are both meaningful and memorable, and these tales are resourcefully fitted into a resplendent design that adroitly accommodates text with a plenitude of captioned photographs, other illustrative items, and sporadic informational sidebars.

Two aspects of this exemplary book that I found both illuminating and moving were the authors' cosmopolitanism and their consciousness of standing on the shoulders of giants. One manifestation of the first quality is the democratic and just attention accorded those of non-Japanese ancestry—people of Chinese, Filipino, and African descent—living and working within the Japantown community. A case in point of the second quality is the dignified homage paid to the late Helen Mineta, whose unfinished history book written for the 1990 Japantown Centennial is not merely repeatedly noted by Fukuda and Pearce, but also judiciously drawn upon by them for excerpts to supplement and enhance their narrative.

In reading *San Jose Japantown* my own personal journey of discovery for this site was expanded and embellished. I found out, for example, that Yuriko Amemiya Kikuchi's mother, Chiyo Amemiya, was a midwife; that Yuriko taught dance (*buyo*) to the Japantown *Nisei* girls; and that the Amemiya home (and midwifery) on North Sixth Street is still standing today. I also discovered that Gary Okihiro, after the publication of his co-authored *Japanese Legacy*, organized a meeting of local institutional representatives and informed them of a need for an organization to preserve San Jose *Nikkei* history, an action leading to the founding of the Japanese American Resource Center by Eiichi Sakauye and others, which in turn morphed into the Japanese American Museum of San Jose, the present book's publisher. I furthermore became aware that the postwar resettlement years were the "peak years of Japantown," and that notwithstanding the migration of the *Nikkei* population to the suburbs, "Japantown was still the center for the Japanese American community." Additionally, I was alerted to the vital role played by the *Sansei* in the 1970-80s reawakening of and rejuvenation of Japantown and Japanese culture. In this connection, I was informed that Roy Hirabayashi, who as a San Jose State student was aligned with Asians for Community Action and helped start Asian American Studies, would afterwards with his wife PJ Hirabayashi (whose 1977 urban studies master's thesis at San Jose State was "the first serious study of San Jose Japantown") fashion San Jose Taiko into a dynamic protean marker of identity for democracy, social justice, civil and human rights, Asian American and *Nikkei* culture, and San Jose Japantown.

I am certain that many other readers will find within the pages of *San Jose Japantown: A Journey* their own reasons for celebration.

CITIZEN INTERNEES: A Second Look at Race and Citizenship in Japanese American Internment Camps
By Linda L. Ivey and Kevin W. Kaatz (Santa Barbara, CA: Praeger, 2017, 277 pp., $48.00, hardcover)

Published in the July 19, 2018 edition of the *Nichi Bei Weekly*.

Each spring semester my wife Debra Gold Hansen, a professor in the online Information School at San José State University, team-teaches a course entitled "History of the Book." One class assignment has students produce a historical paper about a local library of their choice. Since many of the students are from West Coast areas, often these papers deal with libraries serving communities whose Japanese American residents were uprooted and incarcerated during World War II. Had one of my wife's past students opted to focus on the Redwood City Public Library, this person likely would have devoted some space to discussing its Karl Vollmayer Local History Room, including a collection of letters and other documents within it known as the Moorish Collection. Named after Elmer Morrish (1886-1957), a Redwood City banker, this archive consists of a back-and-forth correspondence between Morrish and the Redwood City *Nikkei* camp inmates relative to their wartime finances and property management that resourcefully contextualizes an important and tragic chapter of American history. It is the primary (and sometimes quite personal) documents in the Morrish Collection that served Linda Ivey and Kevin Kaatz, historians at California State University, East Bay, as their principal research data for *Citizen Internees*.

Located on the San Francisco Peninsula in northern California's Bay Area, between the cities of San José and San Francisco, Redwood City is the county seat of San Mateo County. The fortuitous combination of a burgeoning immigrant Japanese/Japanese American population, a temperate climate (cool morning breezes and fog with afternoon warmth and sunshine), flat land, fertile soil, and a comparatively tolerant mainstream population proved ideal for chrysanthemum cultivation in the early twentieth century. This situation eventually led to mid-1920s Redwood City—with its landscape profusely dotted with Japanese flower growers and greenhouses sited mainly on five-acre parcels and a crop generating an annual income of $7 million—to being christened by its Chamber of Commerce as the "Chrysanthemum Center of the World." This story, augmented by the booming floriculture period enjoyed (after the 1929 economic crash) by *Nikkei* in the 1930s, has been well documented—in the 1994

PBS documentary film *Chrysanthemums and Salt* by Dianne Fukami; a 2004 San José State University history master's thesis by Jagruti Patel entitled "Japanese Americans in Redwood City: A Local History;" and the 2017 Japanese American Museum of San Jose presentation "The Proudest of All Flowers: Chrysanthemum Cultivation, Japanese American Community & Suburban Boosterism in Redwood City, California, 1906-1942" by Stanford University doctoral student Paul Nauert.

As stated by Ivey and Kaatz in their opening chapter, their book is not a definitive treatment of the Japanese American World War II social catastrophe, but "rather it is an invitation to explore these letters [in the Moorish Collection] and consider the ways in which people functioned as citizens and legal residents within a state of incarceration." What is meant by this statement is spelled out in the remainder of the book. Notwithstanding that most Redwood City *Nikkei* were essentially stripped of their right to earn a living while incarcerated during the war at the Tanforan Assembly Center in the Bay Area and the Topaz Relocation Center in Utah, they were still expected, as were inmates in other such camps, to exercise to some degree their citizen obligations. These included paying their property taxes as well as federal and state income taxes, which covered earnings coming from outside the camps and the meager sums paid for their work within camp, and to do so promptly in order to avoid being assessed late fees.

The heart of *Citizen Internees* is the steady stream of mailings, numbering some 2,000, transacted between Morrish and the Redwood City inmates, which are excerpted throughout the first half of the book and selectively reproduced in full in the book's closing half. These letters, businesslike but also cordial and sometimes poignant, make it evident that Moorish protected the properties of the imprisoned population, liquidated their holdings and personal possessions with dispatch and distributed the proceeds equitably, oversaw the propriety of the designated wartime tenants' behavior via periodic site visitations, and also collected rents from delinquent tenants as needed and secured new tenants. Moreover, Moorish wrote reference letters and provided testimonies that helped Redwood City incarcerees to leave camp for the purposes of work, education, or military service. When the camps were closing, Moorish stepped in to facilitate his clients-cum-neighbors having as smooth a return as possible under the circumstances to their Redwood City homes and gardens.

A very affecting section of this book is its epilogue, which provides a short history of Elmer Moorish. It details that in 1956, he was honored by the Redwood City Chamber of Commerce naming him as the recipient of its "Man of the Year" award. Although his wartime role vis-à-vis Japanese Americans was not mentioned in this connection, the following year that community pooled their resources and sent Moorish on a round-the-world cruise, including a tour of Japan. A few months later, he passed away at age seventy-one. Arguably, his finest legacy, as *Citizen Internees* exemplifies, is the Moorish Collection, a precious gift that keeps on giving. Is there a similarly bountiful archive in your local library? If so, access it and discover what stories abound in it so that you can learn from them and perhaps later share them with others in the spirit of Linda Ivey and Kevin Kaatz.

HISTORIC WINTERSBURG IN HUNTINGTON BEACH
By Mary F. Adams Urashima (Charleston, SC: The History Press, 2014, 204 pp., $19.95, paperback)

Published in the July 24, 2014 edition of the *Nichi Bei Weekly*.

The most fitting way I can think of to begin this review of Mary Adams Urashima's *Historic Wintersburg in Huntington Beach* is to appropriate and slightly modify what the great American poet Walt Whitman said in relation to his most notable poetic volume, *Leaves of Grass* (1855): "Whoever touches this book touches a [wo]man." A resident of Orange County's Huntington Beach and a passionate advocate of historic preservation, the perfervid desire of Urashima to preserve significant historical structures and sites derives not from her being a fusty antiquarian, but rather from her envisioning preservation as a progressive means to stimulate greater appreciation of America's diverse history and cultures.

This cosmopolitan goal championed by Urashima, a California Association of Human Relations Civil Rights Leadership Award recipient, is personified in her book's poignant dedication: "For my son, Keane Patrick Yoshio Urashima, in whose eyes I see the future." In Orange County, that future promises to be one in which Asian Americans figure prominently, since 600,000 of the county's present total of three million people are of Asian ancestry, placing the pan-Asian population of Orange County ahead of every other U.S. county save those of Los Angeles and Santa Clara. This demographic fact positions Orange County for a strategic leadership role in facilitating the nationwide initiative issued in 2013 by the Secretary of the Interior and the National Park Service to undertake an Asian American Pacific Island Theme Study tasked with investigating the stories, places, and people of Asian American and Pacific Island heritage.

At the heart of Urashima's bountiful book is her engagingly composed, resourcefully documented, and marvelously illustrated story of a 4½-acre parcel of land situated within the onetime agricultural village of Wintersburg, which flourished from the late 1800s until annexation in 1957 by suburbanizing Huntington Beach. It is Orange County's only known pre-Alien Land Law of 1913 property still extant. Owned by the pioneering Japanese American Furuta family, this site during the 1908-47 interval became populated by a complex of six historic structures that, in 2014, are still intact: (1) the 1910 Wintersburg Japanese Presbyterian Mission (Orange County's oldest *Nikkei* church, it was founded in 1904); (2) the 1910 manse, home to Orange County's first ordained clergy of any denomination; (3) the 1912 home of Charles Mitsuji and Yukiko Yajima Furuta; (4) the 1908-12 Furuta barn, Huntington Beach's last pioneer heritage barn; (5) the 1934 Depression-era Wintersburg Japanese Presbyterian

Church; and (6) the 1947 post-WWII home of Raymond and Martha Furuta.

This piece of property, which includes remnants of a goldfish and flower farm, topped the list of the dwindling few remaining *Nikkei* sites of importance compiled in 1986 by the Japanese American Council (JAC) of the Historical and Cultural Foundation of Orange County. Capitalizing on the JAC-sponsored oral history interviews with four pioneering *Issei* (Japanese/English) and one *Nisei* (English only) revolving largely around the historic Wintersburg site, Urashima fashions a compelling argument to support the contention by historians (including myself) that this site, in tandem with a cluster of nearby commercial and public-use facilities, should properly be considered the cradle of Orange County's loosely aggregated—the county has never had a Japantown—Japanese American community.

However, in 2011, Urashima and others (in and out of Huntington Beach and the Japanese American community) became alarmed when the City of Huntington Beach, which in 1996 had listed the "Furuta House" and "Japanese Church" as local landmarks in its Historic Resources Cultural Element of the City's General Plan, now issued an ominous notice. It was for an environmental impact report on behalf of the historic site's then owner, Rainbow Environmental Services (a waste transfer company, a.k.a. Rainbow Disposal), which proposed a zone change from residential to industrial/commercial with an application for demolition of all site structures. At that point, Urashima mobilized a community-wide effort, which she has since chaired, to preserve "Historic Wintersburg." She also initiated an ambitious, highly imaginative, and exceedingly far-reaching "Historic Wintersburg" blog. Her book, which is rooted in but does not replicate this blog, should be seen therefore not as just another local history volume, but instead as the creation of a person of enlarged consciousness and conscience who has employed history as a social and moral force.

On November 4, 2013, the Huntington Beach City Council, by a split vote, duly rezoned the Historic Wintersburg property and approved the demolition of all six of its historic structures. The City Council did give the Historic Wintersburg Preservation Task Force eighteen months (until mid-2015) to save this historic site. On June 23, 2014, the National Trust for Historic Preservation (NTHP) named Historic Wintersburg to its 2014 list of "America's Eleven Most Endangered Historic Places." It is the first historic place in development-oriented Orange County so designated in the twenty-seven-year history of the NTHP list. Preservation of Historic Wintersburg remains a long shot, but that contingency assuredly will not deter Mary F. Adams Urashima from trying to salvage this priceless historical and cultural site. Those of you who read her absorbing blog and/or book will, I think, fathom why Historic Wintersburg is worth saving and perhaps even elect to assist in its preservation for posterity.

ASIAN AMERICANS IN MICHIGAN: Voices from the Midwest Edited by Sook Wilkinson and Victor Jew (Detroit: Wayne State University Press, 2015, 370 pp., $34.95, paperback)

Published in the July 20, 2017 edition of the *Nichi Bei Weekly*.

In 2009 I published an article about Japanese Americans in the Interior West, a field earlier pioneered by two Arizona State University doctoral students, Eric Walz and Andrew Russell. So, I was naturally pleased when the *Nichi Bei Weekly* invited me to review the present book. It, in effect, shifts the venue of the same general topic east to the Midwestern state of Michigan (particularly Detroit's Tri-County area: Wayne, Oakland, and Macomb counties) and broadens its concern from Japanese Americans to Asian Americans. The first book to tackle this subject, "Asian Americans in Michigan," as observed elsewhere by one of its forty-one contributors, Frances Kai-Hwa Wang, "takes a closer look at Asian Americans in the heartland, where because of small numbers, the community's experience is vastly different from that on the coasts, and where cross-cultural multiethnic and multiracial coalitions and community groups have always been a reality."

The intent of this volume is manifestly pan-ethnic, focusing as it does on Michigan's fastest growing racial/ethnic community, which between 2000 and 2010 increased 39 percent to total 289,607 people in nineteen different Asian-derived communities. However, because of the length and breadth of *Asian Americans in Michigan*, the comparative brevity of this review, and its targeted *Nikkei* readership, I will restrict my attention here to those portions of the book devoted to the Japanese American experience in Michigan.

Fortunately, the *Nikkei* story is addressed in three of the book's five parts. In Part One ("Taking Soundings of Asian America in Michigan"), co-editor Victor Jew, an Asian Americanist at the University of Wisconsin-Madison, emphasizes the World War II role of the War Relocation Authority in promoting resettlement among its ten-camp incarcerated *Nikkei* population in Michigan. In addition to persuading onetime West Coast farmers to go to Michigan via a pamphlet entitled "Farming in Michigan," which cited the state's leadership in dry beans, potatoes, sour cherries, celery, and apples, the WRA urged other *Nikkei* to resettle in metropolitan areas such as Detroit (1,649) and Ann Arbor (534).

Within Part Two ("Legacy Keeping and Memory Keepers"), essays by two accomplished retired women, Toshiko Shimoura and Asai Shichi, rivet their attention on Japanese Michigan. In "The History of Nikkei in Detroit," California-born *Nisei* Shimoura, a World War II concentration camp survivor, surveys her subject through three disparate chronological periods: 1900 to 1924; 1944 to 1950; and 1970 to the present. During the first interval, she explains, the few *Issei* pioneers in Detroit were dispersed around the city, and hence neither formed organizations nor coalesced into a Japantown. The years between 1944 and 1950, however, were more consequential. Owing to the government-forced resettlement of wartime incarcerees, a trickle of *Nikkei* (mostly *Nisei*), including families, were drawn to Detroit by its abundance of industrial jobs. While a bona-fide Japantown never materialized, due to governmental discouragement of *Nikkei* clustering into "deleterious" group visibility, a variety of ethnic organizations did emerge, including the 1946 formation of the city's Japanese American Citizens League chapter. In the post-1970 era, says Shimoura, the waning of *Nikkei* immigrants to Detroit was supplanted by a surge of Japanese nationals with business interests, and this resulted for Japanese Americans in an enrichment of Japanese culture, traditions, and cuisine. As for the younger generations of *Nikkei*, on the other hand, it became increasingly customary to marry outside the ethnic group and to sacrifice in-group practices and priorities on the altar of Americanization.

With respect to Asai Shichi's contribution, "From Hammered-down Nail to Squeaky Cog," it pivots on the significance of the 1982 murder of Chinese American Vincent Chin by unemployed auto workers mistakenly believing him to be of Japanese ancestry, and the subsequent lenient sentences given to Chin's killers. As viewed by Japan-born Shichi—who came to the U.S. on a Fulbright Scholarship and studied at Columbia University and the University of California, Berkeley, before teaching at a variety of Michigan universities and serving on numerous boards of *Nikkei* organizations—the "Chin-bashing" progressively altered the *Nikkei* (and Asian American) community outlook in Detroit (and Michigan) from that of passivity in the face of oppression to active resistance to it. Shichi captures this transformed spirit in a dramatic scenario that unfolded at a 1992 public event: "Dr. Kaz Mayeda, a prominent second-generation Japanese American researcher at Wayne State University, got tough, reminding the audience that it was the tenth anniversary of Vincent Chin's murder. 'If we have to, we'll take up arms to prevent this sort of thing from happening again.'"

Part Four ("Life Journeys") provides the most abundant representation of *Nikkei* experience. Lynet Uttal, a University of Wisconsin-Madison professor of human development and family studies and former Asian American Studies Program director, titles her essay "Growing Up Hapa in Ann Arbor." Although her mother was of Japanese heritage and her father of Russian Jewish heritage, as a child Utall was viewed as Chinese by her elementary school classmates, who chased her around the playground with taunts of "Red China! Red China! Red China!" As she came of age, she received mixed messages from her mother, who told her and her siblings that "we were American, not Japanese." Yet, while encouraged to deny her race in public, at home she lived her ethnicity: being served Japanese food and instructed to be humble and hyperaware of others. For Utall, growing up in the Midwest amounted to being "a noticeable, racialized person, yet without any social or political history. Our group story was unknown."

Japan-born (1929) and raised in Japan, Kyo Takahashi, at age fourteen, volunteered for World War II service in the Imperial Japanese Naval Air Force. During the war he witnessed the destruction of Tokyo and his hometown of Yokohama, the burning of his family home, and the bombing of his military base. In 1952 he got work as an artist/designer for a Tokyo advertising agency. In 1963 Takahashi left Tokyo for Los Angeles and enrolled in the Art Center College of Design. He later relocated to New York to work for the J. Walter Thompson Company, then the world's largest advertising agency. Concentrating on the automobile industry, he became a highly successful car illustrator, which took him on business to Detroit. Eventually, Takahashi was offered a lucrative position in Detroit in 1984, which he was reluctant to accept because of Vincent Chin's tragic 1982 murder: "People in Detroit hate Japanese, don't they?" However, upon joining Detroit's Japanese American Citizens League chapter, Takahashi met the son of a JACL member involved as a lawyer in the Vincent Chin case. "If one good thing came out of that tragedy," reflects Takahashi, "it is that the entire Asian community pulled together."

Finally, biracial *Sansei* Dylan Sugiyama, an immigration attorney and former resident of Lansing, Michigan, where he worked as a civil rights representative with the Michigan Department of Civil Rights, exploits the usable past in "My Family's Experience of the Japanese American Internment Camps" to serve as a present and future touchstone. Although his family responded in the affirmative to the key two questions on the 1943 "loyalty oath" administered to the incarcerated *Nikkei* population, writes Sugiyama, some 8,000 chose to be sent to Japan, including many who later renounced their U.S. citizenship in disgust of their mistreatment by the U.S. government. He expresses pride in the actions of those *Nisei* inmates who resisted being drafted from behind barbed wire on constitutional grounds and were then shackled with federal prison sentences. Although some 30,000 Japanese American served with heroic distinction during World War II, mostly in segregated units, there were also, as Sugiyama points out, many other dissenters apart from the draft resisters, "thus refuting the common impression that Japanese Americans meekly and passively accepted their internment." For him, the significance of the "internment" did not end with World War II or even the Civil Liberties Act of 1988 with its governmental apology and reparation payments, but persists into the present relative to the racial and ethnic profiling of other so-called "deviant" Americans.

The editors and other contributors to this multi-vocal anthology are to be commended not only for their estimable scholarship, but also for rendering a formidable service to Asian American community-building in Michigan. This book sets the stage for a full-dress treatment of the Asian American experience in the entire Midwest region.

THE COLOR OF SUCCESS: Asian Americans and the Origins of the Model Minority
By Ellen D. Wu (Princeton, New Jersey: Princeton University Press, 2014, 376 pp., $39.50, hardcover)

SACRIFICING SOLIDERS ON THE NATIONAL MALL
By Kristin Ann Hass (Berkeley: University of California Press, 2013, 280 pp., $29.95, paperback)

Published in the January 1, 2015 edition of the *Nichi Bei Weekly*.

These books by Ellen Wu and Kristin Hass both assess a contested facet of Japanese American studies from a comparative perspective, and both are judiciously conceptualized, skillfully organized, soundly argued, lucidly written, and bountifully documented.

Fortuitously, their chronological spans (Wu, 1940s-60s; Hass, 1982-2004) are sufficiently contiguous to warrant reviewing them jointly. Moreover, by jettisoning their non-Japanese American sections (in Wu, the Chinese American model minority experience; in Hass, three of the four war memorials built in the past three decades on the National Mall in Washington), this review can concentrate on connecting Wu's analysis of the Japanese American model minority image with Hass's evaluation of the National Japanese American Memorial to Patriotism during World War II.

When queried as to her book's most significant contribution, Wu responded that it showed how the conception of U.S. Asians as model minorities (educated, prosperous, moral, lawful, and nationalistic) "is an invented fiction rather than timeless truth. ... [that] certain Asian American spokespersons, government officials, social scientists, journalists and others conjured up ... for various political purposes."

As regards this stereotype's *Nikkei* variant, Wu spotlights the activity of the Japanese American Citizens League (JACL) leadership and its late moving spirit Mike Masaoka (1915-1991). She contends that during and following World War II they forged a governing political-cultural paradigm in which the *Nisei* soldier became Japanese America's face and martial patriotism its default setting.

From its 1929 start JACL was an exclusive organization. Open only to *Nisei*, its leaders were primarily older, university-educated, middle-class businesspeople. The JACL's leadership of political conservatism and deference to white Americans repelled intellectuals, liberals, and progressives. Also, the JACL alienated *Issei* and *Kibei-Nisei* with its flag-waving Americanism, as exemplified in its August 1941 executive secretary appointment of Mike Masaoka, a nationalistic Mormon *Nisei* from Utah.

In 1940, Masaoka orated his chauvinistic "Japanese American Creed" before the U.S. Senate, pledging to actively assume his citizen obligations "cheerfully and *without any reservations whatsoever* [emphasis added], in the hope that I may become a better American in a greater America." Clearly, says Wu, Masaoka aimed this creed "at white opinion makers, legislators, and dignitaries."

Prior to U.S. entry into World War II, the JACL organized the Southern California Coordinating Committee for Defense. Chaired by Mike Masaoka's brother Joe Grant, it gathered information on subversive activities within the *Nikkei* community for Naval Intelligence. After Japan's Pearl Harbor attack, the Los Angeles JACL chapter established the Anti-Axis Committee to expand SCCD's work. Its roundup of *Issei* community leaders and their incarceration in alien internment camps rendered JACL largely anathema to the *Nikkei* majority.

Nonetheless, even before President Franklin Roosevelt's February 19, 1942, signing of Executive Order 9066, JACL had convinced the U.S. government to grant it the power to represent all Japanese Americans. After 110,000-plus West Coast *Nikkei* were confined in ten interior concentration camps, War Relocation Authority (WRA) administrators rewarded JACL for assisting in their community's mass exclusion and imprisonment. But, observes Wu, "the popular perception that JACL leaders had acted as *inu* (dogs or stool pigeons) in their vigorous push to promote *Nisei* loyalty destroyed their credibility among other *Nikkei*." Thus, suspected JACL camp "collaborators" were beaten and/or driven into exile, while the organization's reputation and membership plummeted.

In April 1942, JACL spokesperson Masaoka presented authorities with recommendations for detaining Japanese Americans. Uppermost was having military service for *Nisei*, which the government had terminated, promptly reactivated. Meanwhile, camp JACLers pushed military service for *Nisei* to halt suspicion about their American loyalty, even though this exacerbated the League's toxic unpopularity.

In November of 1942, JACL convened an emergency Salt Lake City meeting with delegates from all ten WRA camps. They voted "to ask the War Department to reclassify *Nisei* 'on the same basis as all other Americans.'" This decision precipitated a bloody riot at the eastern

California Manzanar camp in early December 1942. Coupled with the preceding November 1942 strike at Arizona's Poston camp (likewise triggered by a JACL leader's beating) the Manzanar Riot persuaded authorities to devise a mechanism for segregating "loyal" Japanese Americans from "disloyal" ones, an action for which JACL and Mike Masaoka had long lobbied.

In January of 1943, Secretary of War Henry Stimson announced plans to form an all-Japanese American Combat team of mainland U.S. and Hawai`i volunteers. The JACL endorsed this "Jap Crow" regiment for pragmatic reasons, and Mike Masaoka became its first volunteer. The next month a loyalty questionnaire was given adult camp inmates. Questions 27 and 28 proved controversial: "Are you willing to serve in the armed forces of the United States on combat duty, wherever ordered?" "Will you swear unqualified allegiance to the United States and faithfully defend the United States from any or all attacks by foreign or domestic forces?" Those affirming these "registration" questions were recruited by the army (while negative respondents were remanded to northern California's Tule Lake Segregation Center). However, only 1,181 camp volunteers, far short of the 3,000 anticipated, materialized. Many more volunteered from Hawai`i, since there *Nikkei* had not suffered mass removal and imprisonment. These volunteers constituted the core of the 442nd Regimental Combat Team, which fought in Italy, France, and Germany, while compiling what historian Paul Spickard portrays as "a record of heroism unparalleled in the history of American warfare."

The *Nisei* soldiers' performance jump-started a villainous to valorous reversal in the standing of JACL and Masaoka within the *Nikkei* community. As the 442nd's public relations officer, Masaoka cranked out some 2,700 stories stressing how *Nisei* soldiers had volunteered because they were Americans who deeply believed in democracy, "even though [their] ... families were in detention camps as the result of a wartime aberration." This public relations campaign, opines historian Alice Yang Murray, "helped conceal from mainstream America the history of protest against the government and JACL." On the home front, the same message was sounded to *Nikkei* in and out of camp by the JACL's *Pacific Citizen* house organ and reverberated in JACL-oriented camp newspapers and free-zone vernaculars.

In January of 1944, the War Department announced the military draft's reopening to *Nisei*. Although applauded by JACL and Masaoka and accorded a surprisingly favorable camp *Nisei* reception, this action provoked draft resistance from roughly 300 *Nisei* inmates. JACL joined the WRA and the U.S. government in castigating draft resisters as draft "dodgers" motivated by cowardice and/or pro-Japanism. As for the eighty-five draft resisters at Wyoming's Heart Mountain camp, the JACL-led *Heart Mountain Sentinel* denigrated their constitutional rationale as a rationalization for ducking a fundamental duty of U.S. citizenship. When resisters were convicted for draft evasion and they, along with their Fair Play Committee leaders, were railroaded into federal prisons, the *Sentinel* deemed this scenario as justice duly served.

After the war, JACL hastened its institutional rehabilitation, mostly among resettled *Nikkei* populations living in marginal neighborhoods of interior urban meccas. According to Yang Murray, the JACL strongly desired to distance itself from draft resisters (as well as resisters *within* the military), while a few hard liners wanted JACL to urge the government "to deport immediately those who failed to express loyalty" and to require the No-No population at Tule Lake Segregation Center to carry special identification cards. Instead, JACL decided to conduct a media blitz so exclusively focused upon the *Nisei* soldiers as to "erase the history of ... resistance from public memory by denying its existence."

This tactic enjoyed success for several postwar decades, thanks to JACL public relations efforts like sponsoring heroic *Nisei* airman Ben Kuroki on a national speaking tour, arranging for Arlington National Cemetery reburial ceremonies for *Nisei* soldiers, lobbying the army to name a troop transport after posthumously designated *Nisei* Medal of Honor recipient Sadao Munemori, and collaborating in the 1951 feature film *Go for Broke!* To quote Wu, the moral of this movie, for which Masaoka was a special consultant, "echoed JACL's tale on martial patriotism: that *Nisei* had proved beyond a doubt their Americanism through their 'baptism of blood.'"

By this time the JACL had solidified its hegemonic status as Japanese America's spokesperson organization. Through its Masaoka-headed, Washington, D.C.-based Anti-Discrimination Committee, the League undertook a conciliatory, assimilationist-oriented drive to achieve its legislative and judicial goals (e.g., Evacuations Claims bill, *Issei* citizenship, and equal treatment before the law). Deftly exploiting the *Nisei* soldier to promote these actions, Masaoka was feted by the mainstream and JACL-controlled media as a "lobbyist extraordinary."

As the 1960s-1970s social movements unfolded, however, JACL found its power to shape Japanese American identity and citizenship severely contested by activist *Nikkei*. They took exception to books like JACLer leader Bill Hosokawa's *Nisei: Quiet Americans* (1969). A *Denver Post* editor and a *Pacific Citizen* columnist, Hosokawa was virtually silent about *Nikkei* individuals and groups who fought for social justice and democratic rights. In contrast, Hosokawa's critics honored them, cheering books by historians like Roger Daniels' *Concentration Camps USA* (1971) and Michi Nishiura Weglyn's *Years of Infamy* (1976). Daniels questioned "the [JACL-WRA] stereotype of the Japanese American victim of World War II who met his fate with stoic resignation and responded only with superpatriotism," while Weglyn, writing as "an outraged victim," copiously and empathetically covered all WRA camp resisters and dedicated her book to civil rights lawyer Wayne M. Collins who had spent years restoring U.S. citizenship to some 5,000 Tule Lake renunciants.

Although dissenting progressives within selected JACL chapters ignited the 1970s-1980s redress/reparations movement, the JACL Old Guard only grudgingly came to endorse it. In respect to the cultural style of the major redress organizations, the JACL comported itself the most closely to the model minority archetype, including greater emphasis upon martial patriotism. On August 10, 1988, President Ronald Reagan, a conservative Republican, signed into law the Civil

Liberties Act of 1988. That he did so owed much to do with JACL's *Sansei* strategy chair, Grant Ujifusa, arranging to have the president reminded of his impassioned December 1945 speech in Santa Ana, California. On that occasion, as Captain Reagan, a Democratic liberal, he had first saluted the family of Sgt. Kasuo Masuda of the 442nd—"a true American" who earlier that day had been posthumously awarded the Distinguished Service Cross for his Italian battlefield heroics—and then effused: "Blood that has soaked into the sands of a beach is all one color. America stands unique in the world, the only country not founded on race, but in a way an ideal."

Once redress was law, martial patriotic politics à la Mike Masaoka presented a more daunting challenge for JACL to perform. What during the redress movement had been muffled discontent by *Nikkei* toward the JACL's and Masaoka's wartime betrayal of their community now became a full-throated condemnation. When in 1987 Masaoka, assisted by Hosokawa, published the "saga" of Masaoka's life and career "as a soldier, civil rights leader, and premier Washington lobbyist" in *They Call Me Moses Masaoka*, the book was pilloried by Masaoka's critics. James Omura, the JACL's number one enemy from 1934 throughout the war and slightly after it, was encouraged by younger Asian American supporters and Michi Weglyn to review it, which he did in 1989 for the *Rafu Shimpo*. Omura's opening salvo presaged what would follow: "History indeed is infinitely the poorer and literature thereby greatly diminished by the publication of this fabricated account of the historic Japanese American episode of World War II." This review's damage was compounded by Deborah Lim's finding in her 1990 JACL-commissioned report that, at the JACL's March 1942 Emergency Meeting in San Francisco, Masaoka allegedly had recommended that "Japanese be branded and stamped and put under the supervision of the Federal government."

The upshot of such mortal blows to the reputation of a dying Masaoka and the organization so closely identified with him was that JACL largely treated Omura's review with contemptuous silence and sought, unsuccessfully, to suppress Lim's report. But these criticisms and others raised by *Nikkei* created a chorus of voices demanding that

JACL emulate the U.S. government's precedent by apologizing to Japanese Americans for the wartime misdeeds its leaders perpetrated against their community. Most specifically, this demand took shape in the necessity for JACL to express regret for their egregious maltreatment of the draft resisters who, as "resisters of conscience," had chosen to exercise their American patriotism through clarifying and reclaiming their constitutional rights as U.S. citizens rather than robotically submitting to military service from behind barbed wire.

It is here that Kristin Hass's book becomes relevant. Her concern is with the National Japanese American Memorial to Patriotism during World War II. Through the National Japanese American Memorial Foundation (NJAMF), this memorial's development underwent discussions about its mission statement, site, design, and inscriptions. Only the last item was debated, and then with but a single inscription. There were quotations from California *Nisei* Congressman Norman Mineta (Mike Masaoka's brother-in-law), a child incarceree at Heart Mountain, and *Sansei* Robert Matsui, detained as a child at Tule Lake; Hawai`i *Nisei* Senators Daniel Inouye and Spark Matsunaga, both 442nd Regimental Combat Team veterans; WWII President Harry Truman; as well as two poems, a *tanka* and a *haiku*, by unnamed authors. Of these items, only the *tanka* poem (penned by Bill Hosokawa) was deleted, owing to its meaning being deemed too elusive.

In Hass's words, the white heat of the debate "focused squarely on a [1940] quotation [by Mike Masaoka] celebrating the unquestioning loyalty of some Japanese Americans as a 'creed' shared by all Americans." It declared: "I am proud that I am an American of Japanese heritage. I believe in her institutions, ideals and traditions. I glory in her heritage; I boast of her history; I trust in her future." Both supporters and detractors of the controversial Masaoka on the NJAMF Board agreed to remove the "Japanese American Creed" title for the quote. But this did not resolve the controversy. Three board members, including San Francisco State oral historian Rita Takahashi, wanted the quotation deleted to avoid a perennial "fiasco," and they formed the Japanese American

Voice group to encourage the public to protest its inclusion to the National Park Service. Despite some seven hundred protest letters pouring into the NPS, the NJAMF Board prevailing majority "was not willing to let Masaoka go." One *Sansei* graduate history student at Stanford, Steve Yoda, complained that Masaoka's "blindly patriotic oath fans the model minority myth," while Asian American scholar Larry Hashima fretted that Masaoka's quote "may easily be interpreted to equate acquiescence and capitulation as the benchmark for patriotism." In Hass's opinion, Hashima was right, but his logic did not succeed in removing the "Creed" from the monument. Concludes a disheartened Hass: "It is there on the Mall for perpetuity."

TRANS-PACIFIC JAPANESE AMERICAN STUDIES: Conversations on Race and Racializations
Edited by Yasuko Takezawa and Gary Y. Okihiro (Honolulu: University of Hawai`i Press, 2016, 430 pp., $68.00, hardcover)

Published in the July 18, 2019 edition of the *Nichi Bei Weekly*.

This substantial volume is co-edited by two distinguished *Nikkei* practitioners of Japanese American Studies, one a Japan-based anthropologist, Yasuko Takezawa of Kyoto University, and the other a U.S.-situated historian, Gary Okihiro of Columbia University. Although this work is primarily targeted at other scholars and advanced university students within their common transpacific field of inquiry, its well-grounded and illuminating introduction, fourteen essays, and seven perspectival responses to the book's contents have much to offer a general readership. At bottom, the mission of "Trans-Pacific Japanese American Studies" is to expand and enrich Japanese American Studies by moving this sub-discipline beyond its past preoccupation with the *Issei* and *Nisei* generations and the World War II exclusion and incarceration experience of Japanese Americans and by providing greater attention, through dialogue, to cross-national developments and issues and underrepresented communities and perspectives.

Given the brevity of this review, I will attempt within the rest of it to illustrate how this anthology discharges its intellectual burden with distinction by briefly discussing but four of its essays, one by the pioneering transnational historian Eiichiro Azuma (University of Pennsylvania), and the other three by essayists boasting Bay Area connections: historian Valerie Matsumoto (University of California, Los Angeles); anthropologist Sachiko Kawakami (Kyoto University of Foreign Studies); and Asian Americanist Wesley Ueunten (San Francisco State University).

The essay by Azuma decries that, unlike other Asian communities in the U.S., which thrive on the inclusion of postwar immigrants, present-day Japanese America has virtually no place for people like him, a *Shin Issei* who arrived in the country along with thousands of other *Nikkei* after 1945. Because they are accorded only fleeting attention, the *Shin Issei* suffer a paucity of historical representation and are consigned to the status of "perpetual outsiders." So too, claims Azuma, does the same neglect and attendant "invisibility" apply to those Americans of Japanese ancestry who live in locations other than Hawai`i and the Pacific Coast states, a regional bias that obscures the reality of their encompassing a large percentage of post-WWII immigrants. Indeed, "other than the short period of temporary dispersal [resettlement], Japanese American life 'east of California' holds little attention in the story of the postwar Japanese American experience."

As for Matsumoto, who earned her doctorate at Stanford and wrote her first book, "Farming the Home Place," on northern California's Cortez Colony (which was founded one-hundred years ago in 1919 by founding *Nichi Bei Shimbun* editor Kyutaro Abiko), her essay expands the scope of the Japanese American story by spotlighting not *Issei* and *Nisei* men but rather *Sansei* women, especially those actively engaged within the Asian American Movement during the Vietnam War years.

In the case of Kawakami, the transpacific research emphasis of her essay is "the spatial practice primarily revolving around individual daily commercial and consumption activities of Korean immigrants in San Francisco's Japantown." Through interviews she conducted in Korean/Japanese/English with Japanese-literate men and women seniors who came of age during Korea's colonial period (1910-1945) and also with predominantly male Korean small business owners, she reached two related conclusions: first, that these immigrants, although they lived, worked, and socialized in Nihonmachi, did not represent it as "their" community; and second, that their relationship to Japantown was rather one of a silent "place-based affinity," a concept that Kawakami developed to capture how these immigrants participated "in the lives and communities of others to satisfy their practical needs."

With regard to Ueunten, he conducted participant-observation research within a small cluster of scattered Bay Area Okinawan immigrant women, the Nakayoshi Group, who for some 15 years had been meeting to eat, talk, and sing songs "they own." As cogently summarized by the book's co-editors, Ueunten discovered in his fieldwork that central to these women's experiences as women is violence, extending from the WWII Battle of Okinawa to the persisting U.S. occupation and militarization of Okinawa. Based upon his interactions with the Nakayoshi Group, Ueunten makes the case for "a more inclusive Japanese American history and community that accounts for the voices of all of its diverse members."

Perhaps the most consequential takeaway from this bountiful book is best articulated by Duncan Ryûken Williams, the director of the USC Center for Religion and Culture and the author of this year's most lauded book on the Japanese American experience, *American Sutra,* when he observes in his reaction to the diverse offerings of the essayists that "it is not just that we need to attend to the changing Japanese American community, which will only become increasingly majority multiracial in the future, but we need to attend to families and persons of the multiracial and mixed-roots heritage."

CONJECTURING COMMUNITIES: Ebbs and Flows of Japanese America (A special issue of *PAN-JAPAN: The International Journal of the Japanese Diaspora*)
Edited by Lane Ryo Hirabayashi (Normal, IL: Illinois State University, Spring/Fall 2016, Volume 12, Numbers 1 & 2, 189 pp., $12.50, paperback)

Published in the July 21, 2016 edition of the *Nichi Bei Weekly*.

During my involvement in Japanese American studies, from 1972 to the present, I have been struck by two simultaneous developments. The first is a growing sophistication in theory and methodology among its academic practitioners; the second is a decreasing connection to and concern for the Japanese American community by these same scholars. While I do not see this bifurcated situation—which has been remarked on by many others in the field—as a "crisis" worthy of "alarmist" pronouncements, I do find it a cause for celebration to encounter the work of those academe-based teacher-scholars in Japanese American studies who, like Lane Ryo Hirabayashi, consistently produce and/or engender work that achieves a dynamic equilibrium between the competing demands of intellectual rigor and quality control and those of community enrichment and empowerment. It is precisely for this reason that I feel especially fortunate to review here the Hirabayashi-edited anthology "Conjecturing Communities: Ebbs and Flows of Japanese America" and also to highly recommend it for consumption to *Nichi Bei Weekly* readers.

The content of this special issue of the "PAN-JAPAN" journal is easy to summarize. Bracketed by Hirabayashi's exemplary introduction and judicious afterword, one is treated to seven pieces contributed, in consecutive order, by stellar community-based Japanese American studies scholars (Wesley Ueunten, Eri Kameyama, Kyung Hee Ha, Shigueru Tsuha, Amy Sueyoshi, Lily Anne Yumi Welty Tamai, and James M. Ong). Six of these selections are substantive essays that focus, as per Hirabayashi, "on groups that may, or may very well not, become part of the larger Japanese American community in the twenty-first century": "*Uchinanchu*," or Okinawan Americans; "*Shin Issei*," or new postwar Japanese immigrants; "*Zainichi*," or overseas Koreans born/raised in Japan who are now living in the U.S.; Peruvian Japanese who now live in California; Japanese American members of LGBTQ populations; and immediate-postwar mixed race individuals who came to the U.S. as adoptees. The seventh piece is an annotated bibliography that not only provides readers of the anthology with additional information on the history and experiences of the above noted six groups, but also showcases theoretical and analytic frameworks proposed to study their respective identity formation.

In his introduction, Hirabayashi informs us that he had field-tested the public performances of all of the contributors to *Conjecturing Communities*. He also allows as to how he encouraged them to "express their personal feelings" so that readers "can better understand what issues are important to you [and] ... how you *feel* about those issues." In reading Hirabayashi's introductory essay, we are given proof that he had primed himself to put into practice what he had "preached" to his contributing authors. Indeed, although I have read a great deal of the exceedingly self-effacing Hirabayashi's past writings, I found out in this venue alone more about his professional career trajectory and attendant development as an Asian American studies teacher and researcher than in virtually all of his combined antecedent scholarship.

While each of the six substantive essays abound with significant information based on diverse primary and secondary sources and take shape as polished, perceptive, and challenging interpretive studies, the two I found most infused with personal feelings were Wesley Ueunten's "Okinawan Identity in the Diaspora: A Messy Genealogy" and Amy Sueyoshi's "Why Queer Asian American Studies? Implications for Japanese America." In the case of Ueunten, he asks rhetorically, "But why should I [as a *Sansei* ... Okinawan born and raised in Hawai`i with *Nisei* parents also born and raised in Hawai`i] care about Okinawa?" To which he responds, "[Because] I have an undeniable emotional connection to Okinawa." As for Sueyoshi, in discussing persisting homophobia in the progressive gay city of San Francisco, she writes, "I had a personal stake in this as well, because of my own *Shin-Issei* mother and her circle of *Shin-Issei* friends. Being queer around them is a funny mix of 'we know—we like you—we don't have to talk about it.'" I should add, however, that Shigueru Tsuha, in "Japanese Peruvians in California: Ethnic Identity Formations," utilizes the introductory portion of his essay for autobiographically framing his otherwise standard community case study. Moreover, mention needs to be made here of how James M. Ong, in his superlative "'Re-envisioning' the Contours of the Japanese American Community of the Past and Present: An Annotated Bibliography of Sources and Texts which Expand the Scope of Inclusivity," prefaces on multiple occasions his source recommendations with "I feel."

If you want to get a handle on where the ever-changing Japanese American community is now heading, reading "Conjecturing Communities" is an invaluable starting point for such a journey of discovery.

PART IV

THE ARTS

In the Wikipedia *entry denoting "American artists of Japanese descent," 138 names are listed. Some of these individuals are quite notable, such as Ruth Asawa, Hideo Date, Henry Fukuhara, Masumi Hayashi, George Hoshida, Yasuo Kuniyoshi, George Nakashima, Isamu Noguchi, Chiura Obata, Miné Okuba, Henry Sugimoto, and Taro Yashima, while most of the other names are less well-known. All of them, whether born in Japan or the United States, share an aesthetic that, in some measure or other, combines traditional Japanese and Western perspectives (as codified in an anonymously authored internet posting). Thus, these artists blend a view of art being a way of life, something integrated into all aspects of daily life (traditional Japanese) with art being considered something elevated and separate from most aspects of daily life (Western). As for art-making, these artists of Japanese ancestry intermix the notion of it being an expression of collectivity, ritual, tradition, and obligation to the group (traditional Japanese) with that of being an expression of individuality and personal self-expression (Western). With respect to the worldview of these artists it amalgamates the idea of regarding humanity as harmonious with nature (Japanese) with that of deeming humanity as more important than nature (Western). In terms of design, Japanese-lineage artists intermix an emphasis upon surface design rather than the illusion of depth (traditional Japanese) with the illusion of three-dimension space on a two-dimension surface to indicate depth (Western). Concerning technical qualities, these artists of Japanese heritage mingle a belief in the immediacy and spontaneity of creation (traditional Japanese) with that of idealized perfection (Western).* There are assuredly exceptions to the above formulated generalizations. Nonetheless, they should be kept in mind when reflecting upon the work of the artists referenced within this section of A Nikkei Harvest.

Of the five books reviewed below, three of them feature paintings done by artists of Japanese descent. As for the remaining two, one spotlights a traditional Japanese musical form, taiko, that, in its contemporary Japanese American ensemble incarnation as kumi-daiko, is assayed from a Caucasian perspective, while the other is a Japanese American novel in terms of subject matter whose author is an Asian American of another ethnicity.

ShiPu Wang's The Other American Moderns *utilizes the work of three unheralded Japanese-born artists (Frank Matsura, Eitaro Ishigaki, Hideo Noda) and one American-born/Japanese-raised artist (Miki Hayakawa) to enlarge and diversify the meaning of American modernism, arguing that their perspective as "others" allowed them to infuse the genre with a previously lacking multicultural and cosmopolitan dimension. In Barbara Johns's* The Hope of Another Spring, *she capitalizes on the extraordinary illustrated diary Takuichi Fujii, an Issei, maintained during his WWII incarceration at the Puyallup Assembly Center in Washington and the Minidoka Relocation Center in Idaho, along with a sampling of his striking paintings that grew out of his inked drawings, to convey to readers an authoritative first-person assessment of what some 120,000 Japanese Americans experienced as unjust victims of U.S. government oppression. Similarly, Lily Yuriko Nakai Havey in her memoir,* Gasa Gasa Girl Goes to Camp, *utilizes prose, photographic images, and artwork (including retrospectively rendered watercolor paintings of great power) to represent her pre- and early-adolescence as a* Nisei *inmate at the Santa Anita Assembly Center in California and the Amache Relocation Center in Colorado. In* Drumming Asian America, *Angela K. Ahlgren, a Finnish American teacher-scholar-musician, comments on the highly popular Japanese art form,* taiko *(which took hold in the U.S. in the 1960s primarily among Japanese Americans and Japanese nationals) from the vantage point of a* taiko *participant steeped in dance studies, ethnomusicology, performance studies, feminist theory, and the "corporeality of* taiko *performance." Finally, non-*Nikkei *Asian American Andrew Lam's novel,* Repentance, *which is concerned with the Japanese American World War II experience both within the U.S. concentration camps and on the battlefields of Europe, juxtaposes traditional Japanese values, beliefs, and practices against those Westernized counterparts representative of Americanized Japanese.*

THE OTHER AMERICAN MODERNS: Matsura, Ishigaki, Noda, Hayakawa
By ShiPu Wang (University Park, PA: Pennsylvania State University Press, 2017, 180 pp., $69.95, hardcover)

Published in the July 19, 2018 edition of the *Nichi Bei Weekly.*

I have always been intrigued by the titles that authors select to represent their books, and most especially if they are as deftly apt as that which ShiPu Wang has devised for the volume under review. Whereas the designation "American Moderns" has customarily been used to depict such canonical white artists as Stuart Davis (1892-1964), Alfred Stieglitz (1864-1946), Georgia O'Keeffe (1887-1986), and John Marin (1870-1953), Wang devotes his critical attention to four American Moderns of Japanese ancestry: Frank Matsura (1873-1913), Eitaro Ishigaki (1893-1958), Hideo Noda (1908-1939), and Miki Hayakawa (1899-1953). He resourcefully and strategically uses this quartet of "forgotten" minority artists—perceived by mainstream American society to be "others"—as case studies for two principal reasons. On the one hand, Wang believes that our American cultural heritage is more complex than what can be learned from merely viewing the work of a few privileged artists. On the other hand, he feels that his featured *Nikkei* artists helped reconceptualize American Modernism through playing an active role in the formation of a multicultural and cosmopolitan culture in the United States.

Wang launches his four case studies by a pivotal image within an artist's works so as to "uncover its historical context and underlying commentary on what 'America,' and living in America as a minority, meant to a diasporic artist." For example, Wang's chosen image for Frank Matsura, a Japanese photographic artist in Okanogan, Washington, is *Matsura and Susan Timento Pose at Studio* (ca. 1912), since Matsura frequently integrated himself into his portraits of his Native American and Caucasian clientele. As for New York-based artists Eitaro Ishigaki and Hideo Noda (both, like Matsura, Japan-born), their respective images—*The Bonus March* (1932) and *Scottsboro Boys* (1933)—are used by Wang to show how they depicted heroic African Americans to intervene in and comment upon incendiary social justice issues of the Great Depression. Finally, Wang employs *Portrait of a Negro* (ca. 1926) by U.S.-born/Japan-raised Miki Hayakawa to underscore the multiracial character of the life she and other Asian artists in 1920s San Francisco experienced. Together these artists created what Wang labels "imagery of the Other by the Other," whereby "other" represents not a term of marginality, but rather a position within and a perspective on society.

Readers of *The Other American Moderns* should keep in mind what one of its shrewd reviewers, Samantha Snively, has sagely observed, that the era of American Modernism was one of exclusion (the Chinese Exclusion Act of 1882, *Plessy v. Ferguson* in 1896, the Immigration Act of 1924, among many other racist measures aimed to ascertain who counted as "American"). Small wonder then that artists like Matsura, Ishigaki, Noda, and Hayakawa were left out of the Modernist canon. Given that a new exclusionary era now threatens our country, we need to be vigilant to ensure that we resist every attempt to roll back the pluralistic advances we have made in our society and culture in the last half century under the pernicious banner of making America great once again.

THE HOPE OF ANOTHER SPRING: Takuichi Fujii, Artist and Wartime Witness
By Barbara Johns (Seattle: University of Washington Press, 2017, 334 pp., $39.95, hardcover)

Published in the January 1, 2018 edition of the *Nichi Bei Weekly*.

This altogether beautiful book by noted Seattle-based art historian and curator Barbara Johns strikingly testifies to the oft-stated judgment that a picture is worth a thousand words. The core of *The Hope of Another Spring* is the astonishing illustrated diary that *Issei* Takuichi Fujii (1891-1964) fashioned (almost completely) while confined during World War II with his wife and two daughters at the Puyallup Assembly Center (Washington) and the Minidoka Relocation Center (Idaho) concentration camps. Described in a discerning foreword by renowned historian Roger Daniels as "the most remarkable document created by a Japanese American prisoner during the wartime incarceration," the condensed diary in the book consists of a selection of words (translated into English by Fujii's grandson Sandy Kita with Honda Shojo) and images (inked drawings) amounting to more than half of the record's total contents.

The Hope of Another Spring is anchored by an authoritative multifaceted introduction by Johns that narrates Fujii's life history and situates his work into a strategic historical context. It also includes a sampling of radiant water color paintings that were outgrowths of Fujii's inked drawings, Sandy Kita's movingly personal introduction to his grandfather's diary, a concise statement by the artist about the aim of his painting, an exhibition history covering Fujii's artistic career, a useful compilation of endnotes, a carefully selected bibliography of especially pertinent sources, and a well-crafted subject index.

Two things in particular make the book under review very special. First, it marks the initial time that Takuichi Fujii's World War II illustrated diary and correlated water colors have been made available for public consumption, enjoyment, and edification. Second, and related, is that as a result of the availability of Fujii's inmate work, readers as well as researchers are gifted with the fortuitous opportunity of accessing and assessing the unique perspective of a clear-sighted first-generation *Nikkei* witness to the forced wartime mass incarceration of some 120,000 Japanese Americans.

In reading and viewing the contents of *The Hope of Another Spring*, a trio of critical concerns need to be taken under earnest advisement: 1) What was the type of diary that Fujii maintained when incarcerated at Puyallup and Minidoka? 2) What sort of witness was Fujii to the wartime imprisonment experience of his racial-ethnic community? 3) To what extent, if any, did Fujii's diary constitute an act of resistance to his oppression and that of other confined Japanese Americans? Rather than to disclose my answers to these questions, I will instead simply pose them here as a challenge for the readers-viewers of this remarkable book to ponder and resolve for themselves.

Before even buying or borrowing *The Hope of Another Spring*, I would strongly recommend that people take the time to first consult the magnificent photo essay that the University of Washington Press has thoughtfully provided for prospective patrons, viewable online at https://uwpressblog.com/2017/05/30/photo-essay-the-hope-of-another-spring/.

GASA GASA GIRL GOES TO CAMP: A Nisei Youth Behind a World War II Fence
By Lily Yuriko Nakai Havey (Salt Lake City: University of Utah Press, 2014, 224 pp., $29.95, hardcover)

Published in the July 24, 2014 edition of the *Nichi Bei Weekly*.

Through a sophisticated blend of artwork, prose, and photographic images, plus an assortment of other useful illustrative materials, Lily Yuriko Nakai Havey (b. 1932) has crafted in *Gasa Gasa Girl Goes to*

Camp what is assuredly among the very most exquisite, insightful, and candid memoirs of the World War II Japanese American experience. I vigorously applaud the University of Utah Press's marketing of this volume—which hinges on Havey's pre- and early-adolescence incarceration at the Santa Anita Assembly Center in Southern California and the Amache (or Granada) Relocation Center in southeastern Colorado—as a "creative memoir." While all memoirs (a literary genre that in recent years has mushroomed in popularity) embody creativity, the one under review here does so primarily (though certainly not exclusively) through the prism of its exceedingly talented *Nisei* artist-author's retrospectively rendered watercolor representations of her wartime past in America's concentration camps.

In reading *Gasa Gasa Girl Goes to Camp*, I was reminded of the fictional and non-fictional memoirs penned by a celebrated generational contemporary of Havey's, the British author Penelope Lively (b. 1933). As in the case of Lively, who writes for both adults and children, Havey (whose accessible and engaging memoir will predictably captivate children and adult readers) likewise stresses the supple power of memory and plays up the acute and pervasive tensions between "official" history and personal history.

On the other hand, whereas Penelope Lively's trademark as a memoirist is her championing of the impact of the past on the present, in her memoir Havey not only promotes this proposition throughout her narrative in historical reflections pertaining to her background and that of her extended family members in the U.S. and Japan, but also dramatizes how the dynamic present shapes our interest in and interpretation of the mutable past. "In the 1980s," she explains in her preface, "I learned about armed-service personnel suffering from post-traumatic stress disorder (PTSD) and wondered whether some of my unease with confined spaces ... bright lights, and loud noises might be symptoms of the same syndrome. [So to find out] I painted a series of watercolors about my [wartime] experiences."

Thanks to a remarkably perceptive foreword contributed by

Cherstin Lyon, a rising star in Japanese American studies and public and oral history, readers of *Gasa Gasa Girl Goes to Camp* will be better able to ascertain what this book is ("an artistically written record of one woman's journey into her past"), what it is not ("a factual record of everything that marked the wartime experiences of 120,000 individuals who were caught in a tragic display of intolerance and racial prejudice"), and what, at bottom, is its abiding value ("it intimately shares one woman's memories of the past and, at the same time ... explore[s] issues rarely discussed in any historical or narrative literature about the camp experience, particularly for women").

This is a book that must be read, shared, discussed, taught—and savored!

DRUMMING ASIAN AMERICA: Taiko, Performance, and Cultural Politics
By Angela K. Ahlgren (New York: Oxford University Press, 2018, 177 pp., $34.95, paperback)

Published in the January 1, 2019 edition of the *Nichi Bei Weekly*.

Up until 2004, I was a mere (and rather unreflective) spectator to *taiko* drumming. However, that year I fortuitously became involved as an oral historian in a Japanese American National Museum-sponsored project that culminated in a 2005-2006 exhibition at JANM titled *Big Drum: Taiko in the U.S.* Curated by Sojin Kim, it featured a new documentary DVD of the same name that included parts of the exhibition media installations as well performances by various *taiko* groups and videotaped interviews with key *taiko* leaders and practitioners. The exhibition's July 13, 2005 opening, according to a June 2006 Masumi Izumi review in the *Journal of American History*, attracted 800 people, while on that same day, 600 drummers from the United States, Canada, Japan, and Britain congregated across the street in Los Angeles's Little Tokyo at the Japanese American Cultural and Community

Center for still another opening, that of the 2005 North American Taiko Conference. Clearly, *taiko* as a performing arts ensemble had come of age since its early 1950s origins in Japan and its late 1960s beginnings in California.

At the time of the JANM project, the number of *taiko* groups in North America hovered around 200. Although initially *taiko* in the U.S. emerged as an art form practiced primarily by Japanese Americans and Japanese nationals, the JANM project was enacted when *taiko* ensembles, if still dominated by Japanese Americans, were increasingly peopled by other Asian Americans as well as those from different racial backgrounds. In terms of gender, the number of women had exceeded that of men, yet men were still the main group leaders and the ones designated to play their group's coveted roles as featured soloists. As to the brand of cultural politics undertaken, as epitomized by 1973-formed San Jose Taiko, it primarily consisted of making connections between *taiko* and the politics of the civil rights-inspired Asian American Movement's "ethnic consciousness-raising efforts as well as antiwar demonstrations, education reform, and grassroots activities focused on helping underserved communities," though connections were also forged between *taiko* and women's rights and empowerment.

In contrast, when Angela Ahlgren undertook the 2006-2009 fieldwork for her 2011 University of Texas doctoral dissertation in Performance and Public Practice (upon which *Drumming Asian America*, with some significant updating, is based), dramatic changes in the *taiko* world had already taken root. The number of *taiko* groups had nearly doubled, the proportionate percentage of Japanese American performers had substantially decreased, women (Asian American and non-Asian American) had not only become two-thirds of the *taiko* ranks, but also assumed more prominence as both ensemble leaders and high-profile entertainers. With respect to cultural politics, *taiko* now lent itself to becoming construed in terms of how its performance of "Asian America intersects with race, gender, and sexuality, understanding each of these vectors as both lived experience and as called into being through performances."

It is this cultural-political dimension of *taiko* that assumes prominence, on and off stage, in *Drumming Asian America*. An assistant professor in the Department of Theatre and Film at Bowling Green State University, Ahlgren—a white, blonde-haired, blue-eyed, middle-class woman of Finnish heritage—grew up in an isolated Minnesota community whose population was overwhelmingly Scandinavian and Germanic, and came of age in the 1990s. She describes her perspective on *taiko* being grounded in her "feminist, bisexual, lesbian self," her eighteen years of experience as a *taiko* fan-drummer-teacher-scholar, her research orientation in dance studies, ethnomusicology, performance studies, and queer and feminist theory, and her focus on the "corporeality of *taiko* performance, how players move ... and how those movements make meaning for players and audience."

Not surprisingly, Ahlgren's book "privileges women *taiko* players as interview subjects and gender as a category of analysis," while devoting "attention to groups that have been led or deeply influenced by women *taiko* players." Accordingly, her four core chapters bear out this privileging and devotion. The first of these chapters revolves around San Jose Taiko's co-founder, *Sansei* PJ Hirabayashi, and her group's signature creation and embodiment of the *taiko* folk dance *Ei Ja Nai Ka?* (Isn't it good?), a participatory call-and-response folk dance that pays tribute to the pioneering *Issei* generation, through gesturing and mimicking the manual labor they executed, and thereby linking *Issei* to *Sansei*, past to present, and San Jose Taiko to the Asian American Movement.

The second core chapter shifts from the West Coast to the Midwest and the Minneapolis-based Mu Daiko *taiko* group, whose membership by 2001 had changed from mostly Asian American to half Asian American and half white performers, with women representing half or more of the ensemble, including some queer-identified members. Of special interest is Ahlgren's foregrounding of Korean American adoptees such as Jennifer Weir and Josephine Lee, both socialized apart from other Asian Americans, and how their participation in Mu Daiko complicates the notion of what it means to perform Asian American both for them and for their almost exclusively white Midwestern audiences.

As for the third core chapter, Ahlgren investigates the intersections of gender and race by riveting upon the experience of white and black women *taiko* players, the former of whom in 2016 were pegged at 18 percent of all *taiko* players in North America, while the number of the latter was roughly 2 percent. In this connection, she pointedly explores a question oft-asked in the *taiko* community: how do non-Asian American players fit within an art form like *taiko* that, while open to everyone, is tied to Japanese tradition and Asian American communities? In response, she capitalizes on a song by Mu Daiko's Iris Shiraishi, *Torii*, to suggest how "alienation can be a productive step toward developing cross-racial intimacies."

In her final core chapter, Ahlgren shines her spotlight on Jodaiko, one of the few all-women's *taiko* groups in North America, and among the two or three comprised largely of queer Asian American and Canadian women. In this context she headlines the performance of the group's leader, Tiffany Tamaribuchi, in the piece *Kokorozashi* to explore how Jodaiko "queers North American *taiko* and argues for sexuality as a key lens through which to approach *taiko* performance."

Drumming Asian America is a book that is masterfully written, powerfully theorized, innovatively developed, and richly documented through archival sources and ethnographic fieldwork. Reading it brought me a great deal of pleasure and edification, even though I was challenged mightily at every turn to assay its complex message. Before you tackle it, I would recommend that you listen to the 2016 interview with Angela Ahlgren posted on Bowling Green State University's Taiko Source site, https://taikosource.com/news/new-interview-angela-ahlgren/.

REPENTANCE

By Andrew Lam (North Point, FL: Tiny Fox Press, 2019, 283 pp., $15.95, paperback)

Published in the July 18, 2019 edition of the *Nichi Bei Weekly*.

Andrew Lam, the author of the book under review, studied history at Yale University—where he graduated "summa cum laude"—and afterward became a world-class retinal surgeon. His previous two books consisted of a non-fiction work, *Saving Sight* (2013), honoring renowned practitioners in his specialized medical field, and a WWII novel, *Two Sons of China* (2014), both award-winning bestsellers. His current book, *Repentance*, is a work of historical fiction that is debatably comparable to such classic works of this genre pertaining to the Japanese American historical experience as Jeanne Wakatsuki Houston and James D. Houston's *Farewell to Manzanar* (1973) and David Guterson's *Snow Falling on Cedars* (1994).

All three of these books are what I would characterize as "cinematic novels." Two of them, in fact, have already been made into motion pictures in, respectively, 1976 and 1994, and I would not be surprised, and altogether delighted, if *Repentance* in due time would similarly be transformed into a noteworthy feature film. In keeping with this sanguine forecast, I will devote the remainder of this review to delineating precisely why I believe Lam's volume is not only a remarkable novel in its own right but also one that quintessentially lends itself to silver screen portrayal.

In 2017, novelist and screenwriter Irena Brignull formulated seven tips for prospective writers of cinematic novels: 1) establish a strong premise; 2) think visually; 3) provide a well-made structure; 4) create dramatic tension; 5) employ action and dialogue to reveal motivations; 6) utilize memorable set pieces; and 7) afford fully developed central characters with clearly defined journeys. Although Andrew Lam in all likelihood did not self-consciously set out to produce a cinematic novel per se and almost certainly was unaware of the formulation posited by Brignull, I am confident that she would applaud *Repentance* for artfully embodying all of the elements for success that she itemized.

With respect to the premise or overarching idea of *Repentance*, it is, simply put, to relate the complex WWII Japanese American story as a whole primarily through the experiential lens of one extended family, the Tokunagas. This mission Lam undertakes by linking assorted members of this somewhat dysfunctional kin group with the sacrificial heroics of *Nisei* soldiers in the segregated 442nd Regimental Combat Team, many of whom were Hawai`i and mainland U.S. volunteers with families unjustly incarcerated in American-style concentration camps such as Manzanar.

As regards visualization, *Repentance* is communicated appreciably less through the inner thoughts and feelings of its characters than by the large and close-up settings in which their interactions transpire. The large settings encompass the battlefields of Europe, most especially France, and the imprisoned barracks community of Manzanar, and the close-up ones extend from the emergency room of the University of Pennsylvania Hospital, the "theater of operations" for eminent *Sansei* brain surgeon Dr. Daniel Tokunaga, to the Los Angeles home of his parents, Keiko, a onetime Manzanar inmate, and Ryoji "Ray" Tokunaga, a decorated 442nd veteran from Hawai`i.

In terms of structure, Lam provides a well-planned plot, replete with strategically ordered chapters, scenes, and turning points, all building systematically to a climactic ending, while making room for twists, surprises, and backstories. Most of the chapters alternate in time between the late 1990s and the mid-1940s within far-flung venues, and all are carefully sequenced so as to convey a deftly choreographed narrative that is dynamic, enthralling, multifaceted, and unpredictable.

Concerning dramatic tension, Lam achieves this both through juxtaposing the hopes and dreams of his characters against the obstacles preventing their realization and by pointing out the gap between what his characters and his readers know. Many of the characters in *Repentance* yearn for love, often unrequited, for honor, sometimes elusive, and happiness, frequently thwarted. Because many of Lam's characters are less than forthcoming, their truths are typically shared with readers only incrementally and episodically.

Relative to action and dialogue, Lam makes the former take priority over the latter and mostly uses dialogue to trigger reactions that have striking effects. Instead of deluging readers with mere words, he stimulates their thoughts and feelings by engaging them in reflecting upon the behavior of his characters and their interactions, or lack thereof. For him, it is words with heft as well as charged silences that truly matter.

In the case of set pieces, *Repentance* abounds with big, exciting, memorable moments, ones which stay with readers after putting down the book. Some of these moments foreground significant action, like a tense military incident or an emotional collapse, while others are revelatory, as the discovery of a crucial document or the avowal of a long-withheld secret.

Pertinent to characters and their journeys, Lam's characters, especially his central ones, have discernable goals that readers can get behind and embark on journeys, even emotional and ethical ones, that are normally quite clearly defined. The most important and best personalized of the author's assemblage of characters are Daniel Tokunaga and his presumed biological father, Ray Tokunaga, who throughout the novel wage a cold and, sporadically, hot generational, temperamental, and moral war against one another. While less vividly developed than these protagonists, other notable characters in the novel, such as Daniel's *Nisei* mother, Keiko, his Scandinavian American wife, Beth, his high school *Nikkei* girlfriend, Anne Mikado, and his father's closest wartime buddy, Hiro Fukuda, are imaginatively rendered in Lam's beautifully calibrated prose style. As intimated by the title Lam assigned to his book, *Repentance*, a common theme binding together the majority of his cast of characters is their journey in search of atonement.

This marvelous novel deserves to become a majestic movie.

PART V

WORLD WAR II JAPANESE AMERICAN INCARCERATION CAMPS

During World War II Americans of Japanese ancestry were oppressed by a disaster, not one caused by nature, but rather one that was man-made. This social disaster was promulgated by the U.S. government's unjust 1942 decision, via Executive Order 9066, to evict the entire Nikkei *population from their homes, places of business, and communities on the West Coast—where the overwhelming majority of these U.S. citizens and law-abiding aliens resided—and incarcerate them in concentration camps variously called by their euphemistic terms of "internment centers," "assembly centers," "relocation centers," "isolation centers," and "segregation centers." This mandated policy, which was supported by the leadership of the Japanese American Citizens League's collaborative role, catalyzed a cataclysmic change in every facet of the victimized population's cultural composition. The fabric of family was stretched and torn, the pattern of leadership disturbed, the economic structure dismantled, and the underlying sense of personal, family, and community identity endangered. Infusing and imparting focus to the assorted socioeconomic losses was the psychological conviction of being a threatened people.*

Without question the World War II experience of Japanese Americans is by far the most scrutinized aspect of Nikkei *history, not only by scholars and other writers, but also members of the Japanese American community (including many who personally suffered it directly). Once this topic was broached in the 1970s by such ground-breaking seminal studies as historian Roger Daniels'* Concentration Camps USA: Japanese Americans and World War II *(Holt, Rinehart and Winston, 1971) and Nisei layperson Michi Nishiura Weglyn's* Years of Infamy: The Untold Story of America's Concentration Camps *(William Morrow, 1976), a veritable flood of books have been published that have assayed the WWII camp experience of Japanese Americans in a dizzying array of permutations viewed from a variety of perspectives.*

The fourteen book reviews encompassed in this section of A Nikkei Harvest *showcase volumes that, taken together, neatly illustrate the diversity and innovation of the field of inquiry in recent years to the topic of Japanese American wartime confinement. The most comprehensive treatment of this topic is Susan H. Kamei's* When Can We Go Back to America?, *which piggybacks the experience of the post-WWII redress movement onto a narrative account of the wartime Nikkei experience that extends from Japan's attack on Pearl Harbor to the closing of the assorted incarceration camps. In Claire Sato and Violet Harada's edited work,* A Resilient Spirit, *the long-neglected subject of incarceration facilities in Hawai`i is richly documented and, in the process, augments that already so amply recorded over many years relative to the U.S. mainland. The Train to Crystal City, by Jan Jarboe Russell, focuses on the Crystal City Internment Camp in Texas that boasted the largest and most variegated population (in terms of nationality and ethnicity) of the constellation of WWII internment centers. It is a book that greatly enriches the extant knowledge base about the understudied Department of Justice-administered camps interning Americans of Japanese descent. As for the book by Ronald Bishop, with Morgan Dudkewitz, Alissa Falcone, and Renee Daggett,* Community Newspapers and the Japanese American Incarceration Camps, *it also enlarges the understanding of a mainly neglected historiographical area pertaining to the Nikkei camps. It achieves this end by analyzing how non-Japanese American citizens and local newspapers surrounding nine of the ten War Relocation Authority (WRA)-managed "relocation centers" perceived and interpreted their respective incarcerated neighbors. In the* *case of* Reflecting on WWII, Manzanar, and the WRA, *Arthur L. Williams—the son of the assistant chief of internal security at the Manzanar War Relocation Center in eastern California who himself lived as a teenager at that camp during WWII—stresses the non-*Nikkei *experience of those people who called Manzanar their wartime "home." In so doing, Williams succeeds in filling still another gaping void in camp studies. Two other books that fill gaps in the sphere of the WWII* Nikkei *concentration camps are Stephanie Hinnershitz's* Japanese American Incarceration, *which treats them as sites of enforced labor, and Eric L. Muller's* Lawyer, Jailer, Ally, Foe, *which focuses on the multifaceted work of project attorneys in the ten WRA incarceration centers. With respect to Mike Mackey's* Wyoming Samurai, *he utilizes the Heart Mountain Relocation Center in northwest Wyoming as a pioneering case study in which to explore how the issue of military service in multifarious ways confronted and complicated the lives of* Nisei *inmates in the WRA camps. Another book focused on the Heart Mountain camp is Bradford Pearson's sports-and-society study* The Eagles of Heart Mountain, *in which he relates in dramatic fashion the transformation of the incarceration center's ragtag high school football team into one of Wyoming's best gridiron squads. As for Moving Walls by Sharon Yamato, this daughter of WWII prisoners at the Poston Relocation Center in southwest Arizona fixes her path-breaking focus upon the barracks housing at the Heart Mountain, Wyoming camp to explore the postwar utilization of these alleged temporary wartime quarters as a touchstone artifact at the Japanese American National Museum in Los Angeles and as transformed structures for multiple use by Wyoming homesteaders in the agricultural area surrounding the onetime Heart Mountain camp site. Finally, Walter M. Imahara and David E. Meltzer's edited volume* Jerome and Rohwer *showcases the World War II experiences of the two most neglected of the ten War Relocation Authority camps.*

WHEN CAN WE GO BACK TO AMERICA? Voices of Japanese American Incarceration During WWII

By Susan H. Kamei (New York: Simon & Schuster, 2021, 736 pp., $22.99, hardcover)

Published in the January 1, 2022 edition of the *Nichi Bei Weekly*.

During the 1980s, I was privileged to co-direct the Honorable Stephen K. Tamura Orange County Japanese American Oral History Project (OCJAOHP), jointly sponsored by the Japanese American Council of the Historical and Cultural Foundation of Orange County and the Japanese American Project of the Oral History Program at California State University, Fullerton. In addition to producing fifteen bilingual oral history volumes with pioneering *Issei* and *Nisei*, this project yielded a survey of Japanese American historical sites in Orange County and gave rise to the 1989 publication by Lynx Books of an epic historical novel, *The Harvest of Hate*. Originally written in 1946 by a World War II mathematics teacher at the Poston Relocation Center named Georgia Day Robertson, the published version included a preface by Hiroshi Kamei, who as a high schooler was among the some 2,000 Orange County *Nikkei* imprisoned at the Arizona detention camp. He credited his mathematical class work under Robertson's direction for inspiring both his postwar graduation from Pasadena's California Institute of Technology and his distinguished career as a mechanical engineer and aerospace company manager. Throughout the course of the OCJAOHP, for which Kamei was a prime mover, he exuded great pride in the volunteer work of his attorney daughter Susan as a member of the Japanese American Citizens League's legislative strategy team in the Japanese American redress and reparations movement.

Although I have never met Susan Kamei in person, my reading of her bountiful book here under review redeemed for me the promissory note floated by her late *Nisei* father so many years ago as to her dedication to the cause of placing the landmark World War II Japanese American story into an enlarged and suitable perspective. After a stimulating foreword by Secretary Norman Y. Mineta, the author of *When Can We Go Back to America?* provides a short introduction stressing her father's pivotal role in her career decision as a *Sansei* to become a lawyer and to then work alongside of him (and many others) for over a decade on achieving redemption and modest compensation for those 120,000 Americans of Japanese ancestry who were unjustly evicted from their mostly West Coast homes and incarcerated within inland American-style concentration camps. Kamei then embarks on a five-part series covering 355 pages consisting for the most part of her narrative account of the period spanning Japan's attack on Pearl Harbor on December 7, 1941, and the passage of the Civil Liberties Act on August 10, 1988, interspersed with overwhelmingly Japanese American voiced commentaries relative to differing facets of the WWII Japanese American experience drawn from "previously published works, oral histories, congressional testimonies, or works in the public domain." She next devotes a sixth part of her monumental book, a total of 161 pages, to providing substantial biographical entries relative to those individuals whose first-person voices she has drawn upon to vivify and supplement her third-person overview. She then rounds out her book with a variety of very useful appendices along with other vitally significant informational items.

With respect to her narration, it is superlative in every important respect: well-researched and documented, exquisitely expressed, judiciously reasoned, and self-effacingly represented. Some readers may find the biographies of her "contributors" excessive, but I found each of them both interesting and revealing and I applaud Kamei for generously conferring upon these individuals the status of veritable co-authors of *When Can We Go Back to America?*

Insofar as I have a reservation about this book, which I regard as among the very best comprehensive treatments of its consequential subject matter, it involves Kamei on two occasions presenting moot points as matters of congealed historical fact. In the first instance, she unambiguously writes that "Rosalie [Hankey] Wax, a field worker from the Japanese and American Resettlement Study, made a false allegation against him [Ernest Kinzo Wakayama] to the FBI, claiming he was a ruthless gang leader." In the second case, Kamei unequivocally states that during the December 8, 1945 presentation by General

Joseph Stilwell of a posthumous Distinguished Service Cross to Staff Sergeant Kazuo Masuda at his family's farm in Fountain Valley, California, "Kazuo's mother refused the medal in protest for having lost her son while being incarcerated by the country he'd been serving." Kamei may be correct in these assertions, but I would have liked seeing from her the documentation supporting them, since I believe them to be at this point debatable.

A RESILIENT SPIRIT: The Voice of Hawai`i's Internees
Edited by Claire Sato and Violet Harada (Honolulu: Japanese Cultural Center of Hawai`i, 2018, 100 pp., $25.00, paperback)

Published in the January 1, 2019 edition of the *Nichi Bei Weekly*.

Having previously read with enjoyment and edification a trio of books published by the Japanese Cultural Center of Hawai`i—*Life Behind Barbed Wire* (2008), *Family Torn Apart* (2012), and *An Internment Odyssey* (2017)—I was overjoyed by the prospect of scrutinizing still another sterling JCCH volume. Although not as ambitious in analytical penetration, topical and thematic context, and historical detail as the above noted three works, this slender primer is both more comprehensive in coverage and richer in multi-perspectival representation of a lived wartime ordeal than any of its precursors. Of a piece with the earlier JCCH books, *A Resilient Spirit* acts strategically as an educational vehicle to incorporate the Hawai`i *Nikkei* involvement into the heretofore mainland-dominated World War II uprooting and incarceration story of the Japanese American community.

Upon perusing the book's foreword by Carole Hayashino, retiring president and executive of JCCH, readers will become cognizant of two significant facts. The first of these is the pivotal role played by her organization in rediscovering, between 1998 and 2002, Hawai`i's largest and longest operating WWII civilian internment and prisoner-of-war camp, Honouliuli, in West O`ahu, and the JCCH's subsequent dedication "to forever preserve the history of Hawai`i's confinement sites." The second key fact imparted to readers by Hayashino is that the co-editors of *A Resilient Spirit*, Claire Sato and Violet Harada (both specialists in the field of library and information science), enshrine in their treatment of the wartime internment experience of Hawai`i *Nikkei* the notion long ago vocalized by Edison Uno —the legendary father of Japanese American redress and Hayashino's onetime ethnic studies mentor and colleague at San Francisco State University—that "history must be told by those who lived it."

Consistent with this historical inclination, Sato and Harada organize their book into eleven diverse thematic/topical chapters ("December 7, 1941," "Torn from Their Families," "No Longer Free," "Daily Life Behind the Barbed Wire," "Pastimes," "Mess Hall Meals," "Separation and Longing," "Sorrow in the Camps," "Release with Conditions," "Bittersweet Reflections," and "Resilient Spirit"). Each of these chapters are comprised of a cluster of artfully chosen and exceedingly moving mini-stories communicated by thirty-six internee narrators (whose brief life histories are provided in an appendix). These storytellers, overwhelmingly male *Issei* aliens, speak to the situations prevailing at the multiple internee camp sites (minimally seventeen) within O`ahu and the neighboring islands (which are conveniently mapped in a second appendix). What made Honouliuli unique among the detainment center and internment camps was that in addition to the approximately 360 internees it held at any given time, it imprisoned 3,000 to 4,000 POWs, principally non-combatants who provided the labor force for Japan's South Pacific military holdings.

Thanks in large part to the efforts of the JCCH, in 2015 President Barack Obama proclaimed Honouliuli a National Park Service-managed national monument. It would be a very wise decision for future visitors to that interpreted site to read in advance *A Resilient Spirt*, an action which is bound to convert an eye-and-mind-opening historical encounter into one suffused with palpable feeling and enlarged meaning.

REMEMBERING OUR GRANDFATHERS' EXILE: U.S. Imprisonment of Hawai'i's Japanese in World War II
By Gail Y. Okawa (Honolulu, Hawai'i: University of Hawai'i Press, 2020, 251 pp., $26.00, paperback)

Published in the January 1, 2021 edition of the *Nichi Bei Weekly*.

Back in 1980, very little had been written about the World War II imprisonment experience of more than 5,500 Japanese American aliens (*Issei*) within the hodgepodge of 24 U.S. Department of Justice and U.S. Army internment camps as against what some 120,000 aliens and *Nisei/Sansei* citizens of Japanese ancestry underwent in the 10 War Relocation Authority-administered concentration camps. Accordingly, the former confinement sites were often carelessly dismissed as "those other camps." During the succeeding 40 years, a profusion of studies—the most comprehensive of which was Tetsuden Kashima's *Judgment Without Trial* (2003)—have appeared to provide greater understanding of what internment entailed for the continental population of *Issei* deemed potentially dangerous. But not until the last decade has the internment of hundreds of Hawai'i *Issei* in mainland detention facilities been accorded in-depth autobiographical treatment, such as that found in Yasutaro Soga's *Life Behind Barbed* Wire (2008), Otokichi Ozaki's *Family Torn Apart* (2012), George Yoshio Hoshida's *Taken from the Paradise Isle* (2015), and Suikei Furuya's *An Internment Odyssey* (2017). The beautifully written book under review here by Gail Y. Okawa, a professor emerita of English at Youngstown State University in Ohio, both nicely complements and greatly enriches the content of this quartet of estimable volumes.

Beginning in 2002 and extending over the next 18 years, Okawa devoted herself to tenaciously researching the WWII mainland internment experience of her maternal *Issei* grandfather, Reverend Tamasaku Watanabe, a Protestant minister, along with that of a correlated cadre of Hawai'i-originated prisoners, within an assortment of detention facilities (but primarily the Santa Fe Internment Camp in New Mexico). Driven by her dedication to her family and the Hawai'i Japanese American community, she resourcefully explored a proliferation of archival holdings of primary sources and she undertook interviews with numerous informed people, including a few surviving *Issei* internees, to produce in ordinary language "a multivocal, multigenerational, and multigenre narrative" (p. 7). The targeted readership which she hopes to reach with her book is assuredly not specialists fully conversant with the internment history of the Hawai'i *Issei* deemed "potentially dangerous aliens," but rather those individuals like herself "who want to research personal encounters with such major historical events" (p. 7).

One of the many laudable achievements Okawa scores with her bountiful volume, richly enhanced by a plenitude of illuminating illustrations and maps, is to make clear that those Hawai'i *Issei* men that the U.S. government rounded up, arrested, and imprisoned in the wake of the Pearl Harbor attack by Japan on December 7, 1941—Japanese language teachers; Buddhist, Shinto, and Christian clergy; journalists; and businessmen—were not only leaders of Japanese-ancestry communities in Hawai'i, but they were also "educated and highly literate and understood the significance of the written and spoken word" (p. 105). As a consequence, this "immigrant intelligentsia" developed in their respective camps of confinement a panoply of cultural performances in which to enact their literacy (theater, art, music, *Noh* chanting, funeral services, sermons), to forge expressive communities within camp society, and to mobilize overt and covert forms of resistance to their oppression.

Although Okawa doesn't herself treat the experience of the eight Hawai'i *Issei* women who were interned on the mainland as alien enemies during World War II, she does tell readers that six of them were imprisoned at the camp for women in Seagoville, Texas, with the other two in New Mexico and California, and thus implicitly urges future researchers to pursue this and other neglected dimensions of her research topic.

THE TRAIN TO CRYSTAL CITY: FDR's Secret Prisoner Exchange Program and America's Only Family Internment Camp During World War II
By Jan Jarboe Russell (New York: Scribner, 2015, 416 pp., $30.00, hardcover)

Published in the July 23, 2015 edition of the *Nichi Bei Weekly*.

During World War II there existed eight Department of Justice (DOJ)-administered internment camps. Three states had a single facility: Montana (Fort Missoula Internment Camp); North Dakota (Fort Lincoln Internment Camp); and Idaho (Kooskia Internment Camp). Each are represented by a book: Carol Van Valkenburg's *An Alien Place: The Fort Missoula, Montana, Detention Camp 1941-1944* (1996); John Christgau's *Enemies: World War II Alien Internment* (1985); and Priscilla Wegars's *Imprisoned in Paradise: Japanese Internee Road Workers at the World War II Kooskia Internment Camp* (2010). One state, New Mexico, housed two DOJ camps: the Santa Fe Internment Camp and the Fort Stanton Internment Camp. Neither has gained book-length treatment. Another state, Texas, accommodated three DOJ camps: the Kenedy Internment Camp, the Seagoville Internment Center, and the Crystal City Internment Camp. Only the last has spawned a book—in fact, two books: Karen L. Riley's *Schools Behind Barbed Wire: The Untold Story of Wartime Internment and the Children of Arrested Enemy Aliens* (2002) and the book by Jan Jarboe Russell here under review. While all of these estimable volumes deserve the conscientious attention of general and academic inquirers into the World War II Japanese American confinement experience, in my considered opinion *The Train to Crystal City* is the most comprehensive, compelling, and consequential of the lot.

Russell's capacious 416-page book—replete with aptly-chosen historical photographs, useful chapter sources and notes, and an inclusive bibliography—is comprehensive in several respects and for multiple reasons. On the one hand, the author utilizes a wide-angle lens to portray the World War II era of the Crystal City camp (located 110 miles southwest of San Antonio and fifty miles north of Mexico). This not only permits her representation to include richer detail about people, places, and situations, but also allows her to render selected foreground topics more pronounced and arresting while simultaneously capturing extensive contextual information. On the other hand, Russell employs a panoramic perspective to encompass the full chronological sweep of the Crystal City camp's evolution from prewar origins to postwar denouement. The rationale driving the study's extraordinary depth and breadth stems from the camp's special nature: officially named the Crystal City Enemy Detention Facility and administered by the Immigration and Naturalization Service, it was the largest of the WWII DOJ compounds with some 6,000 internees; its longevity was the greatest, operating from 1942 until 1948; it was the only overtly family camp within (and even outside) the DOJ constellation of wartime internment units for "enemy aliens"; and its confined population was the most profoundly diversified among DOJ camps, given that it included multi-generational internees of Japanese, German, and Italian ancestry drawn from the mainland United States, the Territory of Hawai`i, and numerous South and Central American nations.

What accounts for the book's compelling quality is Russell's journalistic flair for ferreting out interesting and revealing stories and her literary capacity for relating them with the power and grace of an imaginative writer. Also contributing to making her book such compelling reading is Russell's strategic decision to pivot the larger Crystal City camp story upon the shifting fortunes of two teenaged internees, one a Los Angeles, California, *Nisei* daughter of Japanese nationals ineligible for U.S. citizenship (Sumi Utsushigawa), and the other an American-born U.S. citizen female from Strongsville, Ohio (outside of Cleveland), whose German-ancestry parents had failed to secure their U.S. citizenship in a timely prescribed manner. This device imparts "face" and "personality" to an account that might otherwise have taken on the pale cast of a standard-issue institutional history, which however effectively managed would have been far less affecting and transformative for its readers.

But what of the book's consequentiality? In a very real sense, it is prefigured in the book's title, which is both descriptive and metaphorical. While many of the camp's interned population traveled to the Zavala County, Texas, complex by train, a large number of them, lured by the seductive prospects of family unification and hemispheric security, were "railroaded" by the U.S. government in one or another venal way to jettison their freedom, property, civil rights, and dignity and to accept the crushing confinement of high-security imprisonment and forced repatriation to an Axis nation as part of an international exchange for "more important Americans." Moreover, the adult internees at the Crystal City camp involved in this exchange were obliged in advance of their departure to sign an oath promising never to disclose details either of their internment or their exchange.

Insofar as I have criticisms about such an altogether excellent book as *The Train to Crystal City*, they fall into two categories: erroneous facts and overlooked opportunities. With regard to the first category, Russell notes that the Geneva Convention agreement (of 1929) was "signed by many countries, including Japan," but Japan was *not* a party to this agreement. Also, in discussing *Issei* Yoshiaki Fukuda's life in postwar San Francisco, Russell observes that "despite all that he endured during the war, Fukuda became a U.S. citizen in 1951." However, naturalization was *not* extended to *Issei* until the passage of the Immigration Act of 1952. As for missed opportunities, I thought that Russell should have accorded greater attention to the experience of the Latin Americans (and not only Peruvians), both of Japanese and German ancestry, as well as those Japanese Americans from Hawai`i, and the few internees of Italian ancestry from wherever, all of whom get slighted or neglected. Finally, I feel that Russell missed the boat in the case of her discussion of Crystal City *Nisei* internee Edison Uno. While she does a magnificent job depicting his stalwart role as a school-aged spokesman for constitutional rights and characterizing him as "the first Japanese American from inside an internment camp to ask for official redress," Russell should have availed herself of the chance to celebrate at least some of the signal progressive actions Uno took in the postwar years (and delineated by Alice Yang in her *Densho Encyclopedia* entry on him) that catalyzed the successful Japanese American movement for redress and reparations.

COMMUNITY NEWSPAPERS AND THE JAPANESE-AMERICAN INCARCERATION CAMPS: Community, Not Controversy
By Ronald Bishop, with Morgan Dudkewitz, Alissa Falcone, and Renee Daggett (Lanham, MD: Lexington Books, 2015, 372 pp., $100.92, hardcover)

Published in the January 1, 2016 edition of the *Nichi Bei Weekly*.

In the interval between 1973 and 1988, thanks to some enterprising undergraduate and graduate students of mine affiliated with the Japanese American Oral History Project (JAOHP) of the Oral History Program (OHP) at California State University, Fullerton (CSUF), an archive of oral history interviews was compiled with World War II residents of the small towns located in close proximity to four U.S. War Relocation Authority (WRA)-administered concentration camps incarcerating evicted Americans of Japanese ancestry—Manzanar and Tule Lake in California, Poston in Arizona, and Jerome in Arkansas. All of these interviews were later made available to researchers through primarily CSUF history student-edited publications: Jessie Garrett and Ronald Larson's *Camp and Community: Manzanar and the Owens Valley* (1977), and two 1993 volumes, co-edited by Nora Jesch (with me), devoted to the taped reminiscences of "guards and townspeople" in the *Japanese American World War II Evacuation Oral History Project* (1991-1995). Each of the JAOHP interviews within the archive sought to capture the perspectives of nearby community residents from all walks of life toward their respective neighboring camps throughout their wartime duration.

The book under review here, *Community Newspapers and the Japanese-American Incarceration Camps*, both complements the Fullerton research model yet differs markedly from it. First, while it too focuses upon the WRA camps, its purview encompasses nine of the total ten facilities, leaving unexamined only the Poston one. Second, those responsible for the book's production (a Drexel University professor, Ronald Bishop, and three of his former students, Morgan Dudkewitz, Alissa Falcone, and Renee Daggett), while nominally journalism historians, are now (or once were) institutionally affiliated with the Philadelphia-sited Drexel's Department of Communications. Third, although the book's four authors employ interviews as information-gathering research tools, they are far less dependent upon community-based oral history fieldwork for the aggregated data upon which they garner their insights, construct their chapter-by-chapter and overarching narratives, and posit their assorted conclusions. Fourth, and most importantly, the Drexel study pursues, in depth, the sharply delineated objective of assaying how local community journalists (and, to a lesser extent, public relations professionals) covered the wartime period embracing the construction of the WRA camps and their subsequent peopling by *Nikkei* incarcerees.

As the superb introduction by Ronald Bishop makes clear, the book's chapters embody a common mode of inquiry and underscore a preponderantly shared set of research conclusions. With respect to the former, Bishop details the following questions as those guiding him and the other three authors: What main themes about the incarceration and construction of the camps were emphasized by the respective local newspapers covering them? How did the local journalists describe the incarcerated populations upon their arrival at and during their early settlement within the WRA camps? Was the local newspaper(s) coverage of the imprisoned Japanese Americans positive or negative? Did the local journalistic treatment of the confined *Nikkei* "echo the bigoted coverage found in large West Coast dailies?" In compiling their stories, what sources did the local reporters utilize primarily? Did these reporters pay any attention to "the civil rights violation committed against the incarcerees?"

To my mind, the chapters that adhere to these guidelines most faithfully and fully (and hence to better overall effect) are those dealing with the two California camps at Manzanar and Tule Lake, plus the Wyoming and Utah camps of Heart Mountain and Topaz. Likely this qualitative difference is due to a combination of two factors, Bishop's involvement in all four of these exemplary chapters and the availability of considerably more historical documentation and interpretation on these sites as against those of Gila River (Arizona), Minidoka (Idaho), Amache (Colorado), and the two Arkansas camps of Rohwer and Jerome.

With respect to the major research conclusions of the assorted camp chapters they, with some variation, are registered by the book's authors in a remarkably similar vein—that is, while the community journalists (and public relations officials) duly reported on the site selection and establishment of the camps, they did so in a way that permitted them to support their community of service by shoring up its social order, building and sustaining its spirit of operation, promoting its civic and economic sectors, and steering clear of "unpleasant happenings" and controversial issues. At bottom, this provincial orientation reduced journalists into being unabashed community boosters more concerned with consensus as opposed to conflict, tension management rather than constructive criticism, and palatable fictions instead of objective truths. The collateral damage inflicted by this modus operandi was that local journalists and public relations purveyors "rarely wrote about the violation of the incarcerees' civil rights."

Over and beyond its methodology and conclusions, the book under review provides a treasure trove of invaluable new information about the remote rural areas in which the WRA camps were located and in which their local newspapers functioned. It also endows its readership with richly textured life-histories of the publishers, editors, and prominent reporters for these newspapers. This grounded information, in turn, permits academic and lay camp researchers into this topical area to at long last transcend the shallow stereotypes that have heretofore passed muster as "local knowledge."

There are naturally some flaws to be found in such an ambitious undertaking as *Community Newspapers and the Japanese-American Incarceration Camps*. Mostly we find "the devil is in the detail." Several of the camp-sited studies (e.g., the Gila River and Minidoka chapters) are flawed by information that is both excessive and confused. There are also problems owing to inaccurate name and place designations (e.g., Roy Nash, not "Ray" Nash; Darwin, not "Derwin"); factual errors (e.g., the Jerome camp closed on June 30, 1944, not "June 30, 1942"; Amache was not the only camp sited on non-federal land, as Manzanar was situated on land leased by the U.S. government from the Los Angeles Department of Water and Power); irregularities in editorial protocol (e.g., the first names of two significant journalists, Todd Watkins and Henry Dworshak are unmentioned anywhere in the text, only in the index); and incorrect source attributions (e.g., this author is alleged to have refuted a scholarly assessment relative to Manzanar that he never, in fact, did; moreover, the chapter endnotes correlated with this allegation refer not to my work, but rather to that of another Manzanar researcher, Karen Piper). A more consequential concern, one of omission rather than commission, is that this lengthy, closely-argued book lacks any photographs, maps, or illustrations of any kind to aid readers in their digestion and comprehension of its very useful content.

Notwithstanding such comparatively minor liabilities, what demands paramount recognition here are the signal achievements of this book, not the least of which is it being a study that resulted from a truly collegial partnership between a distinguished university professor and his dedicated students, an arrangement that is often lauded in theory yet is at a severe discount in practice.

REFLECTING ON WWII, MANZANAR, AND THE WRA

By Arthur L. Williams (Victoria, B.C.: Friesenpress, 2014, 256 pp., $17.99, paperback)

Published in the July 21, 2016 edition of the *Nichi Bei Weekly*.

Manzanar occupies a special place in my consciousness and conscience. I was first introduced to this eastern California site in 1972 by a California State University, Fullerton (CSUF) History Department colleague and close friend who was a teenage *Nisei* incarceree there during its successive World War II iterations as a *Nikkei* detention center run by the Wartime Civil Control Administration (WCCA) and the War Relocation Authority (WRA). Among my earliest oral history interviews were those done with Manzanar detainees, camp administrators, and appointed staff. My first published article pertinent to the Japanese American wartime experience was on the so-called Manzanar Riot of December 1942, and I later co-authored a book on the central figure in that bloody episode of inmate resistance to oppression. For many years I have participated in the annual Manzanar Pilgrimage. Moreover, accompanied by former *Nisei* Manzanarians, I frequently led my CSUF classes on forays to Manzanar, and these sometimes stimulated the involved students to generate Manzanar-based oral history interviews, term papers, master's theses and public history projects, and even published articles and books. On several occasions, moreover, graduate students of mine collaborated with me in carrying out National Park Service (NPS)-funded grant work as historical consultants relative to Manzanar's past and ongoing development as an NPS site.

    I was understandably intrigued, then, when upon browsing the books for sale in the Los Angeles-based Japanese American National Museum's gift shop some months back, I ran across the volume being reviewed here: Arthur L. Williams' *Reflecting on WWII, Manzanar, and the WRA*. Consisting of an introduction, fifteen chapters, and seven appendices, this energetic and enlightening book amalgamates a personal/family/community memoir with local/regional/national history while also doing service as a reference book on the physical and social character of the Manzanar War Relocation Center in eastern California's Owens Valley. However, readers should be well aware that the emphasis of Williams's "reflections" is decidedly upon the non-*Nikkei* experience of those who made Manzanar their "home base" during World War II. This emphasis is understandable in that the author, a teenager during his Manzanar tenure, was the son of two (of the 200 some) WRA employees: his mother, Mary M. Williams, chief dietician; and his father, Arthur L. Williams, Sr., assistant chief of internal security.

What became clear to me as I read Williams's book was that I was less impressed by the quality of the author's narrative style or the analytical penetration of his historical interpretation than the sheer diligence and dedication of his monumental research into diverse aspects of Manzanar history previously slighted or altogether ignored by other Manzanar historians, including myself. One needs only to list the titles of his appendices to recognize this manifest fact: "Camp Structures," "WCCA Manzanar Personnel," "WRA Employees: Families, Job Titles, Housing Assignments," "WRA Salaries," "Original [Manzanar] Riot Report of Arthur L. Williams, Sr.," "Military [Police] Personnel at Manzanar," and "Military Police Dates and Events of Interest." Readers of Williams's book will also learn much from the carefully selected photos and other illustrations that not only adorn but also illuminate his text. You may take issue with Williams on some of his contentions, but I think you will agree that his book nicely represents what people have in mind when they call a particular book, film, museum exhibit, or other cultural production "a labor of love."

In reading over the promotional literature for *Reflecting on WWII, Manzanar, and the WRA*, I found myself in accord with something attributed to the individual who is arguably Manzanar's finest historian and arguably that camp's most skilled oral historian, former Manzanar ranger Richard Potashin. "Art Williams," opines Potashin, "has presented the reader with a view of WWII Manzanar history from a completely new perspective. ... He has pulled from personal experience and exhaustive research to reveal in-depth the WRA's challenges in providing for the needs of 10,000 Japanese Americans unjustly incarcerated during World War II."

JAPANESE AMERICAN INCARCERATION: The Camps and Coerced Labor During World War II
By Stephanie Hinnershitz (Philadelphia: University of Pennsylvania Press, 2021, 309 pp., $39.95, hardcover)

Published in the July 20, 2023 edition of the *Nichi Bei News.*

Although certainly not an American labor historian per se, I am profoundly abashed that, notwithstanding my having been researching, writing, and teaching about the unjust Japanese American World War II detention for five decades, I never until now paid more than fleeting attention to the predominant focus of the invaluable book under review here by Stephanie Hinnershitz: "the design and implementation of Japanese American incarceration and the centrality of labor to both of these undertakings." In addition to Hinnershitz being the well-deserved recipient of the 2022 Philip Taft Labor History Award for *Japanese American Incarceration,* she should be roundly lauded by practitioners and students alike of Japanese American history for penning the first study that, in the author's own words, categorizes the experiences of *Nikkei* laborers under Executive Order 9066 "as coerced prison work."

In this same vein, the book's publisher, the University Press of Pennsylvania, draws upon the opinions of two giants in the field of Asian American studies, Erika Lee and John Howard, to highlight Hinnershitz's signal achievement. Whereas the former commends her scholarship for exposing "a deeper infringement of Japanese Americans' rights than had been previously understood and compels us to revise how we teach this tragic chapter in American history," the latter makes the claim that Hinnershitz's "bold interpretation" (rooted in rigorous archival research) "forces a thoroughgoing rethink of the American carceral state."

Japanese American Incarceration consists of five chapters which, taken together, present a tripartite scenario: (1) that the utilization (i.e., exploitation) of Japanese American labor in the so-called "assembly centers" and "relocation centers" (i.e., concentration camps) was an important goal guiding the U.S. government's policy of enforced mass incarceration; (2) that the labor extracted from Japanese American inmates was crucial to their assorted mobilizations of resistance to what they deemed as darkly oppressive treatment; and (3) that the state-coerced wartime work of *Nikkei* incarcerees was consistent with the tradition of American prison labor.

Hinnershitz's opening two chapters revolve around how the decisive consideration by the U.S. government to employ Japanese American labor in the camps figured prominently in the decisions about their locations (i.e., replete with neighboring agricultural land contributing to site self-sufficiency), augmented by "convenient" fringe benefits (such as having inmates being granted periodical releases so as to provide inexpensive farm labor employment for privately owned nearby properties). Chapters 3 and 4 are case studies set at one assembly center in California, Santa Anita, and two reception centers/relocation centers, Manzanar in California and Poston in Arizona, all of which witnessed noteworthy manifestations of inmate insurrection. As for the fifth chapter, it explores the entangling of labor and resettlement, whereby Japanese Americans could be released from the camps to secure jobs outside of the West Coast exclusion zones as "parolees" in jobs within a "work-release" program.

Overall, *Japanese American Incarceration* is both an amply researched and a well-written monograph. Its flaws for the most part are comparatively minor ones such as the misspelling of the names of two prominent Japanese Americans, Sue Kunitomi Embrey (p. 275) and Minoru Yasui (pp. 249, 309). A more serious error is Hinnershitz's flagrant mischaracterization of Manzanar's second project director

Roy Nash, charging him with being "more focused on maintaining good relations with the local townspeople than ... the challenges of running Manzanar and implementing better living, working, and self-governing policies," when the reverse situation was in reality the actual case.

LAWYER, JAILER, ALLY, FOE: Complicity and Conscience in America's World War II Concentration Camps
By Eric L. Muller (Chapel Hill: University of North Carolina Press, 2023, 283 pp., $30.00, hardcover)

Published in the July 20, 2023 edition of the *Nichi Bei News*.

As someone who has taught both history and literature classes, I recently had my curiosity aroused by an article in *The New Yorker* magazine (April 24 & May 1, 2023) written by Louis Menand, a professor of English at Harvard University noted for his seminal books in U.S. intellectual history. The article's subject matter, "creative nonfiction," according to Menand, is a relatively new genre that has emerged when biographers and historians "adopt a narrative style intended to make their books read more like novels." However, he concludes, notwithstanding that authors of such books utilize the techniques of fiction (e.g., dialogue, first-person voice, description, and speculation), their final product is nonfiction "as long as it's all fact-based and not make-believe."

Thanks to Menand's formulation, I was in a fully receptive frame of mind when I was given the fortuitous opportunity to read the brilliant book here under review written by Eric Muller, a distinguished professor of jurisprudence and ethics at the University of North Carolina School of Law, and the author/editor since 2001 of a series of award-winning and groundbreaking volumes focused on the Japanese American concentration camp experience during World War II. Described on the book's dust jacket as having an "imaginative narrative deeply grounded in archival evidence," *Lawyer, Jailer, Ally, Foe* is also touted in two promotional peer blurbs as "carefully researched and deeply imagined" (Julie Otsuka) and "a bold experiment in creative historical narration" (Christopher R. Browning).

At the core of his book, Muller presents his readers with a standard-issue historical monograph, albeit one of exceptional quality. Accordingly, he rivets his concern on an important yet understudied topic, the legal system within the War Relocation Authority, the civilian organization in charge of the World War II Japanese American incarceration camps. He then reduces his treatment of this broad topic to manageable proportions by focusing on the corps of lawyers at the ten WRA detention centers charged with the three-pronged task of providing their directors with legal advice, acting as community organization advisors to their respective inmate population, and supplying imprisoned Japanese Americans at their particular camp with guidance in respect to their personal legal worries. To further sharpen his focus, Muller limits his primary attention to three "representative" camp lawyers: Jerry Housel at Heart Mountain in Wyoming, Ted Hass (plus his inmate lawyer associate Thomas Masuda) at Poston in Arizona, and James Hendrick Terry at Gila River in Arizona. In respect to enacting his interpretation, Muller draws upon a rich and previously untapped archival database, the substantive (i.e., not merely statistical) biweekly letters the project lawyers were mandated to send to their boss at the national WRA office in Washington, D.C., Philip M. Glick (as well as to all of the other project lawyers). Finally, and most significantly, Muller organizes his historical inquiry around a bottom-line ethical question: how did the WRA legal staff justify their everyday involvement within an enterprise that perpetuated and exacerbated racial discrimination?

Readers of *Lawyer, Jailer, Ally, Foe* should take the time and go to the trouble of carefully reading Muller's "Preface," "Author's Note," and "Acknowledgments" sections, for therein he painstakingly explains and justifies the imaginative departures he has taken from his otherwise conventional work of non-fiction. I found his rationale in this regard to be exceedingly convincing, but others might conceivably take exception to his infusion of "made-up" material into an allegedly historical manuscript.

My one reservation about this masterpiece by Muller is that he and/or the University of North Carolina Press, for some reason that I cannot fathom, made the decision that the inclusion of an index, something customary in a work of non-fiction, was unnecessary.

WYOMING SAMURAI: The World War II Warriors of Heart Mountain
By Mike Mackey (Cody, WY: Western History Publications, 2015, 181 pp., $18.95, paperback)

Published in the January 1, 2018 edition of the *Nichi Bei Weekly*.

This is Mike Mackey's fifth and, apparently, final book centered on the World War II experience of the Heart Mountain Relocation Center in northwest Wyoming. Mackey, who has made his home in both Powell and Cody, the two communities nearest to Heart Mountain, is exceedingly well informed on the camp's history and passionately dedicated to its historical interpretation and legacy. Accordingly, it has always shocked and saddened me that as a professional historian, Mackey's knowledge and commitment relative to Heart Mountain has not, for one or another reason, been translated into a teaching position for him at Northwest College in Powell and/or an appointment to the staff of the Heart Mountain Interpretive Center.

As for *Wyoming Samurai*, it is a comparatively brief yet highly useful case study of the salient role played by the issue of military service at Heart Mountain—more so, in fact, than at any of the other nine American-style concentration camps for Americans of Japanese ancestry administered by the War Relocation Authority (WRA). Without exception, all of the WRA confinement centers' inmate populations seethed with resentment at the U.S. government's 1942 decisions to discharge American-citizen *Nisei* from the military because of their ancestry, to relegate those remaining in uniform to servile duties, and to downgrade the draft status of *Nisei* to 4C (aliens or any group of persons not acceptable for military service). Then, too, virtually all of the WRA detention camps' incarcerated denizens took umbrage at the War Department's 1943 determination to open army enlistment to Japanese Americans for volunteer service in a segregated unit. Finally, there was fairly widespread opposition within the ten WRA penal colonies to the War Department's 1944 policy of reopening the military draft to *Nisei* as a way of reclaiming some of their lost citizenship rights and offering them a chance to demonstrate their loyalty as Americans.

What made the situation at Heart Mountain qualitatively different from that of its counterpart lockups was first, the degree to which the implementation of the segregated volunteer unit and the resumption of the *Nisei* draft was contested, and second, the character of that contestation. As Mackey points out, whereas the number of volunteers from the WRA camps fell dramatically below government expectations, "the recruiting program at Heart Mountain was among the least successful." In the case of the resumption of the *Nisei* draft, Heart Mountain, percentage-wise, spawned the most *Nisei* who resisted the military draft.

In terms of the type of challenge mounted, respectively, to the segregated volunteer unit for *Nisei* and the subsequent drafting of them into the military, what made Heart Mountain distinctive is that in each instance it was both organized and principled. As regards the former circumstance, the dissent-protest-resistance in early 1943 was led by *Nisei* Frank Inouye, a UCLA senior at the time of his incarceration. It took shape in the formation of an organization called the Heart Mountain Congress of American Citizens. To quote Mackey, "The Congress adopted fourteen resolutions which fell into several categories: clarification of citizenship status, halting [the loyalty] registration until clarification was obtained, and implied consent of the *Nisei* to serve in the Army once their citizenship was clarified." These resolutions were fueled by a burning question: Why should American citizens volunteer to serve in the army of a government that had imprisoned them behind barbed wire?

In respect to the Heart Mountain Fair Play Committee-led *Nisei* draft resistance movement, it was fathered by Kiyoshi Okamoto, a Congress of American Citizens activist, as a one-person operation before morphing into a formal organization, replete with officers and a swelling membership. By March of 1944, the FPC declared that its membership would "refuse to report for their physical examinations or to the induction if or when called in order to contest the issue," and thereupon began taking that precise step in substantial numbers. This activity climaxed in two celebrated trials held in Cheyenne's federal district court, the first in June 1944 for sixty-three draft resisters (in the largest mass trial in Wyoming history), and the second in October/November 1944 for seven FPC leaders on the grounds of conspiring to impede the draft. In both cases, convictions and federal penitentiary imprisonment terms resulted, though in 1945 the FPC leaders had their jail sentences overturned by a federal court of appeals in Denver and in 1947 President Harry Truman granted the *Nisei* draft resisters a full pardon.

While Mackey accords the draft resistance movement at Heart Mountain ample space and judicious respect, the heart of his book—chapters 5, 6, and 7—is devoted to the military participation of Heart Mountain's men and women (although the role of the latter is simply noted and not developed). Much of what is covered in this section of *Wyoming Samurai* represents a condensation of the standard issue version of the heroic record achieved during World War II by Japanese American soldiers of the 100th Battalion, the 442nd Regimental Combat Team in Europe, and the Military Intelligence Service in the Pacific. Mackey wisely accents his war narrative with the notable actions of select Heart Mountain soldiers, and usefully provides an appendix representing an Honor Roll for all of Heart Mountain's many enlistees.

Wyoming Samurai is well written and documented and recommends itself both to a general readership and as an assigned text for high school and lower-division college students. Moreover, it should be made required reading in Wyoming's secondary schools.

THE EAGLES OF HEART MOUNTAIN: A True Story of Football, Incarceration, and Resistance in World War II America
By Bradford Pearson (New York: Simon & Schuster, 2021, 388 pp., $28.00, hardcover)

Published in the July 22, 2021 edition of the *Nichi Bei Weekly*.

For a number of years, I have been working on a sports and society book treating the social and cultural transformation of Southern California in the early Cold War period through the lens of prep football as epitomized by a December 14, 1956, CIF championship game between Downey High School and Anaheim High School played before a record crowd of between 40 and 60 thousand fans at the Los Angeles Coliseum. I sensed that I was stalled in completing it by a fatal flaw, but did not fully realize what precisely that flaw was until I ran across a March 5, 2021, *Washington Post* critical assessment by Samuel Freedman of Bradford Pearson's stunning book here under review. The author of the 2013 book *Breaking the Line* about the conjunction between Black college football and the Civil Rights Movement, Freedman believes *The Eagles of Heart Mountain* to be a brilliant and beautifully written book, one that shrewdly treats the gridiron exploits of the Heart Mountain High School football team within the context of anti-Japanese racism before and during World War II. But he feels that the book suffers from one major liability: "the context crowds out the primary story line." I agree wholeheartedly with Freedman's double-edged assessment.

Pearson's book is organized within three parts. In the first and second chapters of Part I, the author strikingly introduces readers to the two seasoned *Nisei* footballers—star quarterback Tamotsu "Babe" Nomura and stalwart tackle George "Horse" Yoshinaga—who as best friends serve as the protagonists within the book's dramatic account of how a ragtag football squad of largely unproven teenage inmates at the Heart Mountain concentration camp in Wyoming became arguably that state's very best high school team in the 1943-1944 seasons by winning all of its games but one, and aside from that narrow loss, shutting out its other opponents. Pearson then shifts gears in the remaining three chapters of Part I and all seven chapters of Part II, wherein he exquisitely narrates a richly detailed, well-documented, and exceedingly insightful overview of the harshly discriminatory Japanese American historical experience leading up to Japan's December 7, 1941, attack on Pearl Harbor and the subsequent chain of events responsible for the U.S. government's unjust mass eviction of some 120,000 Americans of Japanese ancestry in ten euphemistically named "relocation centers." Although Pearson artfully threads the Nomura-Yoshinaga spearheaded Heart Mountain football saga foregrounded in the book's title through some of these chapters, it only takes center-stage within five brief action-packed chapters of Part III.

The disproportionate structure of Pearson's book is bound to disappoint those readers who understandably will expect that the social and cultural portion of the book should take a back seat to the sports portion. Nonetheless, such readers should be mindful that while the latter section of *The Eagles of Heart Mountain* is far more exhilarating, the former section is far more significant and, accordingly, should not be glossed over or, worse still, skipped entirely.

Personally, my favorite part of the book consists of those superb chapters in Part III wherein Pearson intertwines his football story in conjunction with that of the Heart Mountain draft resistance movement involving 85 youthful *Nisei* (including footballer Tayzo Matsumoto) who supported the position of the inmate Heart Mountain Fair Play Committee (FPC) and refused induction into the military until their U.S. citizenship rights were restored. Thanks in part to the ardent "patriotic" advocacy of Heart Mountain's Caucasian administrators as well as the collaborative staff of the *Heart Mountain Sentinel* newspaper, including sports writer George "Horse" Yoshinaga, both the draft resisters and the FPC leadership were successively tried in the same Cheyenne federal court and meted out multi-year prison sentences. Ironically, in the early 1990s, at a time when Yoshinaga was a quarrelsome columnist for the Los Angeles-based *Rafu Shimpo* newspaper, he engaged in an extended vitriolic press debate with former FPC leader Frank Emi, a black-belt *judoka*, which spilled over into a front-page piece in the *Los Angeles Times*. Whereas Emi characterized the draft resisters as courageous civil rights heroes, Yoshinaga outrightly dismissed them as "draft dodgers" and "chickens." Privately, along with numerous other onetime draft resisters from Heart Mountain and other camps, Emi referred to Yoshinaga as a "Horse's Ass," but he also conceded that "Horse," however inadvertently, had given the resisters the public attention and attendant respect and admiration that they heretofore had lacked.

In spite of *The Eagles of Heart Mountain* being Pearson's first book, it is undeniably a seminal one.

JAPANESE AMERICANS AT HEART MOUNTAIN: Networks, Power, and Everyday Life
By Saara Kekki (Norman: University of Oklahoma Press, 2022, 246 pp., $23.97, hardcover)

Published in the January 1, 2023 edition of the *Nichi Bei News*.

Having read in Saara Kekki's acknowledgements within the book under review that its contents had been favorably vetted by three historians of the Japanese American World War II experience who I greatly admire (Eric Muller, Greg Robinson, and Paul Spickard) and having observed that the latter two of these historical scholars had provided promotional comments on the book's cover attesting to the work's seminal significance, I was utterly thrilled with the fortuitous opportunity to read and review *Japanese Americans at Heart Mountain*. This was especially the case because the Heart Mountain concentration camp had figured so largely in my own published scholarship, particularly in recent years. On the other hand, my enthusiasm relative to Kekki's study was dampened somewhat when I discovered that it was driven by the methodology of dynamic network analysis, something she explains in detail in a concluding appendix that, I admit, largely eluded my quantitative-and-computer-challenged comprehension. As a consequence, I determined to focus my attention here less on Kekki's methodology per se than on the fruits of the findings it generated relative to the Heart Mountain experience.

Although Kekki's network analysis is complemented by her use of traditional historical sources such as letters, diaries, government reports, and oral histories, her foremost concern is with what she characterizes as "big data," which in respect to a historical dataset is one she defines as "too large for an individual researcher to process manually." In this connection, her model for assessing the networks at Heart Mountain is based on a trio of substantial datasets: (1) the responses to form 26, which the War Relocation Authority (WRA) received from all 10,000 or so camp inmates upon entry; (2) the so-called "final roster," which accounted the movement of inmates from camp for indefinite leaves such as education and employment and final destinations; and (3) the content of the camp newspaper, the *Heart Mountain Sentinel*. Utilizing these three networks, Kekki, a postdoctoral researcher at Finland's University of Helsinki, rivets her primary attention on "manifestations of power, agency, and resistance" within the Heart Mountain incarcerated community. Although granting that such themes have been typically studied by historical researchers through narrative documents, Kekki argues that historical big data and dynamic network analysis can "help us see trends and changes in a community that has [previously] received little scholarly attention."

The ten chapters comprising the body of Kekki's artfully written, carefully reasoned, and richly documented book all testify to the truth of her promissory note, although Chapter 8 resonated with me the most, owing to my particular research emphasis upon inmate resistance activity in Heart Mountain and the other camps. Entitled

"Disobedience Behind Barbed Wire: Passive and Active Resistance," this chapter vivified for me the laundry list of claims Kekki makes for the power of dynamic network analysis in her epilogue ("Networks of Power and the Power of Networks"), but most especially her culminating one: "The clear understanding that historical events are not just a series of actions taken by individual 'great men.'"

Saara Kekki has provided a heuristic model for future historical scholars to emulate with respect to the nine other WRA camps.

MOVING WALLS: The Barracks of America's Concentration Camps
By Sharon Yamato (Washington, D.C.: National Park Service, 2017, 64 pp., $19.95, paperback)

Published in the July 19, 2018 edition of the *Nichi Bei Weekly*.

Sharon Yamato is truly a lovely person. She is also a lyrical writer, a seasoned journalist, a capable historian, a skilled interviewer, an accomplished curator, and a talented filmmaker. The daughter of parents who were World War II prisoners in the Poston Relocation Center in Arizona, she was born after the war in the Japanese American resettlement community of Denver, Colorado, and thereafter raised and educated in Los Angeles, California. While coming of age, Yamato shared with many others in the *Sansei* generation an unawareness of her family and racial-ethnic group's unjust wartime exclusion and incarceration experience. In 1976, however, she was awakened to the harsh reality of this event when she read a powerful rendering of it in a landmark book written by a camp survivor, Michi Nishiura Weglyn: *Years of Infamy: The Untold Story of America's Concentration Camps*. This work, plus a personal encounter with Weglyn some years later, catalyzed Yamato's now distinguished career, which includes three documentary films—*Out of Infamy: Michi Weglyn* (2010); *A Flicker in Eternity* (2013); and *Moving Walls: American Night-*

mare to American Dream (2017)—and three books—*Moving Walls: Preserving the Barracks of America's Concentration Camps* (1998); *Jive Bomber: A Sentimental Journey* (2010); and the volume that is here under review. What unites all of Yamato's productions is her fervent desire to enlighten consumers about a very dark episode in America's past, but in a manner that accurately communicates its horrors and ominous forebodings while at the same time offering a positive message of uplift and even triumph.

Yamato's newest book is a prime case in point. It is an updated spinoff from her 1998 book, but significantly different in one major respect. The earlier iteration of *Moving Walls* revolved around the galvanizing community adventure in which a band of intrepid Japanese American volunteers (including Yamato) removed two actual Heart Mountain Relocation Center barracks—wartime "homes"—for imprisoned *Nikkei* from their Wyoming site and transported them to the Japanese American National Museum in Los Angeles, where one of them was installed as the museum's touchstone artifact. By means of a series of intergenerational oral history interviews with the volunteers, Yamato sought to capture what the barracks conjured up in their minds as to their palpable meaning relative to the entire nightmarish World War II removal and confinement experience.

The revised version of the book first tells this story, but then shifts its focus to the after-the-war transformation of onetime Heart Mountain barracks by Wyoming homesteaders and their offspring families into homes, garages and storage sheds, and even apartment buildings, community centers, and a variety of other repurposed structures. To properly communicate this dreamlike story of the adaptive reuse of the Heart Mountain barracks by enterprising postwar pioneers, Yamato undertook intensive fieldwork in the area of Wyoming surrounding the wartime camp. This included locating the renovated structures, clarifying the salient details of the Heart Mountain wartime story and its postwar legacy within Wyoming, and conducting interviews with the current occupants of the transfigured barracks to gather what they today remember, think, and feel about the Heart Mountain camp and, beyond that, the Japanese American incarceration. Fortunately, Yamato has eloquently captured for posterity the content and context of her Wyoming fieldwork, which here merits accession and reflection: http://www.discovernikkei.org/en/journal/2015/6/11/quest-to-find-barracks.

With a foreword by former Wyoming U.S. Senator Alan K. Simpson, who lived cheek by jowl with the Heart Mountain camp during his WWII Cody, Wyoming, boyhood, and a panoply of spectacularly moving photos by award-winning photographer Stan Honda—his *Nisei* parents, like Yamato's, were Poston inmates—*Moving Walls: The Barracks of America's Concentration Camps* is a literary, aesthetic, and historical jewel. Furthermore, this book is now augmented by a film (*Moving Walls: American Nightmare to American Dream*) and a special traveling exhibit (*Moving Walls: Heart Mountain Barracks in the Bighorn Basin*) that opened in September 2017 at the Heart Mountain Interpretive Center in Powell, Wyoming. Community organizations that could mount programs featuring all three of these interrelated and interpenetrating productions would be more than triply blessed.

JEROME AND ROHWER: Memories of Japanese American Internment in World War II Arkansas
Edited by Walter M. Imahara and David E. Meltzer (Fayetteville: University of Arkansas Press, 2022, 228 pp., $22.46, hardcover)

Published in the January 1, 2023 edition of the *Nichi Bei News*.

In 2002-2004, I was honored to serve with two distinguished historical colleagues, Roger Daniels and the late Franklin Odo, as a co-consultant for the Life Interrupted Project, jointly sponsored by the Public History Program of the University of Arkansas, Little Rock, and the Japanese American National Museum. Funded chiefly by the Winthrop Rockefeller Foundation, an organization dedicated to promoting statewide issues of economic, racial, and social justice, this project generated eight new exhibitions, initiated elementary- and secondary-level educational curriculum, produced a new documentary film, and organized a major one-day national conference, "Camp Connections," held at Little Rock in September 2004. As succinctly observed by filmmaker-writer-psychotherapist-social activist Satsuki Ina in her Winter 2006 project review for the *Public Historian*, the Life Interrupted Project's primary purpose was to "educate the citizens of Arkansas and the nation about Japanese Americans in World War II Arkansas, with particular emphasis on the Jerome and Rohwer camps in Arkansas, where Japanese Americans from California were held during the war." Two decades later, the book under review here, judiciously edited by Walter M. Imahara and David E. Meltzer, embodies the very same enlightened mission.

To fulfill this assignment, Imahara and Meltzer have artfully assembled an impressive compendium of recollections of the two camps (the furthest removed and the least documented of the ten World War II War Relocation Authority incarceration facilities for Japanese Americans) provided by former inmates and their close relatives. The majority of the memoirs relate to families whose prewar roots were in cities and towns in California's agricultural San Joaquin Valley. The stories they tell typically (but certainly not always) relate information pertinent to their communities of origin and then proceed to provide significant and very often captivating details about their uprooting and enforced migration to so-called temporary "assembly centers" (fifteen in number overseen by the Wartime Civil Control Administration), followed by their transfer to one of the two more permanent Arkansas WRA "relocation centers." Although most of the WRA-based narratives pertain primarily to life at the Jerome camp as against the Rohwer camp, certainly ample coverage is given to the latter site as well.

While many of the narrators represented in *Jerome and Rohwer* were very young at the time of their World War II incarceration (and even some of them were born after the WRA camps had been emptied of inmates), this fact does not detract from the value of the book. Instead, it points out how increasingly the story of the concentration camps are going to be communicated in the future less on the basis of direct personal experience per se than through the agency of heartfelt and conscientious inter-generational transmission.

The co-editors of this bountiful volume are to be congratulated not only for the meticulous assembly and abundant content of the selected narratives, but also for providing readers with a precise and comprehensive index that will allow them to retrieve topical information in an efficacious manner.

PART VI

WORLD WAR II JAPANESE AMERICAN RESISTANCE

In 1946, anthropologist Alexander Leighton authored a Princeton University Press book titled The Governing of Men: General Principles and Recommendations Based on Experience at a Japanese Relocation Camp. *It richly documented the largely successful November 1942 strike mounted by inmates at the War Relocation Authority (WRA)/Bureau of Indian Affairs (BIA)-administered Poston Relocation Center in southwestern Arizona. Nine years later, in 1955, Norman Richard Jackman produced a doctoral dissertation in sociology at the University of California, Berkeley, "Collective Protest in Relocation Centers," which covered 115 incidents of resistance that occurred throughout World War II in all of the ten so-called "relocation centers" managed by the WRA. Then, in 1970, Douglas Nelson, a University of Wyoming graduate student, wrote a master's thesis, "Heart Mountain: The History of an American Concentration Camp," that focused solely on inmate resistance at the WRA facility in northwestern Wyoming designated in his title. The following year, Nelson's faculty mentor, Roger Daniels, drawing heavily from his student's thesis, released his classic work* Concentration Camps USA: Japanese Americans and World War II *(New York: Holt, Rinehart, and Winston, 1971), which offered a reassessment of resistance in the WRA camps. Both of these two studies placed special emphasis on the 1944 Nisei draft resistance movement at the Heart Mountain camp. The year 1973 saw the appearance of a pioneering article in the fledgling* Amerasia Journal *by Gary Okihiro that posited two theoretical models of Japanese American inmate resistance relevant to the above noted Poston Strike and the "riot" at eastern California's Manzanar War Relocation Center. It was followed up in 1974 with another* Amerasia Journal *article, this one co-authored by Arthur Hansen and David Hacker, that offered a revisionist case study of the "riot" at Manzanar in which it was recast as a "revolt." In the wake of the next year's publication of Nelson's thesis as a book bearing the same title,* Heart Mountain: History of an American Concentration Camp *(Madison, WI: State Historical Society of Wisconsin and the Department of History at the University of Wisconsin, 1975), there appeared within the same decade and that following it two other seminal resistance-themed volumes. The first was Michi Nishiura Weglyn's* Years of Infamy: The Untold Story of America's Concentration Camps *(New York: William Morrow, 1976), the last half of which was devoted to resistance activity at the WRA concentration camp of Tule Lake in northern California. The second was Richard Drinnon's* Keeper of Concentration Camps: Dillon Myer and American Racism *(Berkeley: University of California Press, 1987), which emphasized the resistance movements at the WRA's "isolation centers" in Moab, Utah, and Leupp, Arizona, as well as that at the Tule Lake Segregation Center. Then, clustered around the turn-of-the-century were five more works about resistance. Three were books, and two were films. The books consisted of Eric Muller's* Free to Die for Their Country: The Story of the Japanese American Resisters in World War II *(Chicago: University of Chicago Press, 2001); William Hohri's edited anthology, with Mits Koshiyama, Yosh Kuromiya, Takashi Hoshizaki, and Frank Emi,* Resistance: Challenging America's Wartime Internment of Japanese-Americans *(Lomita, CA: The Epistolarian, 2001); and Frank Chin's documentary novel,* Born in the USA: A Story of Japanese America, 1889-1947 *(Lanham, MD: Rowman & Littlefield, 2002). The two films were Emiko Omori's* Rabbit in the Moon *(Hohokus, NJ: New Day Films, 1999) and Frank Abe's* Conscience and the Constitution *(Seattle: Resisters.com Productions, 2000). All of these productions, in whole or in part, dealt with the draft resistance movement at Heart Mountain.*

The five books reviewed in this section of A Nikkei Harvest, *four of them by women historians, are among the comparatively small but growing number of narrative and cinematic creations that in the opening two decades of the twenty-first century have tackled head-on the issue of WWII resistance. In Japan-born-and-raised Takako Day's* Show Me the Way to Go Home, *she concentrates her commentary on the camp resistance of* Kibei *(U.S. citizen* Nisei *educated in Japan), who were demonized by the government, and even by many* Nikkei, *for their staunch opposition to oppression, both in the "relocation centers," where they were outspoken in their defiance to the ill-worded 1943 "loyalty registration," and at the Tule Lake Segregation Center, where many of them renounced their U.S. citizenship in protest to their mistreatment as American citizens. Cherstin Lyon, in* Prisons and Patriots, *explores the principled resistance to the draft of former inmates at the WRA camps of Topaz in Utah and Amache in Colorado, both within the context of their confinement at the chiefly overlooked Tucson Federal Prison Camp in Arizona's Catalina Mountains and the contested definition of the concept of U.S. citizenship. Similarly, Eileen Tamura's biographical book* In Defense of Justice *foregrounds the voluble denunciation of the U.S. government's WWII eviction and imprisonment of 120,000 Americans of Japanese ancestry by a Hawai`i Nisei and World War I veteran, Joseph Kurihara, at the WRA center of Manzanar, as well as his unswerving resolve to renounce his U.S. citizenship for postwar life in Japan (which he had never previously even visited). As for Mira Shimabukuro, in* Relocating Authority, *she seeks through unearthing seemingly innocuous resistance writings (such as the 1944 letter that the Mother's Society of Minidoka in Idaho sent to U.S. President Franklin Roosevelt opposing the* Nisei *draft) to transfer the authoritative voice for the defining nature of the WWII* Nikkei *incarceration experience from the U.S. government, the WRA, and the collaborative JACL leadership to the inmates of the prison camps (whose resistance she claims was far more widespread and robust than that which has been heretofore represented by public media and word of mouth). Lastly,* Kibei *Tatsuo Ryusei Inouye's* Tule Lake Stockade Diary *consists of the diaristic entries he faithfully and* *frankly compiled while being imprisoned, along with other Tule Lake Segregation Center protesting inmates in that facility's notorious stockade from November 13, 1943, to February 14, 1944.*

SHOW ME THE WAY TO GO HOME: The Moral Dilemma of *Kibei* No No Boys in World War II Incarceration Camps
By Takako Day (Middlebury, VT: Wren Song Press, 2014, 222 pp., $19.95, paperback)

Published in the July 24, 2014 edition of the *Nichi Bei Weekly*.

"What I have attempted to introduce in [*Show Me the Way to Go Home*]," writes Takao Day in the preface to her brilliant, bold, highly significant, if rather sprawling book, "are the lives and the struggles of Japanese-speaking Japanese Americans (known as '*Kibei Nisei*,' a minority within a minority) who survived the tempestuous period of World War II when Japanese was an enemy language." She then proceeds to say that particularly the "No No's" within the *Kibei* population, owing to prejudice, have been silenced, and follows up this shrewd observation with a ringing declaration: "The stories of these men must not remain buried like a dirty secret in Japanese American history. Their voices should be heard."

Let me say first off that I entirely agree with Day. I felt this way as long ago as the mid-1970s when I co-transacted the tape-recorded narratives of two iconic *Kibei* men who were bitter wartime enemies within the Manzanar concentration camp: Karl Yoneda (1906-1999) and Harry Ueno (1907-2004). It pleased me greatly both to witness the 1983 publication of Yoneda's autobiography, *Ganbatte*, and to be involved as a coeditor of Ueno's 1986 life history, *Manzanar Martyr*. I also experienced elation at the appearance in print of *Kibei* Minoru Kiyota's 1997 memoir, *Beyond Loyalty*, which had been translated from Japanese into English. Then, in 2013, I was delighted to discover an unpublished UC Santa Cruz dissertation by Michael Jin entitled

"Beyond Two Homelands: Migration and Transnationalism of Japanese Americans in the Pacific 1930-1955," particularly since it contains a fascinating biographical portrait of the enigmatic prewar journalist and wartime Manzanar inmate David Akira Itami, a *Kibei* who, a few years after supervising court interpreters assigned to indicted Japanese war criminals at the International Military Tribunal for the Far East held in Tokyo, committed suicide at age thirty-nine.

So, I was truly excited to read that Takao Day had identified fifteen men within the U.S. and Japan who had been "considered 'troublemakers,' 'disloyal' to the U.S. during the war, and long stigmatized in the Japanese American community," and that she had not only tape-recorded their recollections, but also had translated them into English. However, I became confused somewhat by her characterizing them as "*Nisei*" rather than "*Kibei Nisei*," and her providing a list of these men (either properly named or indicated with a pseudonym) that added up not to fifteen interviewees, but instead to ten.

Since their stories presumably formed the book's documentary core, I was disconcerted, too, by her enlisting interviewees' names unaccompanied by a description of any sort as to who they were and how their lives had played out. As it turns out, their stories are distributed throughout the entire text, but it is left to the reader to assemble full biographical portraits. That the book lacks an index makes this assembly process inordinately time-consuming and exasperatingly inefficient.

It is disappointing, as well, that Day does not offer her readers more precise overall information as to when and where and under what conditions her interviews were transacted, whether or not they were transcribed in both English and Japanese, whether they have been deposited in a public archive (or at least plans made for such deposit) so that researchers can avail themselves of their contents for purposes other than Day's and/or to assess the context in which she has selectively adduced this material to advance her interpretive argument.

It has pained me to have to dwell on the above shortcoming in what is otherwise a magnificent piece of historical scholarship, one which consumed ten years to materialize and enlisted the services of two professional translators and the skilled editing of her husband Michael Day and still another person. Although the organization of the book's chapters are problematic, the matter within them is consistently pertinent, intelligently approached, richly developed, amply documented, and artfully expressed in clear and compelling prose. One learns a great deal about such previously underdeveloped yet profoundly important topics as: why *Kibei-Nisei* have largely been left out of the master narrative of the World War II Japanese American story; the extent of the *Kibei-Nisei* population and the diversity contained within it; the relationship of *Kibei-Nisei* to the general Japanese American community and, specifically, to the Japanese American Citizens League; the short- and long-range impact of the 1943 registration's loyalty questions on *Kibei-Nisei*; the roles played by family and citizenship in relationship to *Kibei-Nisei* "loyalty" and "disloyalty"; the political climate and cultural dynamics at the Tule Lake Segregation Center and the implications they had for *Kibei-Nisei* in respect to the "resegregation movement" and U.S. citizenship renunciation; and the wartime and postwar experience of *Kibei-Nisei* renunciants, both in the U.S. and Japan, who opted for whatever reasons to sustain their changed status or to restore their U.S. citizenship.

Given the very high-profile importance these days of the *Kibei-Nisei* experience, especially in relationship to the conjoined issues of the Tule Lake Segregation Center and U.S. citizenship renunciation/restoration, *Show Me the Way to Go Home* demands an engaged readership both inside and outside of the Japanese American community.

PRISONS AND PATRIOTS: Japanese American Wartime Citizenship, Civil Disobedience, and Historical Memory
By Cherstin M. Lyon (Philadelphia: Temple University Press, 2012, 233 pp., $30.95, paperback)

Published in the January 1, 2012 edition of the *Nichi Bei Weekly*.

Prisons and Patriots is Cherstin Lyon's first book. Its publication catapults Professor Lyon, a historian at California State University, San Bernardino, into the ranks of the premier scholars of World War II Japanese American protest and dissent. Accordingly, this volume will now assume a place among seminal books like Roger Daniels's *Concentration Camps USA* (1971), Michi Nishiura Weglyn's *Years of Infamy* (1976), Richard Drinnon's *Keeper of Concentration Camps* (1987), Eric Muller's *Free to Die for Their Country* (2001), Frank Chin's *Born in the USA* (2002), and Shirley Castlenuovo's *Soldiers of Conscience* (2008), as well as such similarly consequential documentary films as Emiko Omori's *Rabbit in the Moon* (1999) and Frank Abe's *Conscience and the Constitution* (2000).

Prisons and Patriots originated in the "Tucsonian" Oral History Project that Lyon launched at the 1999 ceremony renaming the Tucson Federal Prison Camp as the Gordon Hirabayashi Recreation Site. During World War II this facility was a minimum-security honor camp for prisoners constructing highways in Arizona's scenic Catalina Mountains above Tucson. In 1943 it detained Hirabayashi, a University of Washington *Nisei* student, Quaker, and conscientious objector who the previous year had resisted U.S. government-imposed curfew and exclusion orders on West Coast *Nikkei* (and then later became a draft resister). In 1944 it confined forty-one other *Nisei*, mostly inmates from the War Relocation Authority-administered concentration camps at Topaz, Utah, and Amache, Colorado, who resisted induction without having their stripped prewar U.S. citizen rights restored. Drawing upon her interviews with Hirabayashi and the other *Nisei* Tucsonians and pertinent archival documentation, Lyon crafts a compelling narrative to convey this multifaceted story about a largely neglected wartime confinement site and those *Nikkei* denizens within it who elected to demonstrate their patriotism via U.S. Constitution-sanctioned civil disobedience as against heeding combined federal government and Japanese American Citizens

League propaganda and pressure to prove their "loyalty" through segregated military service.

The genius of Lyon's book lies less in the stories she recounts than in her placing them into instructive and relevant contexts. The most important of them concerns the nature of citizenship. While seemingly static in "ordinary" times, notes the author, this concept in unstable times (e.g., during World War II and today's roiled global climate) becomes "contested, variable, fluid." Citizenship, Lyon contends, is "not simply a set of rights or obligations to be granted" but instead "the *relationship* between citizens and the state, and [it] is redefined over the life of the individual and in response to the state's changing needs." Building upon this insight, Lyon persuasively advances the grounded argument that over and beyond the Tucsonians, Gordon Hirabayashi, and the several hundred draft resisters within the constellation of Japanese American prison camps, the entire wartime incarcerated population of *Nikkei* mounted a "strong, diverse, and at times well-organized resistance" to both voluntary service and the draft.

While neither the wartime acts of individual draft resisters nor the pervasive community resistance sentiment underlying them has yet attained a popular hold on the American or Japanese American collective memory, *Prisons and Patriots* promises to provide this development with considerably greater traction. Moreover, it very likely will serve the same function for those still demonized Japanese Americans who during World War II renegotiated their U.S. citizenship rights and obligations through expatriation and renunciation.

IN DEFENSE OF JUSTICE: Joseph Kurihara and the Japanese American Struggle for Equality
By Eileen H. Tamura (Urbana, IL: University of Illinois Press, 2013, 228 pp., $40.00, hardcover)

Published in the January 1, 2014 edition of the *Nichi Bei Weekly*.

On the dust jacket of this volume I am quoted as pronouncing it to be "a substantial contribution to Japanese American historiography and collective memory." That reserved opinion was based upon my reading of the penultimate manuscript draft that Eileen Tamura revised into *In Defense of Justice*. Having now read the published version of this work, I am prepared to proclaim it a masterpiece deserving of inclusion in the pantheon of books on Japanese American World War II dissent-protest-resistance along with such earlier classics penned by Roger Daniels (*Concentration Camps USA*, 1971), Michi Nishiura Weglyn (*Years of Infamy*, 1976), Richard Drinnon (*Keeper of Concentration Camps*, 1987), Eric Muller (*Free to Die for Their Country*, 2001), Frank Chin (*Born in the USA*, 2002), Shirley Castlenuovo (*Soldiers of Conscience*, 2008), Cherstin Lyon (*Prisons and Patriots*, 2012), and James and Lane Hirabayashi (*A Principled Stand*, 2013).

In support of this bold contention, I will advance three general points as a baseline for further discussion. The first point involves the controversial subject of Tamura's biography, Joseph Kurihara (1895-1965). At the Manzanar concentration camp this Hawai`i *Nisei* and World War I veteran and American Legion and Veterans of Foreign Wars member not only vociferously denounced the U.S. government's unwarranted eviction and imprisonment of 120,000 *Nikkei* in the wake of Japan's attack on the major American naval base of Pearl Harbor on O`ahu, but allegedly was chiefly responsible for the Manzanar Revolt of December 5-6, 1942, that tragically culminated in military police gunfire killing two (youthful) inmates and wounding nine other prisoners.

Notwithstanding his Manzanar "notoriety," Kurihara prior to *In Defense of Justice* had been understudied (but not altogether neglected) by scholars. Tamura has redressed this shortcoming through a combination of probing research questions and a resourceful engagement with the pertinent primary and secondary sources bearing not merely on Kurihara's actions at Manzanar, but on his entire life.

A second point relates to the nature of the sites where Kurihara was confined before renouncing his U.S. citizenship and moving to

Japan: Manzanar (1942), Moab/Leupp (1943), and Tule Lake (1943-1945). While the government assigned them the respective euphemistic labels of "relocation center," "isolation center," and "segregation center," all were, in fact, War Relocation Authority (WRA)-administered concentration camps. Although dissent/protest/resistance occurred in every one of the WRA prisons (and dramatically so at Poston, Arizona, in 1942, and Heart Mountain, Wyoming, in 1944), the most spectacular inmate opposition to oppression arose in those facilities impounding Kurihara. Even before Tamura's book, this defiance at the California camps of Manzanar and (most especially) Tule Lake had received substantial (if often fitful) critical attention, but in the case of the Moab, Utah, and Leupp, Arizona, isolation centers, documentation and interpretation was minimal. Now, thanks to Tamura, much of the mystery associated with all these penal sites and, particularly, the inmate resistance enacted at them, has been eradicated.

Point three pertains to the place where Kurihara spent his life's final twenty years: Japan. Recently, some scholars—most notably historian John Dower in *Embracing Defeat* (1999)—have written about the Allied Powers Occupation of Japan (1945-1952) under U.S. General Douglas MacArthur's military leadership. But aside from a 2009 *Journal of American-East Asian Relations* article by transnational historian Eiichiro Azuma and a few studies on the Military Intelligence Service's role in Occupied Japan, very little scholarship has examined the vital involvement of Japanese Americans (including renunciants), both from the mainland and Hawai`i, during this transformative interval of postwar Japan. In Tamura's brief and plainly titled "Japan" chapter, she considerably illuminates this topic through her narration of what Kurihara experienced in the process of being transformed from an American national into a Japanese national.

With the above three points as a contextual framework for discussing my lofty evaluation of *In Defense of Justice*, we can now discuss each point in order through specific examples and elaborations. Regarding Tamura's lessening of the limitations in Kurihara's existing life history—heretofore largely restricted to his rebellious actions at Manzanar—it can be prudently declared that she has expanded considerably our knowledge of her biographical subject. To be sure, Kurihara's tempestuous time at Manzanar is at the heart of Tamura's book, taking up as it does two meaty chapters ("Resistance in Manzanar" and "Stepping Back"). However, before even getting to these chapters, Tamura provides three others ("Growing Up American," "A Yank in France, a Jap in America," and "To Manzanar") that fortify readers with crucial background information about Kurihara's familial, educational, and religious (Catholic) background in Hawai`i; his pre-World I mainland sojourn and military training in the Midwest; his short wartime tour of duty in France and his postwar year of extended army service in Germany; his 1920s-1930s interwar living, educational, and vocational activities in Los Angeles; his pre- and post-Pearl Harbor undertakings and misadventures; and his emerging antipathy toward both the U.S. government and the Japanese American Citizens League (JACL) while preparing to depart Los Angeles for Manzanar.

Then, too, Tamura follows up her Manzanar chapters with four others encompassing the balance of Kurihara's World War II incarceration experience as well as his postwar East Asian life ("Isolating Citizen Dissidents," "Turmoil at Tule," "Renunciation," and "Japan"). But even Tamura's two Manzanar-based chapters greatly enhance our insight into Kurihara, for in them he is brought into sharper focus by being considered in relation to both those at the camp who were his allies (primarily Harry Ueno) and those Manzanarians with whom he clashed (Fred Tayama, Togo Tanaka, Karl Yoneda, and fellow WWI veteran Tokutaro "Tokie" Nishimura Slocum).

As to what readers can learn from Tamura's book about the three sites of shame where Kurihara "did time" during WWII and the nature and degree of the dissent-protest-resistance that played out within their corresponding inmate populations, the simple answer is: a great deal. Although it is too great to even attempt to tackle in this review, its extent and richness can be hinted at by selective illustrations. For instance, in connection with the Manzanar Revolt, Tamura offers a footnote juxtaposing two explanations by historians for what underlay the conflict between the anti-administrative protesters and the pro-administrative JACL leadership that precipitated the explosive event, and then provides her own interpretation. Writes Tamura: "Lon Kurashige [2001/2002] challenges the emphasis on cultural differences [by Arthur Hansen and David Hacker, 1974] and instead highlights differences in class backgrounds. ... My view is that social class interacted with and fed into the different cultural perspectives of the *Nikkei*." In respect to the Moab and Leupp "isolation centers," I have recommended Tamura's book to a filmmaker, Claudia Katayanagi, who is doing a documentary film on these facilities established by the WRA for so-called "troublemakers." One thing she will learn from Tamura is the exceedingly deep and very dangerous divide at Moab separating the Harry Ueno-led anti-administration faction of former Manzanarians and those ex-Manzanarians, including Joe Kurihara, who cooperated with Moab's director, Raymond Best (who would later assume the same position at Leupp). Regarding the Tule Lake Segregation Center, what readers of *In Defense of Justice* will derive from reading Tamura's book (aside from the fact that at this high-security prison Ueno and Kurihara became reconciled as friends and both pledged their cooperation with Best, who left Leupp to direct Tule Lake), is being treated with a cogent overview of both Tule Lake's complex and conflicted political environment and its attendant resegregation and renunciation movements. It is obvious from what Tamura writes about Tule Lake that she has capitalized not only on such classic works on this camp by Weglyn and Drinnon, but also newer studies such as those by Barbara Takei, Martha Nakagawa, and Sachiko Takita-Ishii, all of which appeared in *A Question of Loyalty*, the 2005 anthology on Tule Lake published by the Shaw Historical Library. For this reason, I have urged filmmaker Brian Maeda to consult the Tamura volume as part of his preparation for his forthcoming Tule Lake documentary.

Perhaps the best way to illustrate what readers of *In Defense of Justice* can gain about the part played by Japanese Americans in Occupied Japan is to share some relevant quantitative and qualitative information offered by Tamura. "From August 1945 to April 1952," she states, "the U.S. Army recruited as many as 6,000 *Nisei* and *Kibei-Nisei* civilians from the U.S. west coast and Hawai`i. ... and many like Kurihara who had only recently renounced their citizenship. In all, a total of almost ten thousand *Nisei* and *Kibei-Nisei*—soldiers and civilians—worked at some point for the U.S. military during the occupation." The employment of these Japanese Americans in postwar Japan—in what can plausibly be argued to have served as a (semi-colonial) resettlement area for *Nikkei* in the same way (though far better) as mainland cities like Chicago, Cleveland, Denver, and Salt Lake City—allowed Japanese Americans (and to a lesser extent those who had renounced their U.S. citizenship) to enjoy "abundant nutritious foods, get their hands on all they wanted in the form of commissary supplies, and visit places of recreation and entertainment," while Japanese nationals "lived their everyday lives in hunger and deprivation."

Beautifully written in accessible language and elegantly and efficiently organized, *In Defense of Justice* is much more than the biography of Joseph Kurihara. Rather, what Eileen Tamura has achieved in her powerful and persuasive book, which is by turns passionately partisan and objectively balanced, is to clearly set forth the importance of one notable dissident leader as a quintessential personification of the transformation of Japanese Americans from patriots to protestors as a consequence of their unjust World War II eviction and imprisonment.

RELOCATING AUTHORITY: Japanese Americans Writing to Redress Mass Incarceration
By Mira Shimabukuro (Boulder, CO: University Press of Colorado, 2016, 248 pp., $26.95, paperback)

Published in the July 21, 2016 edition of the *Nichi Bei Weekly*.

In his essay for a 1999 Mike Mackey-edited anthology, *Remembering Heart Mountain*, Lane Hirabayashi cautions Japanese American Incarceration scholars not to over-generalize about Japanese American "resistance" to oppression within the War Relocation Authority (WRA)-administered concentration camps. However, he then quickly subdues this prudent warning by declaring: "My reading of the archival record confirms, repeatedly ... the frequency and tenacity of resistance on multiple occasions and multiple levels." Four years earlier, in his edited volume of Richard Nishimoto's writings pertaining to WWII resistance activity at the Poston detention camp in Arizona, *Inside an American Concentration Camp*, Hirabayashi explored, extended, and enriched the concept of "popular resistance to mass incarceration," which Gary Okihiro had earlier pioneered relative to Japanese American studies via seminal articles in *Amerasia Journal* (1973), *Journal of Ethnic Studies* (1977), and *Phylon* (1984). This backstory makes it very understandable and appropriate as to why the present book under review here, Mira Shimabukuro's *Relocating Authority*, appears within Hirabayashi's *Nikkei in the Americas* series for the University Press of Colorado.

Although this study is published by an academic press (albeit one atypically attentive to non-academic authors and audiences) and its intellectual scaffolding—particularly within its opening chapter, *Writing to Redress: Attending to Nikkei Literacies of Survivance*—is larded with scholarly terminology and source references, Shimabukuro succeeds admirably in rendering her theorizing user-friendly for a general readership by a combination of sparkling prose and irradiating examples. As for the author's close-grained articulation of her very significant and often quite insightful argument, I have chosen here to jettison it as being beyond the scope of a brief review like this one, and instead to limit myself to summarizing and domesticating the main components, conclusions, and consequences of her erudite treatise.

Certainly, the two key components of Shimabukuro's book—and properly so—are encapsulated within its imaginatively strategic title, *Relocating Authority*, and subtitle, *Japanese Americans Writing to Redress*

Mass Incarceration. In keeping with the recent terminological shift in Japanese American studies away from traditional euphemistic terms like "relocation" shrouding the harsh reality of the *Nikkei* WWII experience, Shimabukuro aims to transfer the authoritative voice for the defining nature of that experience from the U.S. government, the WRA, and the collaborative Japanese American Citizens League (JACL) leadership to the inmates within the assorted incarceration centers. Allied with this aim, Shimabukuro seeks interpretive answers through ferreting out and "attending" to heretofore largely buried or ignored written/verbal material (e.g., contemporary correspondence, notes, manifestos, and retrospective oral histories) emanating from the imprisoned population, with the intention of setting the record straight—that is, "redressing"—both their unconstitutional victimization and the terms of its rectification.

Among Shimabukuro's conclusions, two that resonated powerfully with me are these: 1) that although the source material for supporting the "relocation of authority" sought can be found in university and other "official history" repositories, the more bountiful (and accessible) venues for facilitating this quest are community archives such as the comprehensive brick-and-mortar Hirasaki National Resource Center at the Japanese American National Museum (HNRC-JANM) in Los Angeles and the Seattle-based Densho online collection of oral histories, government records, photographs, encyclopedia entries, and course syllabi; and 2) Japanese American resistance to oppression, as Okihiro, Hirabayashi, and other Japanese American researchers have registered, was far more widespread and robust among their wartime prison denizens than it has been represented both by public media and word of mouth. In this connection, Shimabukuro offers her readers three instructive appendices: the March 1944 manifesto of the Heart Mountain Fair Play Committee as to its support of draft resistance, and two contrasting Minidoka Relocation Center letters reacting to the impending draft of *Nisei* (the February 12, 1944, draft version penned by Minoru Yasui for the Mother's Society of Minidoka, and the more pointed February 20, 1944, revised version authored by the Mother's Society and mailed to U.S. President Franklin Roosevelt).

Respecting the consequences of *Relocating Authority*, the one I found most far-reaching was that the post-World War II unearthing and/or re-assessing of invisible or seemingly innocuous wartime resistance writings, although not figuring per se in redressing oppressive wrongs during the period of *Nikkei* incarceration, later served during the 1970s-1980s to fuel and fortify the collective community-based movement of Japanese Americans for redress, reparations, social justice, and human dignity. As the daughter of redress activist Bob Shimabukuro, who authored the passionate 2001 book *Born in Seattle* on the Japanese American redress campaign, and the stepdaughter of Alice Ito, a prime mover in the dynamic Tom Ikeda-led Densho community organization, Mira Shimabukuro, in *Relocating Authority*, pays forward a family and community legacy of *Nikkei* resistance activity. In so doing, she also has gained a place for herself in the pantheon of Japanese American resistance historiography.

TULE LAKE STOCKADE DIARY: November 13, 1943-February 14, 1944
By Tatsuo Ryusei Inouye (Los Angeles: Nancy Oda Publishing, 2020, 256 pp., $40.00, hardcover)

Published in the July 21, 2022 edition of the *Nichi Bei Weekly*.

There now exists a richly diverse number of publications devoted to the World War II concentration camp for Japanese Americans called generically Tule Lake. This penal facility was initially known as the Tule Lake Relocation Center when it opened on May 27, 1942. However, in the wake of an ill-conceived "loyalty questionnaire" imposed on all ten of the "relocation centers" administered by the War Relocation Authority (WRA) in early 1943, it alone—thanks to pressure applied jointly by the U.S. government, the U.S. Army, and the Japanese American Citizens League—was transformed on July 15, 1943, into the high-security prison re-named the Tule Lake Segregation Center. Its primary purpose was to incarcerate so-called "disloyal" Americans of Japanese ancestry and, presumably, ready them for a future life in Japan. Around 2000, and rightly so, by far the major attention of investigators of this penal facility has been accorded to the post-1943 compound, since it was typified by military oppression of the camp's inmate population and their resistance to that oppression. The quintessential representation of the struggle between these two combatants was the Tule Lake stockade, a prison within a prison, which assumes centerstage in this remarkable diaristic volume under review.

Until the *Tule Lake Stockade Diary*, there existed no extensive autobiographical record that encompassed the day-to-day experiences of those roughly 200 *Nikkei* who, without a hearing or a trial, were locked up for months on end in the crude, grimy, and densely populated army-run stockade on the unsubstantiated basis of being camp "troublemakers." Fortuitously, one of them, thirty-four-year-old *Kibei* Tatsuo Inouye, had the prescience to maintain for posterity what he experienced and observed within the three-month span from November 13, 1943, to February 14, 1944, in which he was a stockade prisoner.

A fourth-degree black belt *judo* master, the stoic, introspective, but forthright and conscientious Inouye was born in Laguna Beach, California, and educated in Japan before he and his *Nisei* wife Yuriko and their two young *Sansei* daughters, in May 1942, were excluded from their West Coast home in Lancaster, California, and incarcerated in the Poston concentration camp in southwest Arizona. It was there where Inouye's negative and neutral responses to the highly controversial two key questions on the "loyalty questionnaire" landed him and his family in the Tule Lake Segregation Center, where he continued his *judo* instruction. In short order, because he became a member of an inmate negotiating committee to protest for improved living and working conditions and against the camp director's overreaction to this development by ordering tanks and soldiers with bayonets and declaring martial law, Inouye was summarily remanded to the hastily constructed stockade.

Inouye's riveting daily entries in his diary run the gamut from the skimpy meals, spartan amenities, and punitive treatment meted out to the escalating number of prison denizens to reflections on such philosophical concerns as honor, respect, patriotism, family values, and human dignity. Participants in the moving and illuminating launching program for *Tule Lake Stockade Diary* held at the Japanese American National Museum on December 11, 2021, discussed all of these topics and more. This "Conversation on *Tule Lake Stockade Diary* by Tatsuo Ryusei Inouye" merits viewing on the JANM YouTube channel by readers of this brief review.

The prime mover in the production of *Tule Lake Stockade*—a truly stunning, powerful, and invaluable volume in every major respect—is Kyoko Nancy Oda, a *Sansei* social activist who was born in Tule Lake Segregation Center shortly before the Inouye family returned to Southern California from Tule Lake. The Inouye diary was skillfully translated into English by Professor Masumi Izumi of Doshisa University in Kyoto, Japan, edited proficiently by notable Japanese American *Sansei* journalist Martha Nakagawa, and illustrated with dazzling artwork created by Ernie Jane Masako Nishi, the middle *Sansei* daughter of Tatsuo and Yuriko Inouye.

PART VII
ASIAN AMERICAN MOVEMENT

On May 8, 2017, the Seattle-based Densho organization posted a piece on their site, "Yellow Power: The Origins of Asian America," which cogently captures the essence of the subject denoted by the piece's subtitle. Its prologue commands attention in this connection.

Prior to the social and political upheavals of the 1960s, there was no "Asian America"—at least not as we know it today. While Americans of Asian descent had joined forces on the picket line and plantation field throughout history, their identities and struggles were mostly defined along distinct ethnic lines. But amidst the tumult of the civil rights movement, young people united their communities to forge a new identity based on their collective experiences as Asian Americans.

At the time that the Asian American Movement coalesced in the 1960s, it was not surprising that Japanese Americans assumed a prominent position within its activities. For one thing, this was because Japanese Americans then represented the largest Asian-ancestry group in the United States. For another thing, it made eminent sense that an ethnic group having been victimized so unjustly just two decades earlier by government oppression and having suffered an attendant loss in human and civil rights should now speak out boldly on behalf of those same rights for all Americans of Asian *descent. Accordingly, Japanese Americans, especially those of the* Sansei *generation (as well as younger* Nisei*), many of whom had been children in the World War II concentration camps, emerged as leaders of Asian American studies programs at colleges and universities, spearheaded Asian American Movement publications and productions, and took up the reins of pancommunity leadership in public debates, demonstrations, and creative endeavors.*

The four historical books about the Asian American Movement that compose this section of A Nikkei Harvest *make clear the significant role that Japanese Americans continue to play today in this movement—notwithstanding that within the five decades since the 1960s the* Nikkei *have become one of the smallest Asian American populations, while the movement's leadership has diversified to encompass many other Asian-ancestry groups deriving from East Asia, Southeast Asia, and the Pacific Islands. The first two books are authored by* Sansei *activists Daryl J. Maeda and Karen L. Ishizuka. In Maeda's* Chains of Babylon, *he pays tribute to late 1960s/early 1970s Asian American radicals who contested notions concerning their race and national inclusion and "articulated a new form of Asian American identity as a multiethnic formation," one binding together, with the two chains of U.S. racism and imperialism, Americans of all Asian ethnicities and those Asians "struggling against American hegemony in Asia." Although concerned that the term "Asian American" has been somewhat corrupted from its earlier progressive connotation of resistance to capitalist exploitation to now become both a mere demographic designation and one implying a pragmatic adjustment to self-promotion and profiteering, Maeda takes heart in a renewal among Asian American activists of the radical progressivism of their principled early predecessors who sought a more just world within the framework of an enlightened global consciousness. In this spirit, Ishizuka's* Serve the People *lauds not only the historical achievements of the youthful early movers and shakers in the Asian American Movement who challenged their country's oppression of human rights both at home and internationally, but also the usable legacy these progenitors have conferred upon succeeding generational cohorts of progressive Asian Americans. As for* The Oxford Handbook of Asian American History, *co-edited by David K. Yoo, the Korean American author of the landmark volume* Growing Up Nisei: Race, Generation and Culture among Japanese Americans of California, 1924-49 *(Urbana: University of Illinois Press, 2000), and Eiichiro Azuma, the Japan-born, U.S.-raised and educated* Shin-Issei *best known for his ground-breaking transnational volume* Between Two Empires: Race, History, and Transnationalism in Japanese America *(New York: Oxford University Press, 2005), its publication signifies the historical coming-of-age of Asian American history. Among its twenty-seven essays devoted to detailing in-depth the scholarship in multiple fields of inquiry within Asian American history, eight are contributed by renowned Japanese American research specialists, seven of whom are* Nikkei, *with the most pertinent in the present context being that written by Daryl Joji Maeda on "The Asian American Movement." The fourth volume in this category is Catherine Ceniza Choy's revisionist volume entitled* Asian American Histories of the United States, *in which she encompasses the 150-year historical experience of diverse Asian American communities in a non-linear manner from a first-person and second-person perspective as well as the more traditional third-person perspective, while contending that Asian American history has more than one origins story.*

CHAINS OF BABYLON: The Rise of Asian America
By Daryl J. Maeda (Minneapolis: University of Minnesota Press, 2009, 213 pp., $20.00, paperback)

Published in the July 25, 2013 edition of the *Nichi Bei Weekly*.

At California State University, Fullerton, I taught History, Asian American Studies, and American Studies courses. My favorite class was an American Studies offering developed in the mid-1970s: "American Cultural Radicalism." If now teaching it, I assuredly would assign Daryl Maeda's *Chains of Babylon*. The best study on the Asian American Movement's origins and early ascent, it also brilliantly showcases U.S. cultural radicalism's robust tradition.

While cultural radicalism can be defined variably, "one of its central characteristics," according to cultural historian Jesse Battan, "has been the emphasis on subjective or personal forms of liberation." Whereas *political* radicals "seek to regenerate society through the redistribution of wealth and political power," *cultural* radicals "rely on the transformation of consciousness as their precondition for the creation of the ideal society." By using Battan's formulation to guide our reading of Maeda's riveting volume, we can arguably better assess its nature and measure its significance. At the same time, however, we need to be mindful that "cultural politics" transcends the narrow formal boundaries of both "culture" and "politics" and encompasses, as media scholars Ian Angus and James Davison Hunter have noted, "the complex process by which the whole domain in which people search and create meaning about their everyday lives is subject to politicization and struggle."

Maeda's introduction ("From Heart Mountain to Hanoi') draws on the historical experience of *Sansei* Pat Sumi, a late 1960s/early 1970s "luminary," to manage his book's fundamental burden: explaining how Asian American radicals during this interval, such as Sumi, "challenged prior ideas about their race and national belonging and articulated a new form of Asian American identity as a multiethnic racial formation." Maeda uses the introduction as well to interpret Sumi's 1970 *Gidra* poem "To My Asian American Brothers" in relationship to the line within it—"Chains of Babylon/bind us together" —that inspired his book's striking title. What Sumi meant by Babylon, clarifies Maeda, was American racism and imperialism, the twin chains binding Americans of all Asian ethnicities together along with those Asians "struggling against American hegemony in Asia."

Before delineating the development of a new Asian American consciousness through four diverse yet overlapping and interpenetrating case studies (Chapter 2-5), Maeda devotes his first chapter, "Before Asian America," to two tasks: 1) surveying the racialization of Asians in the pre-1960s-1970s U.S. through the dynamics of discriminatory immigration policies, legal and legislative measures, and socio-cultural representations; and 2) depicting how Asian groups countered this oppression through Asian-specific nationalism, assimilationist Americanization, and the twin "Old Left" stratagems of labor unionism and political progressivism.

Maeda assigns to each of his strategically selected and astutely titled case studies a primary theme to exemplify within his comprehensive multi-faceted thesis. Thus, Chapter 2 ("'Down with Hayakawa!' Assimilation vs. Third World Solidarity at San Francisco State College") accents Asian Americans' struggles against whiteness; Chapter 3 ("Black Panthers, Red Guards, and Chinamen: Constructing Asian American Identity through Performing Blackness") highlights the rise of Asian American identity relative to blackness; Chapter 4 ("'Are We Not Also Asians?' Building Solidarity through Opposition to the Viet Nam War") stresses how Asian American opposition to the Viet Nam War nurtured transnational compassion for Asians in Asia; and Chapter 5 ("Performing Radical Culture: A Grain of Sand and the Language of Liberty") emphasizes the enactment of Asian American identity through cultural performance.

Maeda's thought-and-conscience provoking conclusion ("Fighting for the Heart of Asian America") articulates and critically reflects upon what he perceives to be the tripartite legacy of the Asian American movement: 1) the term "Asian American" embracing U.S. Asians of whatever ethnicity; 2) a usable past for visionary Asian Americans; and 3) a transnational perspective. On the one hand, Maeda is troubled by the corruption of "Asian American" from a politically charged progressive term connoting an oppositional stance toward capitalist exploitation into one now largely descriptive of demographic factors (e.g., race, ethnicity, and nationality) and betokening a pragmatic accommodation to business practices enhancing individual advancement and maximizing profits. On the other hand, Maeda is heartened both by the way activists in newer Asian American populations have located themselves within the radical tradition established by older Asian American radicals to renew and extend their dream of a more just world, and by the deepened commitment by Asian Americans in the current era of globalization to think and act progressively outside the box of national boundaries.

Chains of Babylon is a book that not merely treats readers to a clear, colorful, and absorbing account of how the Asian American Movement was socially constructed, but also signposts in a broad sense what is required both now as well as in the future to redeem and revitalize its revolutionary promise.

SERVE THE PEOPLE: Making Asian America in the Long Sixties By Karen L. Ishizuka (London: Verso, 2016, 288 pp., $29.95, hardcover)

Published in the January 1, 2017 edition of the *Nichi Bei Weekly*.

In commemoration of the seventy-fifth anniversary of Japan's attack on Pearl Harbor, which prompted the U.S. government to imprison 120,000 Americans of Japanese ancestry (two-thirds U.S. citizens) in concentration camps, a double-edged protest march was staged on the night of December 7, 2016, in Los Angeles's Little Tokyo community. Among the protestors was eighty-year-old *Sansei* activist Jim Matsuoka, who at age seven was impounded with his family and 10,000 other Japanese Americans at eastern California's Manzanar, one of ten War Relocation Authority (WRA)-administered World War II *Nikkei* concentration camps. Like the other protest participants, Matsuoka voiced his and his community's solidarity with the U.S. Muslim community—presently under assault and threatened with governmental registration by President-elect Donald Trump—through chanting "Say it loud, say it clear, Muslims are welcome here." To Matsuoka, little had changed in the last seventy-five years: "There was racism then and there is racism now." Therefore, he could not—and would not—stand idly by and let what had happened to Japanese Americans now happen to Muslim Americans.

In *Serve the People*, Karen Ishizuka pays tribute to those mostly youthful Asian Americans of the 1960s and early 1970s who, like Jim Matsuoka, self-consciously and purposely coalesced into what progressively took shape as the Asian American Movement, replete with a correlative new identity for its movers and shakers. Embracing activist individuals and groups across America, this movement spearheaded a multi-faceted and multicultural struggle for democracy, social justice, and dignity within the U.S. and challenged their country's oppression of human rights both at home and throughout the world. Notwithstanding that this movement has been heretofore overshadowed by those of other contemporary activists of color and still others linked together within a variety of different social categories, Ishizuka makes a powerful case for the importance of the Asian American Movement both in terms of its consequential historical deeds and in the usable legacy it has bestowed upon future generational cohorts of progressive Asian Americans. Still, as Jeff Chang reminds readers in his insightful foreword to Ishizuka's book, "while [she is] committed to telling the story of her peers and her time, she is hardly a triumphalist. She is critical where the story demands it."

Along with many others, I have long been impressed by the artistic and intellectual productions in which Karen Ishizuka (a *Sansei* pioneer in the movement she depicts in *Serve the People*) has played such an instrumental role. I first witnessed her brilliance in a trio of outstanding Japanese American National Museum (JANM) documentary films, all directed by her visionary husband Bob Nakamura and for which she served as the producer and writer: *Something Strong Within* (1994), crafted entirely out of home movie footage taken by inmates in the WRA detention camps; *Looking Like the Enemy* (1996), focused on the wartime experiences of Japanese American veterans in World War II, Korea, and Vietnam; and *Infinite Shades of Gray* (2001), centered on the iterations of acclaimed *Issei* photographer Toyo Miyatake's career. I later witnessed the fruits of Ishizuka's historical scholarship in her 2006 University of Illinois classic volume *Lost and Found: Reclaiming the Japanese American Incarceration*, in which she related through history and memory how a critically acclaimed 1994 JANM exhibition she curated, *America's Concentration Camps: Remembering the Japanese American Experience*, was consumed and confronted by former inmates and visitors. In this volume, she also pondered "how the dual act of recovering—and recovering from—history necessitates private and public meditation between remembering and forgetting, speaking out and remaining silent."

With this background in mind, my expectations for *Serve the People* were exceedingly high. But Ishizuka far surpassed them. The sagacity of the questions she poses and the manner in which she responds to them, the sophistication of her critical analysis, the animation and precision of her prose, the depth and breadth of her research sources, the vibrancy and diversity of her illustrative material, and the ethical force that sustains and consecrates her inquiry—all of these harmoniously combine to render what Gary Okihiro has correctly styled *Serve the People*: "a work of immense significance."

THE OXFORD HANDBOOK OF ASIAN AMERICAN HISTORY
Edited by David K. Yoo and Eiichiro Azuma (New York: Oxford University Press, 2016, 544 pp., $150.00, hardcover)

Published in the January 1, 2018 edition of the *Nichi Bei Weekly*.

This impressive volume, published at the semi-centennial of Asian American Studies, serves admirably as an authoritative marker of Asian American history's coming of age. Edited by two stalwarts in the field, David K. Yoo and Eiichiro Azuma, it consists of a masterful overview introduction by them plus twenty-seven in-depth historiographical essays penned by leading scholars representative of this vibrant multifarious branch of U.S. history. All but one of these scholars are Asian Americans of various ethnicities, with the exception being notable *Nichi Bei Weekly* columnist Greg Robinson.

In addition to Robinson's insightful essay on Asian American Legal History, the handbook includes probing cutting-edge essays by seven highly reputed Japanese American research specialists:

Eiichiro Azuma ("Internment and World War II History"); Daryl Joji Maeda ("The Asian American Movement"); Lon Kurashige ("Theory and History"); Amy Sueyoshi ("Queer Asian American Historiography"); Scott Kurashige ("Race, Space, and Place in Asian American Urban History"); Franklin Odo ("Public History and Asian Americans"); and Eileen H. Tamura ("Asian American Education History").

Structured into four parts—"Migration Flows," "Time Passages," "Variations on Themes," and "Engaging Historical Fields"—each of the book's essays succeed in different yet overlapping and interpenetrating ways to "complicate" (that is, render more complex, precise, and enriched) the mosaic of Asian American history. Typically, this process of complication is attributed by the respective authors of the essays to a combination of salient factors, such as new source material, new theories, new research methods, new approaches, new technologies, new circumstances, new practitioners, and new target audiences.

Virtually all of the writers in the volume emphasize that the field of Asian American history as a whole as well as within its assorted sub-fields has moved from being less provincial and more cosmopolitan as a consequence of being transformed from its earlier focus on the experience of Japanese Americans, Chinese Americans, and Filipino Americans, to its expanded concern with those Asian Americans endowed with a multiplicity of other lineages and backgrounds. In addition, many of the scholars place a premium upon how Asian American history has been illuminated and enhanced through being viewed from a transnational, hemispheric, global, or comparative perspective.

With respect to the writing style employed by the essayists in the handbook, it varies from being very accessible for the general reader to being somewhat less so for those outside of academe who are unversed in its conceptual conventions and discourse. It probably would have leavened the loaf for non-academic readers had provision been made for photographs and other illustrations, such as the arresting Mine Okubo 1942 cover painting, *Planting Trees*, to be infused within the volume to temper its dense tide of text, notes, bibliographies, and index (though I suspect that this format was not permitted for an Oxford University Press handbook).

While *The Oxford Handbook of Asian American History* will assuredly find a home in most relevant institutional libraries, its steep price should not restrain its purchase and selective use by serious scholars of Asian American history both inside and outside of the academy, for it is an altogether invaluable resource. Indeed, its editors and contributors should be saluted for bringing this exemplary work to fruition.

ASIAN AMERICAN HISTORIES OF THE UNITED STATES
By Catherine Ceniza Choy (Boston: Beacon Press, 2022, 206 pp. $26.95, hardcover)

Published in the July 21, 2022 edition of the *Nichi Bei Weekly*.

In the mid-1990s, while teaching history classes at Cal State Fullerton, I was asked to join with a professor from the Education Department to design an academic minor curriculum for the university's new Asian American Studies Program. Since neither of us had taught Asian American Studies classes, we relied heavily in our collaboration upon the curricular models then in use at other universities in California. The most influential for us was the University of California, Santa Barbara, one designed by the celebrated scholar Sucheng Chan. Moreover, when I was tasked with teaching the introductory course for our fledgling program, I chose to use Chan's 1991 survey book, *Asian Americans: An Interpretive History*, as the primary text. Deeply researched, meticulously documented, and pellucidly written, this outstanding book covered its topic for the period extending from the mid-nineteenth century to the present in a linear manner expressed chiefly from a third-person perspective.

In striking contrast to the style employed by Chan is that utilized so innovatively and effectively by Catherine Ceniza Choy in *Asian

American Histories of the United States. A seasoned professor in Ethnic Studies at the University of California, Berkeley, of Filipino American heritage, Choy treats the 150-year socio-historical experience of eleven diverse Asian American communities (together comprising the fastest growing group in today's United States) in a non-linear fashion. In so doing, she writes about it in the first and second person as well as the more traditional third person (that is, more like a drama or other artistic work than a traditional historical narrative) with a premium placed upon vibrant storytelling to render the still elusive Asian American story more palpable and consequential to readers.

It is Choy's contention that Asian American history lacks a single origin story, having instead multiple ones stretching "back as well as forward in time and space." Accordingly, she rivets upon a series of distinctively significant origin stories that have been somehow lost within standard histories of the United States, and opines that when viewed together as a constellation, they can reclaim their former resonance. To cite but one example of such a landmark Asian American origin story, Choy references the 1975 plight of Southeast Asian refugees from Vietnam, Laos, and Cambodia that in time led to their resettlement in all fifty U.S. states. In fleshing out such far-reaching origin stories, Choy grapples resourcefully and brilliantly with the overriding question of just how and why in the current time it is that Asian Americans find themselves, notwithstanding their lengthy history, the target of so much hate in this country. In response to this rhetorical question, she lays emphasis as an impassioned feminist activist upon three salient themes of Asian American histories: violence, erasure, and resistance.

My one concern with this exemplary book is its lack of an index. For a non-linear work such as Choy's, this poses an inordinately thorny problem for readers in terms of efficient information retrieval.

To better grasp Choy's reasons for writing this book at this particular juncture, I strongly recommend that readers access Professor Choy's April 11, 2022, videotaped interview transacted by Asia Society president Kevin Rudd: https://asiasociety.org/video/author-catherine-choy-lessons-asian-american-history.

PART VIII

JAPANESE AMERICAN REDRESS MOVEMENT

One of the finest published historical studies of the Japanese American Redress Movement is Alice Yang Murray's Historical Memories of the Japanese American Internment and the Struggle for Redress *(Stanford: Stanford University Press, 2007). Some years after its publication, writing as Alice Yang, she supplied a superb "Redress Movement" entry for the authoritative* Densho Encyclopedia. *Her overview summary at the outset of the entry reads as follows:*

The Redress Movement refers to efforts to obtain the restitution of civil rights, an apology, and/or monetary compensation from the U.S. government during the six decades that followed the World War II mass removal and confinement of Japanese Americans. Early campaigns emphasized the violation of constitutional rights, lost property, and the repeal of anti-Japanese legislation. 1960s activists linked the wartime detention camps to contemporary racist and colonial policies. In the late 1970s three organizations pursued redress in court and in Congress, culminating in the passage of the Civil Liberties Act of 1988, providing a national apology and individual payments of $20,000 to surviving detainees.

The campaign for redress and reparations began institutionally at the 1970s national Japanese American Citizens League (JACL) convention.

There JACL renegades sought to extend their work on repealing the Emergency Detention Act of 1950 by introducing a resolution to seek compensatory legislation. That resolution and similar ones proposed at successive JACL conventions provoked resistance from delegates fearful of rocking the boat at a time when Japanese Americans were lauded as a "model minority." Still, the JACL formed a committee on redress, and in 1979 the organization decided against demanding individual payments for each incarcerated victim and urged instead a government commission to study the matter and recommend remedies. This action by the JACL catalyzed the formation of two other redress organizations, the National Council for Japanese American Redress (NCJAR) and the National Coalition for Redress/Reparations (NCRR), both of whom opposed the JACL's commission proposal. Notwithstanding this opposition, in 1980 Congress created the Commission on Wartime Relocation and Internment of Civilians (CWRIC), which set the stage for CWRIC's 1981 public hearings conducted across the United States.

*At these hearings the commission heard testimony from over 750 witnesses. Some were former high-ranking civilian and military government officials, non-*Nikkei *employees at the War Relocation Authority (WRA) camps such as teachers, physicians, and social workers, and Japanese American Incarceration (JAI) scholars, journalists, and concerned citizens. But overwhelmingly the witnesses were West Coast Japanese Americans who had experienced incarceration. Their passionate testimonies shattered four decades of self-denial and silence. Clearly, the CWRIC hearings had served Japanese Americans as a community catharsis. Moreover, the hearings were followed by the commission's 1982 findings that exclusion and detention had not resulted from military necessity, but rather from race prejudice, war hysteria, and a failure of political leadership, and, in the succeeding year, called for the aforementioned public apology to the Japanese American community and tax-free payments of $20,000 to each camp survivor.*

The very next year William Hohri wrote a report on the redress movement, Repairing America: An Account of the Movement for Japanese-American Redress *(Pullman: Washington State University, 1984), as seen from the perspective of NCJAR, the organization that he led via a 1983 class-action lawsuit. It remained until after the signing of the Civil Liberties Act of 1988 for the publication of other volumes covering this subject to appear:* Leslie T. Hatamiya, Righting a Wrong: Japanese Americans and the Passage of the Civil Liberties Act of 1988 *(Stanford: Stanford University Press, 1993), which focused on the JACL's congressional approach to gain redress; and* Mitchell T. Maki, Harry H. L. Kitano, and S. Megan Berthold, Achieving the Impossible Dream: How Japanese Americans Obtained Redress *(Urbana: University of Illinois Press, 1999), which emphasized the JACL redress activity in Congress, but also encompassed NCJAR's judicial orientation and the NCRR's grass-roots mobilization strategy. The same situation as with* Achieving the Impossible Dream *prevailed for Janet D. Tanaka's much later and very accomplished documentary film,* Right of Passage *(Cypress, CA: Nitto Films, 2016). Still another book, Robert Sudamu Shimabukuro's* Born in Seattle *(Seattle: University of Washington Press, 2001) provided a powerful oral history-based exploration of a significant and consequential 1960-1990 redress movement.*

However, it was Yasuko I. Takezawa's Breaking the Silence: Redress and Japanese American Ethnicity *(Ithaca: Cornell University Press, 1995), a case study that like the Shimabukuro volume also focused on the redress movement in Seattle, which persuasively accounted for how the World War II incarceration experience of* Nikkei *got mobilized into ethnic community politics and transformative power in the 1970s and 1980s. Coming to the U.S. from her native Japan in 1982 to enroll in the doctoral studies program in anthropology at the University of Washington, Takezawa commenced fieldwork for her dissertation the next year. The heart of her fieldwork research consisted of sixteen open-ended interviews with both* Nisei *and* Sansei *of both genders. Her deepest concern with these interviews was what they would reveal about the two generations' historical experience of ethnic identity and how those experiences shaped their differing reactions to redress.*

Before WWII the Nisei, *who lived simultaneously in the distinct worlds of their ethnic subculture and the mainstream society, experienced both positive and negative ethnic consciousness, but the trauma and shame of their wartime incarceration inclined them to suppress their ethnic heritage after the war. Without giving up the ethnic pride implanted in them in childhood*, Nisei "*made extra efforts to be accepted by the dominant society and tried to Americanize and assimilate.*"

The Sansei, *unlike the* Nisei, *came of age when mainstream society was receptive to them and circumstances conducive to their upward social mobility. The majority of* Sansei *were not conscious of their ethnic identity as young children, though they sometimes regarded things Japanese (e.g., language and food) as bad or shameful, and at times they even regretted not being white. But in the late 1960s and early 1970s, college-age* Sansei *concurrently enrolled in Asian American Studies courses and involved themselves in community agencies and activities. "Redress," explained Takezawa, "was a perfect rallying point for the Asian American Movement, intent as it was on breaking the image of the quiet Asian, on opposing white 'Americanization,' and challenging racism and social injustice." Some* Sansei *were mad at their* Nisei *parents for not resisting Executive Order 9066, the exclusion order, and for not talking to them about their wartime experiences, but many more directed their anger at the governmental injustice and societal racism that caused and sustained the JAI.*

The Sansei's *refashioned social awareness and ethnic identity precipitated an intergenerational dialogue with their* Nisei *parents centering on redress. Initially, many* Nisei *resented their sons and daughters' bringing back bad memories and advised them to forget the past and attend to the present and future. But many more* Nisei *appreciated the* Sansei *efforts to exhume the corpse of the JAI and actively to pursue redress. In the fifteen years before the 1988 redress bill, argued Takezawa, "Japanese Americans underwent a transformation in their ethnic identity, feelings about camp, intergenerational relationships, and some of their norms and values."*

In planning and executing her interviews and using data derived from them, Takezawa concerned herself with the community, as well as individual, memory. What those data suggested, according to her, was that, through fighting the battles of the redress campaign together, Nisei *and* Sansei *overcame their divisive generational perspectives and reconfirmed their common ethnic identity. Moreover, she concluded, "in this process, the feeling of shared suffering, which had previously constructed the subconscious core of the* individual *identity, was transformed into the core of the* collective identity of Japanese Americans." At the same time, since the redress movement was waged as an American issue, using American symbols and acting through American institutions, it strengthened not only the ethnic identity but also the national identity of Japanese Americans.

Two of the three book reviews constituting this section of A Nikkei Harvest involve publications in which Lane Hirabayashi—a Sansei UCLA professor of Asian American Studies who had come of age during the struggle for Japanese American redress—played a key role. One person whom Hirabayashi relied upon heavily in editing the assorted papers making up his 2011 publication Neglected Legacies was Sansei Grant Ujifusa, who performed a pivotal role as the JACL's redress strategy chair both in making redress palatable for those in the 1980s Congress of all political persuasions and in convincing a previously recalcitrant President Ronald Reagan to sign into law the Civil Liberties Act of 1988. Emphasizing not his role or that of any other Sansei in the redress victory, Ujifusa instead heaped praise on two Nisei women activists by name and calling them, along with four other such Nisei women, the core of redress in Japanese American communities. In this same spirit, several of the contributors to Neglected Legacies depict as indispensable the previously understated importance of Nisei and Sansei women within the ranks of the three major redress organizations that led to the movement's success. As for NCRR, this 2018 volume, which at long last centered on the critical importance of the National Coalition for Redress/Reparations to the passage of the Civil Liberties Act of 1988, was spearheaded by an editorial team of seven NCRR veteran stalwarts (five of them Nikkei women), with Lane Hirabayashi serving as the lead editor. This collective account of NCRR's vital grassroots struggle for Japanese American redress and reparations makes it abundantly clear to readers that the organization's success relied upon the intergenerational cooperation of the Nisei and Sansei generations. The third and last redress book in this section, John Tateishi's Redress, published in 2020, assays the conflicted but successful two-decade campaign for redress and reparations from the insider perspective of a progressive and deeply committed Japanese American Citizens League movement leader and legislative lobbyist.

NEGLECTED LEGACIES: Japanese American Women and the Redress/Reparations Movement (A special issue of *PAN-JAPAN: The International Journal of the Japanese Diaspora*)
Edited by Lane Ryo Hirabayashi (Normal, IL: Illinois State University, Spring/Fall 2011, Volume 7, Numbers 1 & 2, 197 pp., $12.50, paperback)

Published in the July 25, 2013 edition of the *Nichi Bei Weekly*.

In this 2011 *PAN-JAPAN* special issue, guest editor Lane Ryo Hirabayashi, an Asian American Studies Department professor at UCLA (where he is also the George & Sakaye Aratani Chair in Japanese American Incarceration, Redress, and Community), acknowledges that in (resourcefully) editing the papers comprising *Neglected Legacies* and in writing up his published (and very perceptive) introduction to them, he benefitted from his interactions with three notable *Sansei* activists.

One of these third-generation *Nikkei*, Grant Ujifusa, was a key national player in the Japanese American redress movement that culminated in the Civil Liberties Act of 1988. The legislation awarded monetary damages to the survivors among the 120,000 American victims of Japanese ancestry whom the U.S. government forcibly imprisoned in concentration camps during World War II. Indeed, on January 26, 2012, the Japanese government bestowed upon Ujifusa the *Order of the Rising Sun*, the equivalent of a knighthood, for his pivotal role as redress strategy chair for the Japanese American Citizen League, both for developing a justification for redress that appealed to liberals and conservatives alike in the 1980s Congress and for his behind-the-scenes, eleventh-hour stage management that helped persuade President Ronald Reagan to reverse his public opposition to the redress bill, which he signed into law on August 10, 1988.

In formally accepting his high honor, Ujifusa was silent about his own part in the success of redress, choosing instead to champion the consequential activities of six other *Nikkei*, including two comparatively unheralded second-generation women (Seattle small business woman Cherry Kinoshita and Philadelphia social worker Grayce Uyehara). Lauding them as people for whom redress was total *isshou kenmei*, full-throttle and non-stop, Ujifusa emphasized that without these six individuals the effort to secure Japanese American redress would have failed.

As far back as summer 2008 Ujifusa struck a very similar note in a *Nichi Bei Times* commentary, reminding readers of the indispensable redress contributions made by individuals at the time marginalized and nearly forgotten. More specifically, Ujifusa would later observe in a *Hokubei Mainichi* opinion piece that *Nisei* women such as Cherry Kinoshita and Grace Uyehara were at the core of redress in Japanese American communities, since they were often more willing than *Nisei* or *Sansei* men to lobby the issue in face-to-face encounters with politicians, not only on the West Coast, but all over the country. This observation led Lane Hirabayashi to encourage Ujifusa to write a semi-academic piece on this topic, to which he replied, "Lane, you do it."

The impressive edited anthology under review here confirms that Hirabayashi accepted Ujifusa's challenge in full measure. Consisting of two substantial historical monographs (Elissa Kikuye Ouchida's "*Nisei* Employees vs. California State Personnel Board: A Journal of *Ex Parte Endo*, 1942-1947" and Susan Nakaoka's "'Typical' *Nisei*: An Intersectional Approach to Interpreting the Lives of Five Japanese American Women Activists"), one short commemorative biography (Phillip Tajitsu Nash's "Michi Nishiura Weglyn: A Friend's Reflections, a Decade Later"), and a modest-sized oral history interview (Edna Horiuchi's "An Interview with Lillian Nakano: *Sansei* Artist and Activist"), *Neglected Legacies* certainly qualifies as a semi-academic work. As such, it is consonant with PAN-JAPAN's statement of purpose, most particularly its avowed interest "in occasional pieces that do not fit the strict definition of academic discourse" since they "can sometimes tell stories that scholarly articles cannot." What makes the combination of mixed-genre contributions to this anthology so laudable is their inter-textual compatibility. In short, they all work toward the same end in a manner that ensures that the work's value as a whole exceeds the mere sum of its parts.

In his preface, Don Nakanishi, the UCLA Asian American Studies Center's distinguished former director, captures this purpose when he writes that "the articles [in *Neglected Legacies*] do far more than highlight and analyze the indispensable roles that *Nisei* women played during one of the most significant periods in Japanese American history. They also provide us with detailed, nuanced accounts of the compelling 'back stories'—personal histories and private beliefs and motives—behind the actions they took."

While all of the stunning selections in *Neglected Legacies* are noteworthy in terms of redeeming the promissory note suggested by Ujifusu and brought to fruition by Hirabayashi, the jewel in this anthology's crown is assuredly the Susan Nakaoka article. For in it, she deftly employs the multi-dimensional theory of "intersectionality," which is that "the fact that race, gender, class, culture, immigration status, and other 'identity' create a unique confluence that shapes how women of color experience the world," to understand, via in-depth oral history interviews, the emergence during the 1980s of five second-generation and third-generation *Nikkei* women activists (Sue Kunitomi Embrey, Chizu Iiyama, Cherry Kinoshita, Chiye Tomihiro, and Grayce Uyehara) as leaders of the Japanese American redress/reparations movement. It is fervently hoped that this very significant article, adopted by Nakaoko from her UCLA master's thesis, will become the basis for a published book.

NCRR: The Grassroots Struggle for Japanese American Redress and Reparations
By Nikkei for Civil Rights & Redress (Los Angeles: UCLA Asian American Studies Press, 2018, 400 pp., $30.00, paperback)

Published in the July 19, 2018 edition of the *Nichi Bei Weekly*.

In recognition of my modest role in the conception and organization of this stellar volume, I received a complimentary copy by post from Lane Hirabayashi, the lead editor for the robust NCRR editorial team (the others being Richard Katsuda, Kathy Masaoka, Kay Ochi, Suzy Katsuda, and Janice Iwanaga Yen). Along with the book, Hirabayashi attached a short note: "This project exemplifies what Asian American Studies is about for me. From, through, and reflecting grassroots knowledge." Having had the good fortune to read a substantial portion of his prodigious scholarly output during his thirty-five-year academic career at San Francisco State, the University of Colorado at Boulder, the University of California at Riverside, and UCLA, I was not surprised by Hirabayashi's message, since virtually all of his writings have been rooted and nurtured in both the concept and the reality of community. Rather than *NCRR* being the exception that proves this rule, it is instead a quintessential depiction of it.

According to the Manzanar blog of Gann Matsuda, whose powerfully evocative photo of the NCRR delegation at the 1989 Day of Protest in Little Tokyo graces the book's cover, the book's Little Tokyo launch on June 16, 2018, was "a wonderful event." I altogether agree with what Matsuda had to say (in so many words) in his posting: that NCRR was and remains a wonderful organization and that *NCRR* is a wonderful book. My evaluation of both the organization and the book is contingent upon the content, character, and the layout of *NCRR*. Put a slightly different way, the message I have taken away about the organization derives largely (but not exclusively) from my ardent immersion in the medium per se of their "ethnobiographical" book—"that is, a collective, or a people's 'account,' in their own words, of the life history of the NCRR."

This is a book that enshrines virtually everything noteworthy about NCRR: its freely voluntary and vitally active constituency; its perfervid commitment to community (not alone in terms of Los Angeles's Little Tokyo and Japanese America, but also of "common" people everywhere who are engaged in a fearless and resolutely perpetual struggle for an expansion of democracy, human rights, civil liberties, and social justice); its enlightened dedication to cultivating a broadly inclusive non-sexist and multi-generational membership both for present and future objectives; and its collaborative decision-making process.

NCRR is comprised of two parts. The first begins by showcasing Glen Kitayama's 1993 UCLA master's thesis, "Japanese Americans and the Movement for Redress: Grassroots Activism in the National Coalition for Redress/Reparations, Los Angeles Chapter." This work written from an impassioned participant-observer perspective is comparable in quality to such other exemplary theses as, say, those done in 1970 by Douglas Nelson at the University of Wyoming on the Heart Mountain Concentration Camp and in 2007 by Kara Miyagishima at the University of Colorado, Denver, on *Nikkei* in twentieth-century Colorado. The study by Kitayama, a former NCRR activist, succeeds so well in the volume because it supplies a "valuable context for the emergence of the NCRR and the larger political and social climate of its founding [in 1980] and, at the same time captures the diverse nature of NCRR's membership ... students, educators, truck drivers, IRS workers, retired persons, and housewives." In addition, it documents that many of the NCRR faithful emerged from the 1960s-1970s Asian American Studies Movement and involvement in community-based resistance activity against the redevelopment of Little Tokyo. The study concludes with the passage of the Civil Liberties Act of 1988 and the transition, two years later, to a new name for NCRR, *Nikkei* for Civil Rights & Redress, and a repurposed organizational agenda.

Part One continues with ten complementary oral history interview excerpts done with noted NCRR activists (all of the book's editorial team, except Hirabayashi, plus Miya Iwataki, Jim Matsuoka, Bert and Lillian Nakano, and Alan Nishio). These probing and palpable conversational narratives with *Nisei* and *Sansei* activists clarify the familial and other experiential reasons leading to their respective affiliation with NCRR and explain how they were able to contribute to its collective development as a democratic/egalitarian organization.

The second part of *NCRR*, titled "Voices of Transformation: Community Organizers and Activists," covers seven chapters. In addition to a moving overarching prologue by Jim Matsuoka, each chapter includes an introduction. The titles of these chapters are an index to the nature of the always inspiring and often quite emotional personal testimonies that they embrace: "Roots of the NCRR"; "Gathering Voices to Speak for Redress"; "Rallying the Community and Building the Movement"; "The People Go to Washington"; "The Role of Art and the Media"; "The Civil Liberties Act of 1988"; "Creating Linkages in the Quest for Justice"; and "A New Generation of Activists." Reading and then ruminating upon the fifty variegated selections within these chapters is what best imparted to me the essence of NCRR and its organizational mission and accomplishments.

Rounding out the volume, Lane Hirabayashi provides both a trenchant "conclusion" and a very useful section entitled "For Further Thought and Readings." The first of these items is distinguished by his articulation of five theses that emerge from *NCRR*: (1) that NCRR was simultaneously broad-based and multi-generational; (2) that credit for Japanese American redress "should not be ascribed to one key organization, or one key set of individuals"; (3) that the NCRR redress movement "made all the difference" in terms of the passage of the Civil Liberties Act; (4) that beyond the passage of the CLA, NCRR continued struggling "to make sure that justice promised became justice effectuated"; and (5) that with the CLA passage, "Japanese American history continues to be deeply relevant to understanding various dimensions of contemporary struggles for social justice." The second closing contribution by Hirabayashi focuses on written and filmic works on the redress movement that readers might consult in order to provide an enlarged context within which to appraise the achievement of NCRR as conveyed in *NCRR*.

Among the back matter in this book one finds helpful sections on acronyms, a glossary of terms, an encyclopedic NCRR chronology by Jim Matsuoka of events spanning from 1955 to 2015, acknowledgements, and a detailed subject index.

This is a book—designed so dynamically by Qris Yamashita and strategically festooned with a remarkable array of photos and other images—that deserves to be read cover to cover. Moreover, the volume merits being devoured not simply as a historical document, but also as a primer for how to mount and sustain a principled and consequential grassroots movement to counter the oppressive nature of our nation's current political system.

REDRESS: The Inside Story of the Successful Campaign for Japanese American Reparations
By John Tateishi (Berkeley, CA: Heyday, 2020, 385 pp., $28.00, hardcover)

Published in the July 16, 2020 edition of the *Nichi Bei Weekly*.

The topic of the Japanese American Redress Movement has been abundantly rewarded by its parade of prominent chroniclers. Those authored or edited volumes which I have been privileged to read and, in some cases, to critically review, are: William Minoru Hohri, *Repairing America* (1988); Leslie T. Hatamiya, *Righting a Wrong* (1993); Yasuko I. Takezawa, *Breaking the Silence* (1995); Mitchell T. Maki, Harry H. L. Kitano, and S. Megan Berthold, *Achieving the Impossible Dream* (1999); Robert Sadamu Shimabukuro, *Born in Seattle* (2001); Alice Yang Murray, *Historical Memories of the Japanese American Internment and the Struggle for Redress* (2008); and Lane Hirabayashi et al., *NCRR* (2018).

I have been drawn to this genre of Japanese American historical literature because of my specialized research field of *Nikkei* resistance to their unjust World War II oppression by the U.S. government. To my mind, however, the most important resistance mounted by Japanese Americans against their mistreatment was not that which, during the war, sporadically manifested itself in individual and group acts of rebellion—as notable and heroic as many of these deeds were —but rather that mobilized during the protracted postwar redress movement. It not only embraced a far greater number of passionately engaged (yet non-violent) participants within the Japanese American community, but also culminated in consequences more far-reaching in terms of personal/collective dignity, social justice, civil liberties, constitutional rights, and the clarification of what precisely it means to be an American.

My reading of John Tateishi's page-turning *Redress* book has deepened my conviction of the astonishing significance of the Japanese American redress movement. For me, Tateishi's hybrid history-and-memoir tome is a masterpiece. In conveying "the inside story of the successful campaign for Japanese American reparations" and his role as the dedicated but oft-confrontational and controversial redress director for the national Japanese American Citizens League (JACL) arm of this ten-year campaign, Tateishi employs a narrative style of enviable verve, perspicacity, candor, and bite. Strategically organizing his book into seven topical-chronological parts ("Beginnings," "Launching the Campaign," "The Strategy," "The First Legislative Fight," "The Commission," "The Final Stage," and "Lessons from the Past"), Tateishi readily acknowledges the myriad contributions of his allies, treats those in opposition to him with respect, and renders transparently (leastwise for the most part) the bases, reservations, and justifications for his decisions in his dual role as the JACL's all-around point-person and legislative lobbyist for redress.

The spot in Tateishi's book where his transparency is arguably problematic comes about in its penultimate part. There the author makes two cases: (1) that the rationale for the 1984 takeover of the JACL leadership by a faction coalescing around the insurgent Legislative Education Committee (LEC) and the attendant loss of his role as legislative lobbyist to the LEC came about because the LEC "breakaway group" wanted the JACL, a purportedly civil rights organization, to devote itself exclusively to the single issue of winning redress; and (2) that he and his JACL cohort group felt that this development would be "myopic and would be rightly viewed as self-serving at a time when the Asian American community had so many [other] pressing needs." This situation led to Tateishi resigning his post in 1986, leaving the Grayce Uyehara-led LEC to direct the legislative campaign that eventuated in the Civil Liberties Act of 1988.

Grant Ujifusa, LEC's chief strategist, has publicly differed with Tateishi both as to why the JACL leadership had pulled back on their commitment to redress and why Tateishi's account of the redress campaign during its concluding—and crucial—two years is anything but that of an "insider." Accordingly, it is fully expected that Ujifusa will author a forthcoming redress book. Whether or not this partic-ular book materializes, John Tateishi has set an exceedingly high bar for *all* future authors of redress volumes.

PART IX
INTERNATIONAL NIKKEI

In 2002, the International Nikkei Research Project (INRP) of the Japanese American National Museum (JANM) produced two books as companion volumes that addressed the topic of Nikkei globalization. The first of these volumes was entitled New Worlds, New Lives: Globalization and People of Japanese Descent in the Americas and from Latin America in Japan *(Stanford: Stanford University Press, 2002); it was edited by three Japanese American anthropologists: Lane Ryo Hirabayashi, James A. Hirabayashi, and Akemi Kikumura-Yano. The second volume,* Encyclopedia of Japanese Descendants in the Americas: An Illustrated History of the Nikkei *(Walnut Creek, CA: AltaMira Press, 2002), was edited by Akemi Kikumura-Yano. Three years later, in 2005, inspired by Kikumura-Yano, with funding from the Nippon Foundation, JANM launched the Discover Nikkei international project, which provided online postings in four languages: English, Japanese, Spanish, and Portuguese. Discover Nikkei's mission statement read: "Discover Nikkei is an international network that celebrates cultural diversity and explores global and local identities. The project connects generations and communities by sharing stories and perspectives of the* Nikkei, *people of Japanese descent who have migrated and settled throughout the world." The definition of*

Nikkei *employed by Discover Nikkei was based upon the findings of the INRP, which during a three-year period involved more than 100 scholars from ten countries and fourteen participating institutions. Accordingly, for Discover Nikkei the term* Nikkei, *per its site homepage, "has multiple and diverse meanings depending on situations, places, and environments.* Nikkei *also include people of mixed racial descent who identify themselves as* Nikkei. *Native Japanese also use the term* Nikkei *for the emigrants and their descendants who return to Japan. Many of these* Nikkei *live in close communities and retain identities from the native Japanese. Currently there are 2.6 to 3 million people of Japanese descent living throughout the world. Most live in the Americas, where they have established families and communities and, in the process, transformed themselves and the societies where they have settled."*

Each of the nine books reviewed in this final section of A Nikkei Harvest *can be broadly construed to fall within the province of the global* Nikkei *experience. In the case of* Daughters of the Samurai, *by Janice P. Nimura, the focus is upon the late-nineteenth century migration and "settlement" in the United States of five Japanese girls who the Japanese government sent there on a decade-long mission to assist their country's Westernization, particularly in terms of women's education. In* Redefining Japaneseness, *sociologist Jane Yamashiro explores how Japanese Americans living in Japan complicate the binary of "Japanese"* (Nihojin) *and "Foreigner"* (Gaijin). *Both of the next two books, Julie Checkoway's* The Three-Year Swim Club *and Suikei Furuya's* An Internment Odyssey, *treat the U.S. mainland experience of Hawai`i* Nikkei; *the first does so within the context of the participation of plantation-trained swimmers from the island of Maui in the London-based 1948 Olympic Games, while the second rivets upon the World War II imprisonment odyssey of a Hawai`i* Issei *businessman, community spokesperson, and progressive haiku poet, Kumaji "Suikei" Furuya, within a veritable gulag of mainland U.S. internment camps. The fifth book, Mary Jo McConahay's* The Tango War, *highlights the WWII cleansing by the Peruvian government of its Japanese-ancestry citizens and the kidnapping of some 1,800 of them, with the complicity of the U.S. government, to imprison them in American internment camps as potential hostages in trades with Japan for U.S. pris-*

oners of war. The sixth review in this section is for Shin Issei Eiichiro Azuma's In Search of Our Frontier, *a book that (along with his equally magisterial 2005 volume* Between Two Empires), *assays the neglected experience of the pioneering* Issei *generation from an intelligently theorized and lavishly documented transnational perspective. This section's next review is Michael R. Jin's* Citizens, Immigrants, and the Stateless, *which explores in depth the transnational stories of second-generation Japanese American emigrants at the crossroads of U.S. and Japanese empires before, during, and after World War II. The penultimate review in this section is Naoko Wake's transpacific study* American Survivors, *which is rooted in oral histories and focuses on the previously largely neglected experiences of American survivors of the U.S. atomic bombings of the Japanese cities of Hiroshima and Nagasaki in 1945. This section's closing review is Jolyon Baraka Thomas's* Faking Liberties, *which explores in a historical perspective the subject of religious freedom in American-Occupied Japan.*

DAUGHTERS OF THE SAMURAI: A Journey from East to West and Back
By Janice P. Nimura (New York: W. W. Norton, 2015, 336 pp., $26.95, hardcover)

Published in the January 1, 2016 edition of the *Nichi Bei Weekly.*

Over the years I have been honored to be privy to the transnational stories both of Japanese women who lived in the United States and Japanese American women who resided in Japan. Some were students of mine at California State University, Fullerton (Mariko Yamashita, Chiaru Kawai, and Reiko Katabami), others I interacted with as peers through the Japanese American Council of the Orange County Historical and Cultural Foundation (Yasko Gamo, Masako Hanada, and Yukiko Sato), a few were Japanese American National Museum colleagues (Eriko Yamamoto and Yoko Nishimura), several more shared membership with me in the Japan Oral History Association (Kayoko Yoshida, Ann Sado, and Dale Sato), while one I befriended primarily via pilgrimages to California's Manzanar and Tule Lake concentration camps (Sachiko Takita-Ishii). In reading and reflecting upon Janice P. Nimura's extraordinary new book, *Daughters of the Samurai*, the tales all these *Nikkei* women related about their respective overseas experiences acquired enhanced resonance for me.

In fact, a major reason why *Daughters of the Samurai* transcends being simply a praiseworthy historical account of the transpacific journeys of her three Japanese female protagonists—Sutematsu Yamakawa (1860-1919), Shige Nagai (1861-1908), and Umeko Tsuda (1864-1929)—is because the present-day experiences of the author (an American daughter-in-law of a Japanese family who, with her husband, spent three post-collegiate years living and working in Japan) match up with those of her Meiji Era (1868-1912) subjects in Victorian America. This situation permits Nimura to empathize at a fundamental level with the far more challenging undertaking of Yamakawa, Nagai, and Tsuda when, in 1871, the Japanese government sent them (along with two other girls from *samurai* families, Tei Ueda and Ryo Yoshimasu, between the ages of six and fourteen) to the United States on a mission to not only live and study there, but also to immerse themselves in Western society and culture and thereafter return to Japan and share what they had learned, most specifically in terms of women's education, to assist their country's Westernization.

This three-part volume is blessed with the author's deeply probing research into primary and secondary research and is expressed through a novelistic, even cinematic, narrative. Part One provides the larger Meiji Japan context in which the girls' ten-year American sojourn, as a small part of the Iwakura Mission (consisting of about fifty rising male stars, average age of thirty-two, drawn from Japan's new leadership), was conceived and enacted. Part Two is set across the Pacific and it encompasses the mission's rapturous and sometimes rambunctious American reception, especially in respect to the five girls, followed largely by the East Coast educational experience of the three youngest girls who completed their decade-long mission (the two fourteen-year-olds, Ueda and Yoshimura, chose to abandon their mission and return home to Japan). Part Three examines Yamakawa, Nagai, and Tsuda during their post-American-mission lives in their native Japan.

In some ways *Daughters of the Samurai* is a historical tragedy. For one thing, when Yamakawa, Nagai, and Tsuda left Japan for America in 1871, Japan was caught up in a Westernization fever, but by the time of their return home in the early 1880s, the pendulum had swung toward resisting Westernization and reconnecting with traditional Japanese ideas, values, and customs. Thus, the girls discovered that their acquired fluency in Western language and manners was not embraced to the extent that they had anticipated. Secondly, while in the United States the command of Japanese language for Yamakawa and Nagai had become rusty, while for Tsuda it was now non-existent. On the other hand, to quote Nimura, "despite this dismaying shift, these young women still managed to make significant and lasting contributions to the progress of women's education in Japan."

Most notably, Umeko Tsuda, who returned to the United States in 1889 to secure her higher education at Bryn Mawr College, would later, in 1900, found one of the first private institutions of higher education for women in Japan. To date, Tsuda College has graduated more than 27,500 women, many of whom have taken an active role in one or another sector in Japanese society. As for Sutematsu Yamakawa, whose graduation from Vassar College made her the first Japanese woman to earn a bachelor's degree *anywhere*, she married the emperor's minister of war, Iwao Oyama, in 1883, and after 1884 became Countess Oyama. Being married to one of Japan's most powerful men afforded her the opportunity to influence (from behind the scenes) the cause of women's education. In the case of Shige Nagai, who in 1882 married Sotokichi Uriu, she became a music teacher at the Women's Higher Normal School and, per Nimura, "juggled seven children and a teaching career generations before the phrase 'working mother' was coined."

Notwithstanding these signal achievements, it is sobering to discover from one reviewer of Nimura's book (James Hadfield) that

Japan, a century after the closing of the Meiji Era, is currently "languishing at 104th place in the Global Gender Report."

Because this cursory review only hints at the bountiful contents of Janice Nimura's brilliant book, readers are advised to view the remarkably illuminating C-Span conversation with Nimura on *Daughters of the Samurai* that another transpacific author, Marie Mutsuki Mockett, author of *Where the Dead Pause, and the Japanese Say Goodbye* (2015), had with her on May 12, 2015 (http://www.c-span.org/video/?326132-1/janice-nimura-daughters-samurai).

REDEFINING JAPANESENESS: Japanese Americans in the Ancestral Homeland
By Jane H. Yamashiro (New Brunswick, NJ: Rutgers University Press, 2017, 216 pp., $27.95, paperback)

Published in the July 20, 2017 edition of the *Nichi Bei Weekly*.

In spite of being involved in researching and writing about Japanese American history for forty-five years, I have only been to Japan once, and then for but a week in the Tokyo-Yokohama area. My purpose was to participate in a conference of the Japan Oral History Association. I was accompanied to this gathering at Tokyo's Rikkyo University by a Japan-born, U.S.-educated colleague at the Japanese American National Museum; she had served an extended professorship at a Japanese university and was a notable specialist in both Japanese and Japanese American history. Throughout the conference I was chaperoned to dinners, cultural institutions, and sporting events by a coterie of distinguished conferees, all either Japanese Americans who were longtime Japan residents or Japanese nationals who had lived and/or worked at length in the United States.

I also interacted with a number of Japanese American conferees who claimed variable degrees of familiarity with Japan and its language and customs. Furthermore, they looked quite like their

Japanese counterparts. For the most part, too, they had been born and raised on the U.S.'s West Coast, but to a lesser extent as well in the country's interior region, on the East Coast, and in Hawai`i. Had *Redefining Japaneseness* been available in 2004 to these conferees, it likely would have been somewhat helpful to them in negotiating even their brief sojourn to their "ancestral homeland." But its value to me would have been chiefly academic, since I am not of Japanese descent, bear no resemblance in appearance to Japan's predominant population, neither speak Japanese nor understand it whatsoever, and have but a rudimentary grasp on Japanese mores and manners. Still, being made aware in *Redefining Japaneseness* that my situation as a white, English-speaking American professor could probably facilitate my reception in Japanese society assuredly would have been useful knowledge for me to acquire.

The working premise of sociologist Jane Yamashiro's luminous book is that Japanese Americans in Japan "complicate" the binary (that is, duality) of "Japanese" and "Foreigner" (whereas someone like me does not, since I am so manifestly a member of the "Foreigner" category). To better understand this premise and its implications before even reading Yamashiro's remarkably enlightening and engaging volume, it would be a wise idea to view her Rutgers University Press-sponsored YouTube posting: https://www.youtube.com/watch?v=B0u43MQWZAg. For therein, Yamashiro addresses such significant questions as: 1) How do Japanese Americans complicate the binary of "Japanese" [*Nihonjin*] and "Foreigner" [*Gaijin*] in Japan? 2) How do Japanese Americans living in Japan vary and does this change their experience? and 3) What is the difference between a Japanese American from Hawai`i and a Japanese American from the continental U.S. in Japan?

Yamashiro is eminently qualified to address these questions and related ones. A *Sansei-Yonsei* raised in San Francisco, she is highly proficient in the Japanese language, as spoken within multiple areas in Japan, where she has lived for protracted periods as a student, researcher, and university professor. She has also lived in Hawai`i (where she received her advanced degrees at the University of

Hawai`i) and the Southern California cities of San Diego (where she did her undergraduate studies at UC San Diego) and Los Angeles (where she has served as a visiting scholar at USC and UCLA as well as being a Loyola Marymount University teaching fellow).

More pertinently, between 2004 and 2009 she conducted for her book more than fifty tape-recorded formal interviews, and many more informal ones, with long-term residents of Tokyo, her cosmopolitan study site. Mostly her informants were "lawyers, businesspeople, and other highly educated white-collar workers," but Yamashiro also interviewed a complement of exchange students and teachers whose stay in Tokyo was of at least one-year duration. In addition, in the decade spanning 2005 and 2015 she conducted thirty-two more formal interviews, plus countless off-the-record ones, with Japanese Americans who were living in the United States after having returned from Japan. Seven of these interviews were follow-ups of ones done by her previously in Tokyo, with two of them being transacted in Honolulu. For the edification of readers, Yamashiro provides a useful appendix that lists all of her project's formal interviewees, who overwhelmingly are assigned pseudonyms to protect their privacy.

So, what, then, is the yield from Yamashiro's prodigious and meticulous ethnographic fieldwork? It is twofold. On the one hand, as a scholarly treatise, *Redefining Japaneseness* breaks new and important ground in sociology, Asian Studies, and Asian American Studies, specifically with regards to extending and illuminating the global phenomena of transnational and ethnic identity construction. On the other hand, to quote the author, "by studying ancestral homeland migration experiences in Japan and showing how they come to redefine Japaneseness through encounters in Japanese society, we gain a better understanding of ... what it means to be Japanese in Japan."

My guess is that while scholars will applaud the first yield of Yamashiro's study, it is the second one that will most command the attention of *Nichi Bei* readers, especially those *Nikkei* who have already endured the complex process of negotiating their ancestral identity as residents of Japan and those who are planning to do so in the future and feel the pressing need and strong desire for a reliable guidebook to ease the burden of their journey of discovery.

THE THREE-YEAR SWIM CLUB: The Untold Story of Maui's Sugar Ditch Kids and Their Quest for Olympic Glory
By Julie Checkoway (New York: Grand Central Publishing, 2015, 432 pp., $27.00, hardcover)

Published in the January 1, 2016 edition of the *Nichi Bei Weekly*.

My favorite Southern California bookstore is in Santa Barbara. Although located in a commonplace strip mall on the outskirts of this picturesque, Spanish-themed resort community, Chaucer's Bookstore is an enchanted place. This is in part owing to its employees, who are not only lovers of people and books, but also dedicated to nurturing a fruitful relationship between them. But this independent bookstore's enchantment is due as well to the cosmopolitan makeup of its stock, which goes well beyond the standard-issue best-selling fiction and non-fiction books typifying most chain bookstores. Consequently, I rarely visit Chaucer's without going home grasping at least one newly published offbeat volume that perfectly suits my taste. Such was precisely the case when, during a recent trip to Chaucer's, I chanced upon Julie Checkoway's *The Three-Year Swim Club*.

Two things prompted me to buy this book. One was the book's subtitle, which linked Maui youth—most, presumably, of *Nikkei* ancestry—with potential athletic stardom. I had simultaneously become attuned to this connection through interviewing professional football-baseball great Wally Yonamine (1925-2011), the son of sugar beet workers near Lahaina, who launched his legendary sports career as a student boarder at historic Lahainaluna High School (see clip on the Japanese American National Museum's Discover *Nikkei* website: http://www.discovernikkei.org/en/interviews/clips/326/), and by closely following the fabled three-year collegiate baseball performance at Cal State Fullerton of future American League All-Star Kurt Suzuki (b. 1983), an alum of the Maui city of Wailuku's Baldwin High School.

My second reason for purchasing Checkoway's book was this accented passage on the cover's flyleaf: "*For readers of* Unbroken *and* The Boys in the Boat *comes the inspirational, untold story of impoverished children who transformed themselves into world-class swimmers.*" Having read and relished both Laura Hillenbrand's 2010 depiction of Olympic Games track star Louis Zamperini in *Unbroken: A World War II Story of Survival, Resilience, and Redemption* and Daniel James Brown's 2013 rendering of the proletarian University of Washington regatta squad in *The Boys in the Boat: Nine Americans and Their Epic Quest for Gold at the 1936 Berlin Olympics*, I was hungry for more of the same genre of engaging sports-and-society history.

It is far from hyperbolic for me to declare that *The Three-Year Swim Club* not merely falls within the same tradition as *Unbroken* and *The Boys in the Boat*, but that it likewise deserves the sort of critical and public acclaim enjoyed by them. What Checkoway narrates in vibrant yet disciplined prose in her superbly documented volume is focused on the span from 1937 to 1948, beginning on the island of Maui's north shore-situated Pu`unene sugar plantation and culminating at the Empire Pool during the "Austerity Olympics" in London. Her book revolves around the vision, dedication, and inventiveness of an idiosyncratic non-swimmer *Nisei* teacher-cum-swim coach, Soichi Sakamoto. His version of "turning a sow's ear into a silk purse" consists of miraculously transforming, within a scant three-year period, a mixed-race band of ragtag plantation boys and girls swimming recreationally in concrete irrigation ditches into formal entrants in duly authorized and highly prestigious swimming competitions (held largely at American mainland venues) as a prelude to participation on the USA team at the 1940 Olympic Games scheduled for Tokyo.

While both Coach Sakamoto and his aquatic charges were hamstrung by bureaucratic restrictions, as well as constrained by a shortfall in proper practice facilities and limited access to adequate public and private pools (due to racial and class prejudice), the Three-Year Swim Team (3YST) achieved a widespread reputation for excellence in its sport. Moreover, selected team members (most notably, Keo Nakama, Halo Hirose, and Fujiko Katsutani) won national championships and/or established world records in their specialty events, and all of these individuals were destined to be Olympic performers, had not international wars caused the cancellation of both the 1940 and 1944 Olympic Games. World War II also was responsible for many 3YSTers joining with thousands of other Japanese Americans in the highly-decorated ranks of the segregated 442nd Regiment and 100th Battalion who waged war against the Axis Powers.

By the time that the 1948 Olympics in London rolled around, Sakamoto had taken a position as coach of the University of Hawai`i swimming team, and only Bill Smith, a twenty-four-year-old Irish-Hawaiian freestyler who had become a 3YST affiliate in 1940, was left to redeem the history and legacy of the club and its embattled mentor, which he did in sterling fashion by winning two gold medals and, in the process, setting new Olympic and world records.

As an epigraph to her "Author's Notes," Julie Checkoway quotes the late Rutgers University cultural historian Warren Susman: "The past is not preserved for the historian as his private domain. Myth, memory, history—these are three alternative ways to capture and account for an allusive past, each with its own persuasive claim." I can think of very few works that so exquisitely balance the claims of these three ways in the service of establishing historical truth as does *The Three-Year Swim Club*. Whether you buy it or borrow it, be sure to do yourself a huge favor and read it.

AN INTERNMENT ODYSSEY: *Haisho Tenten*
By Suikei Furuya (Honolulu: Japanese Cultural Center of Hawai`i, 2017, 416 pp., $26.00, paperback)

Published in the January 1, 2018 edition of the *Nichi Bei Weekly*.

In mid-October of 2017, my longtime and highly regarded colleague at the Japanese American National Museum (JANM), Allyson Nakamoto, regretfully notified me that she had accepted a new educational position at the Japanese Cultural Center of Hawai`i (JCCH). At the same time, however, I was elated to discover that she was going to be employed by an organization, the JCCH, that had been responsible for publishing three remarkable books—*Life Behind Barbed Wire* (2008); *Family Torn Apart* (2012); and *An Internment Odyssey* (2017). My parting advice to Allyson was to read all of these enlightening books immediately.

Taken together, these bountiful volumes have simultaneously achieved the following three ends: 1) substantially enlarged the Japanese immigrant perspective on the World War II Japanese American detention experience; 2) strategically incorporated the Hawai`i Japanese involvement in the heretofore mainland-dominated narrative of that experience; and 3) considerably enriched the limited fund of information pertaining to the WWII alien enemy internment camps.

Like its predecessor volumes within the JCCH's Hawai`i internment story series, *An Internment Odyssey* provides a fascinating wartime participant-observer memoir of an *Issei* leader-writer, in this case via Kumaji "Suikei" Furuya (1889-1977), a prominent Honolulu businessman, community spokesperson, and progressive *haiku* poet. Like the protagonists of the two other series volumes, Yasutaro Soga (1873-1957) and Otokichi Muin Ozaki (1904-1983), Furuya was among the targeted group of 391 persons of Japanese ancestry arrested by the FBI on December 7 and 8, 1941, in the wake of Japan's Pearl Harbor attack. Having been previously identified as "dangerous persons," these men were first detained and interned in Hawai`i facilities and thereafter in a series of mainland prisoner-of-war compounds. In common with Soga, who published his memoir in Japanese (in 1948 as *Tessaku seikatsu*) before it was translated into its 2008 English-language version, Furuya initially released his autobiographical work in Japanese (as *Haisho Tenten* in 1963) prior to the 2017 English translation by Tatsumi Hayashi presently under review.

While the scholarship associated with all three of the volumes noted above is impeccable and the organization of material both ingenious and reader-friendly, I was particularly captivated by certain features of *An Internment Odyssey*. It opens with a heartfelt, insightful, and lyrical foreword by Hawai`i-born-and-bred Gary Okihiro, who during his four-decade scholarly career as a historian on the U.S. mainland has arguably done more than anyone else to advance the cause and repute of Asian American and Japanese American studies. Next comes the introduction by Brian Niiya and Sheila Chun. Like everything else that Niiya has been associated with over his long and productive career in Hawai`i and on the mainland, it is an encyclopedic tour de force. In addition to providing a cogent and authoritative overview of the World War II Japanese American social disaster, this essay richly details the life history of Furuya: as an immigrant leader and poet; his wartime internment experience; his family's life in Hawai`i during the war under martial law; his postwar return to Hawai`i; and his later memory and representation of his wartime detention.

The piece de resistance of *An Internment Odyssey*, naturally enough, is Furuya's memoir. It is primarily organized in chapters devoted to the eight internment camp sites in which he was detained between December 7, 1941, and November 13, 1945: Immigration and Naturalization Service Station (Honolulu, Hawai`i); Sand Island Internment Camp (Honolulu, Hawai`i); Angel Island (San Francisco, California); Camp McCoy (Sparta, Wisconsin); Camp Livingston (Livingston, Louisiana); Fort Missoula (Missoula, Montana); and Santa Fe Internment Camp (Santa Fe, New Mexico). Each stop on Furuya's zigzagging wartime odyssey through seven states and across 11,000 miles is punctuated by his keen observations about the setting, the organization of the facility, the relationships between inmates and camp authorities, and the day-to-day activities of the inmates. These observations are rendered not only in concise and candid prose, but also in illuminating bursts of *haiku* poetry. As aptly noted by Niiya and Chun in their coauthored introduction, Furuya's translated accounts are "virtually the only English-language descriptions of some of these camps [namely, McCoy, Forrest, and Livingston] from the perspective of an internee."

Over and beyond the above items, this book includes many value-added bonuses, such as information about the translator and the translation, a map delineating Furuya's wartime odyssey, a chart indicating the days he spent at each internment camp, a photo section that abounds with fresh images of the internment experience, lists of those incarcerated at several of the camp sites, four varied supplemental appendixes, and endnotes that are both precise and in-depth. Readers of this volume are also in for a rare treat: internee-drawn maps of the Sand Island and Santa Fe internment camps that are published for the very first time.

Let me close this review by reiterating to prospective readers of *An Internment Odyssey* the same advice that I gave to Allyson Nakamoto: read this book, as well as its two companion JCCH volumes, *Life Behind Barbed Wire* and *Family Torn Apart*, as soon as possible.

THE TANGO WAR: The Struggle for the Hearts, Minds, and Riches of Latin America During World War II
By Mary Jo McConahay (New York, NY: St Martin's Press, 2018, 336 pp., $29.99, hardcover)

Published in the July 18, 2019 edition of the *Nichi Bei Weekly*.

Some *Nichi Bei Weekly* readers may well wonder why this book by seasoned Latin American journalist Mary Jo McConahay is being reviewed here for their consumption, consideration, and contemplation. After all, its focus, as the volume's title intimates, is the World War II shadow war for the Western Hemisphere pitting the Axis against the Allies for popular support, military advantage, and natural resources, one in which each side "closely shadowed the steps of the other, like dancers in a tango."

While *The Tango War* certainly fills a gap in the history of World War II, is painstakingly researched and documented, conveys a dynamic narrative, and achieves a balance between being edifying and enjoyable, the overriding rationale for reviewing it in this particular venue is due to the inclusion in the book of what British historian Susan Carruthers depicts as its "two most poignant chapters"— Chapter Six, "In Inca Country, Capturing 'Japanese,'" and Chapter Seven, "Inmates: A Family Affair." Together these chapters assay the causes and consequences of the U.S. government-concocted scheme nicknamed "Quiet Passages" to kidnap Latin American residents (mostly, but not exclusively, Peruvian males of Japanese ancestry, both aliens and, to a lesser degree, citizens) and to dragoon them (some 1,800 Peruvian Japanese out of a total of 2,200 Latin American Japanese) into U.S. internment (a.k.a. concentration) camps.

Chapter Six concentrates mainly on the causation of the Peruvian Japanese catastrophe, which consisted of a combination of factors. Chief among these, according to McConahay, were the U.S.'s fervent need for "Japanese" prisoners to exchange for Americans held captive by Japan; the Peruvian government's escalating anti-Asian prejudice and alleged fear of sabotage, subversion, or espionage by members of its 30,000 Japanese population; and the economic success of Japanese Peruvians and the attendant jealousy about and resentment for this achievement by Peru's white European-oriented business community.

In the next chapter, McConahay turns her major attention to the consequences or costs of the wartime ethnic Japanese cleansing of Peru, which was enacted by its complicit leaders in conjunction with the "Machiavellian" maneuvers of U.S. governmental officials exercising their country's hemispheric overlord powers. As the Peruvian Japanese "captives" boarded ships that would take them to the U.S. at either New Orleans, Louisiana, or San Pedro, California, they were mandated to relinquish their passports, "so they would land in the U.S. as 'undocumented aliens, subject to arrest.'" Then, en route to their destinations, their ships sailed through imperiled waters infested with prowling U-boats. Thereafter, upon arrival at their American ports of entry, the involuntary passengers were interrogated by FBI agents who apprised them that they were subject to arrest because of lacking proper travel documents. In addition, captives and family members were forced to undergo not only the indignity of stripping, but also to endure having attendants spray them with DDT. Following a darkened train ride from New Orleans or San Pedro to the small southern Texas town of Crystal City, the bedraggled passengers were deposited as prisoners of war at a 290-acre site girded by ten-foot fences and guarded by armed sentry towers in a U.S. Immigration and Naturalization Service-administered facility called the Crystal City Internment Center (which remained in operation until 1947). Although McConahay provides a superb overview, replete with personal reminiscences, of this prison, readers interested in a fuller treatment of this site of shame will be well served by checking out Jan Jarboe Russell's 2016 book *The Train to Crystal City: FDR's Secret Prisoner Exchange*. Arguably, the best treatment of the short- and long-term causes and consequences of the pernicious WWII experience of Peruvian Japanese is Lika C. Miyake's January 2002 *Asian American Law Journal* article entitled "Forsaken and Forgotten: The U.S. Internment of Japanese Peruvians During World War II," which is available online.

IN SEARCH OF OUR FRONTIER: Japanese America and Settler Colonialism in the Construction of Japan's Borderless Empire By Eiichiro Azuma (Berkeley: University of California Press, 2019, 353 pp., $75.00, hardcover)

Published in the July 16, 2020 edition of the *Nichi Bei Weekly*.

In recent years historians have increasingly moved away from writing about the history of a single nation state, so-called "mononational" history, to writing an innovative variety of international history known as "transnational" history. Unlike traditional international history, which focused on the formal relations between two nation-states, this new form of historical inquiry seeks instead to illuminate how the events and developments that occurred within two countries overlapped and interpenetrated one another. Unfortunately, such an approach has been at a discount in Asian American and Japanese American historical scholarship. Nonetheless, one brilliant practitioner of these historical subfields, Eiichiro Azuma of the University of Pennsylvania, has been responsible for the publication of two landmark books enshrining the practice of Japanese American transnational history.

In 2006, Azuma authored *Between Two Empires: Race, History, and Transnationalism in Japanese America* (Oxford University Press). Then, in 2019, Azuma saw into print the book presently under review. Together, these books entailed twenty years of painstaking research by Azuma into archives in the United States and Japan. The hallmark of these remarkable books is this: Whereas most extant historical scholarship treating the pre-World War II Japanese American experience has been limited to the theorization of transnational history, what Azuma has done in his publications is to go beyond theory and present, as he wrote in *Between Two Empires*, the "actual events and concrete forces, both in Japan and the United States, as well as within their communities, that influenced the ideas and practices of the *Issei*." It is this difference that makes all the difference, in that it renders both of Azuma's books reader-friendly and, moreover, of compelling interest—not merely to other scholars in his field, but also to general readers, most especially those of Japanese ancestry.

In *Between Two Empires*, Azuma aimed to show how the *Issei* immigrants from Japan to the American West forged a unique collective community identity as aliens ineligible for U.S. citizenship, while being simultaneously oppressed by white American racism, on the one hand, and, on the other hand, Imperial Japan's view of them as patriotic agents of its nationalistic expansionist and militaristic goals. While writing that monograph, Azuma was struck by the examples of a significant number of *Issei* who gave up on the American West as a colonial settlement destination because of its racism and returned to Japan to champion more promising worldwide sites of colonization, such as the non-western U.S., Mexico, Manchuria, Taiwan, and Korea. This then becomes the burden that Azuma attends to in the eight detailed chapters that comprise *In Search of Our Frontier*. In so discharging this burden, according to Michael Thornton's authoritative in-depth *Journal of Asian Studies* review, Azuma seeks to bridge two historical traditions: "that of domestic U.S. ethnic studies, which divorces Japanese Americans from the history of Japan, and that of the Japanese empire (and modern Japanese history more generally), which tends to disregard Japanese communities elsewhere in the world."

Well-written, richly documented, and passionately and persuasively argued, *In Search of Our Frontier* is a work of historical artistry.

CITIZENS, IMMIGRANTS, AND THE STATELESS: A Japanese American Diaspora in the Pacific
By Michael R. Jin (Stanford: Stanford University Press, 2022, 223 pp., $30.00, paperback)

Published in the July 20, 2023 edition of the *Nichi Bei News*.

I feel a close kinship with this remarkable book by Michael R. Jin. In 2013, I was privileged to read his pioneering UC Santa Cruz dissertation, which he completed under the able mentorship of Alice Yang and that became the basis for the 2022 Stanford University Press book here under review. It is included within the press's Asian American series edited by Gordon Chang, the same series in which Yang (then Yang Murray) contributed her stunning 2008 work, *Historical Memories of the Japanese American Internment and the Struggle for Redress*, and I, in 2018, had published my edited volume, *Nisei Naysayer: The Memoir of Militant Japanese American Journalist Jimmie Omura*.

Citizens, Immigrants, and the Stateless is a groundbreaking transnational historical inquiry into the diasporic experiences (many quite challenging and even dangerous) of some 50,000 *Nisei* (second-generation Americans of Japanese ancestry, representing about one-fourth of that cohort group's total population in the U.S.) who, within the first half of the twentieth century, left their native country to settle in either Japan or the territories of the Japanese Empire. Designated as *Kibei-Nisei* (or just simply *Kibei*), their life course, too often suppressed in the standard literature, was not only at variance with that of those *Nisei* who remained in the U.S. (and whose trajectory have been highlighted in both academic and popular accounts), but arguably, according to Jin, less the generational exception than the norm.

Based upon his extensive research into archival and published sources in both the English and Japanese languages, Jin's study consists of six chapters: two of them devoted to *Kibei-Nisei* in pre-World War II Japan, two treating their incarceration in U.S. concentration camps, and two on those who were trapped in wartime Japan. All of these chapters are propelled by case studies that, taken together, illuminate the diversity of *Kibei-Nisei* encounters and personalities embedded in a Japanese American identity. The first two chapters explore the variegated reasons responsible for *Nisei* migrating to Japan (e.g., family, education, employment, and career development), but do so in terms that are perhaps a mite too generic rather than compellingly personal. The middle two chapters, while depicting in broad terms how *Kibei-Nisei* were demonized by the U.S. government, camp authorities, and even certain sectors within the *Nikkei* inmate populace, misfires somewhat on the fortuitous opportunity afforded to provide an in-depth depiction of the *Kibei-Nisei* camp narrative (a topic that badly needs to be seriously addressed and redressed in the future by scholars of the Japanese American WWII incarceration). The final two chapters focus on the following two subjects, both of which are richly documented: (1) the 20,000 *Kibei-Nisei* stranded during the Pacific War in the Japanese Empire, particularly those who either served in the Japanese military or performed non-combatant intelligence gathering; and (2) the *Kibei-*

Nisei victims of the atomic bomb (*hibakusha*)—most especially, those 3,000 living in the city of Hiroshima—who went unacknowledged by the U.S. government and were deemed ineligible for medical care because their war story challenged the prevailing American narrative relative to the nuclear bombing.

My above reservations about Jin's masterpiece are assuredly debatable and decidedly minor in nature. Overall, he has produced a book that is dramatically innovative in terms of its topic and one that is exceedingly well-written, astutely documented, and deserving of reaching a wide audience of engaged readers.

AMERICAN SURVIVORS: Trans-Pacific Memories of Hiroshima & Nagasaki
By Naoko Wake (New York: Cambridge University Press, 2021, 392 pp., $29.05, hardcover)

Published in the July 21, 2022 edition of the *Nichi Bei Weekly*.

In 1974, Betty Mitson and I co-edited a modest and virtually self-published and crudely fabricated book titled *Voices Long Silent: An Oral Inquiry into the Japanese American Evacuation*. It was conceived and developed as way to open up discussion about a World War II event that had heretofore largely been muted by the general U.S. public and even the Japanese American community: the *Nikkei*'s wholesale and unjust eviction by the U.S. government from their predominantly West Coast homes and subsequent incarceration in inland concentration camps. The principal methodology used in this pioneering book was oral history interviews, mostly ones conducted with victims of Executive Order 9066, an action which embodied President Franklin Roosevelt's brazen disregard for the civil liberties and human rights of Americans of Japanese ancestry.

Now, almost a half-century later, a Japan-born-and-raised historian at Michigan State University, Naoko Wake, has turned a spotlight, via her exceedingly brilliant, voluminous, and prestigious Cambridge University Press book, on another previously marginalized topic pertinent to the World War II experience of Americans of Japanese ancestry. It is that of the American survivors of the 1945 atomic bombings of the Japanese cities of Hiroshima and Nagasaki. In addition, she makes clear in her introduction that, in the absence of a research archive devoted to this subject, much of her "inquiry into the U.S. *hibakusha* relies on oral history interviews that I [86 altogether, two-thirds with women] and a handful of others have conducted [a total of 46] with [a rapidly diminishing number of] U.S. survivors, their family members, community supporters, and physicians in Japan and America."

Framed by a helpful stage-setting introduction and an epilogue that looks both backward and forward, *American Survivors* consists of six chapters, chronologically ordered, with the common core for each being "the remembering of the bomb derived from the oral histories." Chapter 1 describes Hiroshima and Nagasaki as historically "immigrant cities" whose World War II populations included many Japanese Americans and colonized Koreans, all with layered memories connecting them to their respective homelands. Chapter 2 examines how these memories shaped the response of *hibakusha* to the catastrophe that beset them in August 1945 in Hiroshima and Nagasaki. Chapters 3 and 4 focus on how, culturally, Japanese American *hibakusha* recoupled with their families in the fifteen years after 1945, first in Japan and then, post 1947, after their return to the United States mainland (preponderantly California) and Hawai`i. Chapters 5 and 6 examine how in the 1960s-1980s era the 1980s *hibakusha* forged a collective identity as survivors by working in tandem with Asian American civil rights activists, chiefly women (even though the *hibakusha* fell far short of gaining the public acknowledgment and redress perquisites accorded World War II Japanese American concentration camp inmates).

American Survivors ranks among the very best books I have encountered over my half-century of historical inquiry into the World War II Japanese American experience, most of which has been fueled by the methodology of oral history. It is, however, a difficult volume to assess in a compact review. In reading it and trying to fathom it, I found myself relying on three very helpful internet sources. The first two were interviews with Naoko Wake: "Asian American History 101: Interview of Professor Wake on American Survivors of Hiroshima and Nagasaki" (1882 Productions, 2021) and "An Interview with Naoko Wake" (New Books Network, 2021). The third was ten of Naoko Wake's interviews relative to American survivors that are available online in the Densho Digital Repository. I highly recommend these sources to readers of this review.

FAKING LIBERTIES: RELIGIOUS FREEDOM IN AMERICAN-OCCUPIED JAPAN
By Jolyon Baraka Thomas (Chicago: University of Chicago Press, 2019, 336 pp., $32.50, paperback)

Published in the July 18, 2019 edition of the *Nichi Bei Weekly*.

Although only an assistant professor of religious studies at the University of Pennsylvania, Jolyon Baraka Thomas has already published one remarkable book, "Drawing on Tradition: Manga, Anime, and Religion in Contemporary Japan" (University of Hawai'i Press), and is presently working on a third book with the tentative title of "Difficult Subjects: Debating Religion and Public Education in Japan and the United States." As for the volume under review here, Thomas's second book, it is a brilliantly conceived, deeply researched, tightly argued, and elegantly composed comparative and transnational inquiry into the concept and practice of religious freedom, with particular emphasis upon Japan's Meiji era and its post-WWII Allied (mainly U.S.) Occupation period.

Because the content and character of "Faking Liberties" defies my powers as a non-specialist to summarize in a short review, perhaps at this juncture the wisest path for me to pursue to stimulate your interest in and facilitate comprehension of Thomas's book is to permit the author to provide you with a summary in his own well-chosen words: https://www.youtube.com/channel/UCKDr29Aepo8m Qo_a-Wy9Kng.

Having heard from Thomas about his book, I would next recommend that you read his very personal and probing seven-page epilogue, "Songs of Freedom," before tackling the book per se. When you do, you will be exposed to his family background. His white mother was reared in a small town in Iowa as the offspring of parents with religious ties, a cosmopolitan outlook, a regard for civil rights, and a proclivity for social justice, while his black father was brought up in South Side Chicago and then educated in rural Iowa at the small liberal arts college of Grinnell, where he met his future wife and, additionally, was placed on an FBI watch list for his activities as co-founder of the Concerned Black Students campus organization—which left him cynical about the U.S. promise of freedom and afterwards led him to teach Jolyon and his brother "to be suspicious of authority and keenly aware of the double standard that all black men face in America" (p. 262).

You will also be informed about Thomas's coming of age in the 1980s in the overwhelmingly white city of Des Moines, during which time he absorbed the lesson that some people were more free than others (punctuated at age seventeen during a stopped car incident by a cop threatening to kill him while treating his accompanying two wealthy white friends deferentially)—which prompted him to move to Japan after 9/11, where he stayed for two stints (2002-4 and 2005-7) and experienced racial profiling both from Tokyo police officers and, on trips back to the U.S., by American airport officials.

Furthermore, reading Thomas's epilogue will alert you to how, during research in Japan in 2013 for *Faking Liberties*, he was harassed at Tokyo nightclubs by police patrols cracking down on "unseemly fraternization between local Japanese people and American service members" (pp. 263-4), a legacy from the 1945-52 Allied Occupation. It will also inform you that when Thomas was writing his book in the U.S. at a time when the police murder of black people was on a steep upsurge and the Black Lives Matter movement was rising in response, he agonized internally as to how his "academic inquiry into the politics of religious freedom could fit with the ongoing project of perfecting liberty in America" (p. 264).

For many years I taught a graduate seminar in history at California State University, Fullerton, titled "History and Historians." What this course emphasized was that the historical writings of historians were powerfully shaped by their sociocultural experiences. In the case of Jolyon Thomas, his "long-standing curiosity about rights, freedom, and America's protean definitions of personhood dovetailed with . . . [his] enduring professional fascination with the conundrum of how the categories of 'religion' and 'not-religion' have operated and continue to operate in modern Japan and elsewhere" (p. 266).

AFTERWORD

On September 8, 2022, University of Texas historian Steven Mintz posted on Twitter a timely essay entitled "The Decline of the Book Review: The State and Fate of Book Reviewing." In this meditative piece, Mintz explained that the "stand-alone newspaper book section [in the United States] is on the verge of extinction," with that of the *New York Times Book Review* being the sole one still currently published. He then adduced at length the multiplex reasons for this sad state of affairs. What most captured my attention, however, is the advice Mintz, albeit inadvertently, offered to those book reviewers (like myself) who are fortunate enough to have a reputable forum (like the *Nichi Bei News*) to publish our reviews. What we should do, accordingly, is to avoid "the steamroller approach" whereby we are predisposed to "demolish or critique every work we read [and review], paragraph by paragraph," and instead to regard our role of "assessment as a form of connoisseurship, consisting of informed and discriminating judgment tempered with critical understanding and an acute awareness of context."

It is my fond hope that readers of *A Nikkei Harvest* will agree after reading the sundry book reviews contained within it by Wayne Maeda and myself that we have honored in practice the spirit of Mintz's sage formulation.

ABOUT THE AUTHORS

Arthur A. Hansen (b. 1938), a third-generation American of Irish-Norwegian descent, was born in Hoboken, New Jersey, and came of age in Santa Barbara, California. He earned all of his academic degrees at the University of California, Santa Barbara, and is now a professor emeritus of History and Asian American Studies at California State University, Fullerton (CSUF). From 2001 to 2005 he served as the senior historian at the Japanese American National Museum. Between 1991 and 1995 he edited for publication the six-volume *Japanese American World War II Evacuation Oral History Project*. In 2007, the Association for Asian American Studies presented him its Distinguished Lifetime Achievement Award. Most of his scholarly writings over the past half century have focused upon the resistance Japanese Americans mounted against their community's World War II oppression by the U.S. government and the Japanese American Citizens League leadership. His most notable recent publications embody this focus: an edited Stanford University Press volume, *Nisei Naysayer: The Memoir of Militant Japanese American Journalist Jimmie Omura*; an authored University Press of Colorado book, *Barbed Voices: Oral History, Resistance, and the World War II Japanese American Social Disaster*; an edited University Press of Colorado memoir of Yoshito Kuromiya entitled *Beyond the Betrayal: The Memoir of a World War II Japanese American Draft Resister of Conscience*; and an authored University Press of Colorado book, *Manzanar Mosaic: Essays and Oral Histories on America's First World War II Japanese American Concentration Camp*.

Wayne H. Maeda (1947-2013), a third-generation Japanese American, was born in Dayton, Ohio, and raised in Sacramento, California. Maeda received his academic degrees from Sacramento City College and the California State University, Sacramento (CSUS). He later taught at both of these institutions as well as at the University of California, Davis. After serving as a faculty member at CSUS for forty years, he retired in 2011. During his CSUS tenure, Maeda was one of the founding faculty of its Ethnic Studies Program and an advisory board member of numerous organizations. Between 1995 and 2013, he was the lead book reviewer for the *Nichi Bei Times* and its successor, the *Nichi Bei Weekly*.

Kenji G. Taguma (b. 1969), a third-generation Japanese American, was born in Sacramento, California, raised in the countryside of West Sacramento, and graduated in 1995 from California State University, Sacramento. An innovative nonprofit media professional and award-winning San Francisco journalist, Taguma has led the transformation of the first nonprofit ethnic community newspaper of its kind in the country, rising out of the ashes of the historic *Nichi Bei Times* (1946-2009) and *Nichi Bei Shimbun* (1899-1942) legacy. In 2009, he launched the *Nichi Bei Weekly* (now the *Nichi Bei News*), for which he is the editor-in-chief, under the aegis of the Nichi Bei Foundation, over which he presides as its president. In this latter capacity, Taguma initiated the annual Films of Remembrance, a day-long showcase of films about the World War II concentration camp experience of Japanese Americans—screening more than 140 films in San Francisco, Sacramento, New York, and San Jose over 12 years. He also instigated the Nikkei Angel Island Pilgrimage, which to date has brought more than 2,000 people over five pilgrimages to learn about the nearly forgotten legacy of Japanese immigrants detained at the site. Additionally, he spearheaded three unprecedented pilgrimages to the former Wakamatsu Tea and Silk Farm Colony site, the first sizeable settlement of Japanese in America.

ACKNOWLEDGEMENTS

I am exceedingly grateful to the Nichi Bei Foundation for publishing *A Nikkei Harvest*. I am also profoundly indebted to Sharon Yamato and Kurtis Nakagawa for encouraging its publication. In addition, I extend my heartfelt thanks to Kenji Taguma and Naomi Hirahara for taking the time from their very impacted work schedules and going to the trouble of overseeing the arduous task of converting my manuscript into a book. My appreciation extends to three very exacting professionals for discharging their respective roles with distinction: cover designer Patricia Wakida, copyeditor Alec Yoshio MacDonald, and indexer Lee Gable. Finally, I would like to thank the authors of all of the volumes included in this book on the Japanese American experience and legacy that I have had the great privilege of reading and reviewing.

INDEX

Note: page numbers in bold indicate reviews.

AAAS. *See* Association of Asian American Studies
Abe, Frank, 166, 171 Abe, Masao. *See Masao* (Vea)
Abiko, Kyutaro, 111
ABMC. *See* American Battle Monuments Commission
Achieving the Impossible Dream (Maki, Kitano, and Berthold), 197, 206
Across Two Worlds (Shibata), 60
activism by Japanese Americans: importance of historical knowledge for, 44–45; importance of words and, 27; intersectionality and, 202; against model minority image, 107; opposition to JACL's agenda, 107. *See also* Asian American Movement; radicalism, Asian American; redress and reparations movement
Adamic, Louis, 30
After Camp (Robinson), **14–15**
Agnew, Spiro, 26–27
Ahlgren, Angela K.: online interview with, 127. *See also Drumming Asian America* (Ahlgren)
Akimoto, Johnny and Victor. *See When the Akimotos Went to War* (Elms)
Alaska-Yukon-Pacific Exposition of 1909, 81
Alien Land Law (California), 84, 96
An Alien Place (Valkenburg), 140
Allied Translator and Interpreter Section (ATIS), Japanese American service with, 54–55
Altered Lives (Fugita and Fernandez), 80
Amache Relocation Center, 118, 123, 145, 146, 167, 171
Amemiya, Chiyo, 91
Amerasia Journal, 166, 178
American Battle Monuments Commission (ABMC), 56

Americanization/assimilation: books on, 15; and decline of Japanese Americans' group orientation, 25; forces contributing to, 76–77, 100; of Japanese American in Michigan, 100; and Japanese family model, 49–50; as prewar norm, 198; radicalization of *Sansei* in 1960s-70s and, 198
American Survivors (Wake), 211, **228–30**
American Sutra (Williams), 112
Angel Island Immigration Station, 2, 221
Angus, Ian, 186
"An Interview with Lillian Nakano" (Horiuchi), 201
Aoki, Richard: Maeda's memories of, 18; as subject of Fujino's *Samurai Among Panthers*, 13, 18–19
Arlington National Cemetery honoring of Japanese American soldiers, 106
Armes, Ethel, 20
Army, U.S., Japanese Americans in, 35–36. *See also* World War II military service by Japanese Americans
Asian American Histories of the United States (Choy), **192–94**
Asian American Movement: books on, 18, 19, 184–85; Ishizuka on, 188–90; Japanese Americans and, 183–84; Maeda on, 186–88; origin of, 183, 189; platform of, 189; radicalization of *Sansei* in 1960s-70s and, 198; redress and reparations movement and, 198; solidarity with Muslims in U.S., 188; and *taiko* drumming, 126. *See also* radicalism, Asian American
"The Asian American Movement" (Maeda), 185
Asian American Pacific Island Theme Study, 96
Asian Americans: hate directed at, currently, 193; *Nikkei* as declining percentage

of, 184; original radicalism implied in, 184, 187; origin of concept, 183
Asian Americans (Chan), 192–93
Asian Americans in Michigan (Wilkinson and Jew, eds.), 78, **98–102**
Asian American Studies: Association of Asian American Studies (AAAS), 29; and *Oxford Handbook of Asian American History*, 185, 190
Asians for Community Action, 92
assimilation. *See* Americanization/assimilation
Association of Asian American Studies (AAAS), 29
atomic bombing of Japan: accounts of American survivors of, 228–30; books on, 55, 64; *Kibei Nisei* and, 227–28. *See also* Hiroshima
Azuma, Eiichiro, 111, 174, 185, 211. *See also Between Two Empires* (Azuma); *In Search of Our Frontier* (Azuma); *The Oxford Handbook of Asian American History* (Yoo and Azuma, eds.)

baseball. *See Transpacific Field of Dreams* (Shimizu)
Battan, Jesse, 186
Beginnings (Misawa), 90
Bend with the Wind (Shibata), 51, **58–61**
Berthold, S. Megan, 197, 206
Best, Raymond, 176
Between Two Empires (Azuma), 185, 211
Beyond Loyalty (Kiyota), 168
"Beyond Two Homelands" (Jin), 168–69
Bidell, Jay, 55
Big Drum: Taiko in the United States project, 90
Bishop, Ronald, 144. *See also Community Newspapers and the Japanese American Incarceration Camps* (Bishop et al.)
Black Panthers. *See Samurai Among Panthers* (Fujino)

Blindsided (Mihara), 26, **40–41**
The Bonus March (Ishigaki), 120
book reviews: as connoisseurship, not criticism, 233; decline of, in newspapers, 9–10, 233
Born in Seattle (Shimabukuro), 80, 180, 197, 206
Born in the USA (Chin), 166, 171, 173
The Boys in the Boat (Brown), 218
Breaking the Line (Freedman), 156
Breaking the Silence (Takezawa), 79, 197–99, 206
Brignull, Irena, 128–129
Briones, Matthew M., 29. *See also Jim and Jap Crow* (Briones)
Brown, Daniel James, 218
Browning, Christopher R., 152

Cable Act of 1922, 20
California: Alien Land Law, campaign against, 84; desegregation of schools in, 65–66. *See also Historic Wintersburg in Huntington Beach* (Urashima)
Camp and Community (Garrett and Larson), 143
"Camp Connections" (2004 conference), 163
Camp Harmony (Fiset), 80
Camp Livingston (Louisiana), 221, 222
Camp McCoy (Wisconsin), 221, 222
Carruthers, Susan, 223
Castlenuovo, Shirley, 171, 173
Chains of Babylon (Maeda), 184, **185–88**
Chan, Sucheng, 192–93
Chang, Gordon, 226
Chang, Jeff, 189
Changing Season (Masumoto), 51, **67–70**
Checkoway, Julie. *See The Three-Year Swim Club* (Checkoway)
Chicago, Japanese Americans resettled in, 31–32
Chin, Frank, 166, 171, 173
Chin, Jeffrey, 83
Chin, Vincent, 100, 101
Chinese Exclusion Act of 1882, 120

Choy, Catherine Ceniza: online interview, 194. *See also Asian American Histories of the United States* (Choy)
Christgau, John, 140
Chrysanthemums and Salt (1994 film), 93–94
Chun, Sheila, 221, 222
cinematic novels, tips for writing, 128
Citizen Internees (Ivey and Kaatz), **92–95**; subject of, 77–78, 94–95
Citizens, Immigrants, and the Stateless (Jin), 211, **226–28**
citizenship: books on, 141; Cable Act and, 20; contested definition of, 167, 172; Heart Mountain inmates' demands on, 154, 157; JACL and, 107; and military service, 106, 154; removed from disloyal Japanese Americans, 37–38, 107. *See also* renunciation of U.S. citizenship
Civil Control Administration (WCCA), 147
Civil Liberties Act of 1988, 102, 107–8, 135, 195, 197, 199, 200–201, 204, 207
civil rights: activists for, 48, 77, 83–84, 229; Asian American Movement and, 183; books on, 36, 47; draft resistance and, 158; internment camps as violation of, 142, 145; redress and reparations movement and, 195; valuing security over, 87–88. *See also* discrimination against Japanese Americans
Claiming the Oriental Gateway (Lee), 77, **79–82**
Coffman, Tom: books by, 63. *See also Tadaima! I Am Home* (Coffman)
Collective Protest in Relocation Centers (Jackman), 165
Collins, Wayne M., 107
The Color of Success (Woo), 78, **102–10**
Commission on Wartime Relocation and Internment of Civilians (CWRIC), 28, 196
community, Japanese American: books on,

77–78; change over time in, 71–77; future status of now-marginal groups, 113–15; in Hawai`i, 19th century, 72; in Hawai`i, 20th century, 73; impact of World War II on, 74–75; individuals' actions as reflection on, 71, 72; and intermarriage, 73; on mainland, prewar, 73–74; origin in Meiji-era farming villages, 71–72; postwar evolution of, 75–77; preservation efforts, book on, 95–98; pre-war, books on, 80–82, 86–87, 88–89, 90, 93–94; prewar, cultural themes of, 25; San Jose Japantown, 90–92; suburbanization, intermarriage, and assimilation, 76–77, 100; turn to family focus, 74. *See also Asian Americans in Michigan* (Wilkinson and Jew, eds.)

Community Newspapers and the Japanese American Incarceration Camps (Bishop et al.), 132, **143–46**

Concentration Camps USA (Daniels), 107, 132, 165–66, 171, 173

Conjecturing Communities (Hirabayashi, ed.), 78, **113–15**

Conscience and the Constitution (2000 film), 166, 171

Cortez Colony, 111

cosmopolitanism: of Fukuda and Pearce's *San Jose Japantown*, 91; of Japanese American community, 45; of Japanese American modernist artists, 118, 120; of *Nichi Bei Weekly/Nichi Bei News* readers, 11; of *Oxford Handbook of Asian American History*, 191; of public schools in Seattle, 81–82; of Urashima, 96

Country Voices (Masumoto), 67–68

critical race theory, 67

Crystal City Internment Camp, 132; books on, 140–43; South American Japanese in, 224

cultural heritage, American, complexity of, 119
cultural radicalism: as all-inclusive domain, 186; definition of, 186; Hansen's course on, 185–86
culture, Japanese American: focus on group welfare in, 25–26, 50, 72; and shame (*haji*), 72
CWRIC. *See* Commission on Wartime Relocation and Internment of Civilians

Daggett, Renee, 132, 143, 144
Daniels, Roger, 14, 107, 121–22, 132, 162, 165–66, 171, 173
Daughters of the Samurai (Nimura), 53, 210, **211–14**
Day, Michael, 170
Day, Takako. *See Show Me the Way to Go Home* (Day)
Day of Protest (Little Tokyo, 1989), 203
"The Death of the Book Review" (Palattella), 9–10

"The Decline of the Book Review" (Mintz), 233
Densho Digital Repository, 230
Densho Encyclopedia, 143, 195
Densho organization, 35, 183
Department of Justice internment camps of, 132, 138–39, 140–41
desegregation of schools in California, 65–66
Dickinson, Saeko Higa, 84
Difficult Subjects (Thomas), 230
Discover Nikkei project (JANM), 209–10
discrimination against Japanese Americans: books on, 157; internment and, 152; JACL Anti-Discrimination Committee, 107; Maeda on, 187; military's mistreatment of American-citizen soldiers, 153–54; miscegenation laws and, 20–21; in Seattle, 82; U.S.-Japan Gentlemen's Agreement and, 74. *See also Jim and Jap Crow* (Briones); racial

discrimination; *entries under* Immigration Act
Distant Voices (Masumoto), 67–68
Divided Destiny (Takami), 79–80
DOHO (Hansen and Larson), 83
Doho newspaper, 83
Dower, John, 174
Drawing on Tradition (Thomas), 230
Drinnon, Richard, 166, 171, 173, 176
drumming. *See taiko* drumming
Drumming Asian America (Ahlgren), 118–19, **124–27**
Dubrow, Gail, 80
Dudkewitz, Morgan, 132, 143, 144

The *Eagles of Heart Mountain* (Pearson), 133, **156–58**
Ei Ja Nai Ka? folk dance, 126
Elms, Matthew. *See When the Akimotos Went to War* (Elms)
Embracing Defeat (Dower), 174
Embrey, Sue Kunitomi, 150, 202

Emergency Detention Act of 1950, 196
Emi, Frank, 158, 166
Encyclopedia of Japanese Descendants in the Americas (Kikumura-Yano, ed.), 209
Enemies (Christgau), 140
ethnic studies: Maeda and, 2–5; states mandating, 67; Uno and, 137
Eto, Margaret Hisayasu, 59
Eto, Masaji, 59
Eto, Take Yanahara, 59
Eto, Tameji, 59
Evacuation and Resettlement Study (JERS), 29, 31–32
Executive Order 9066, 42, 104, 131, 149, 198, 228

Faking Liberties (Thomas), 211, **230–32**
Falcone, Alissa, 132, 143, 144
"Fallow Field" (Okihiro), 89
family, Japanese American: books about, 50–51; individuals' actions as reflection on, 71, 72; influence of traditional Japanese model on, 50

family, traditional Japanese model of, 49, 50; Americanization and, 49–50; ongoing influence of, 50
Family Torn Apart (Honda, ed.), 13–14, **16–17**, 136, 138, 220
Farewell to Manzanar (Houston and Houston), 128
Farming the Home Place (Matsumoto), 111
fear of Japanese Americans, article on, 27–28
Fernandez, Marilyn, 80
Fiset, Louis, 80
A Flicker in Eternity (2013 documentary film), 160
Forced Out (Kawamoto), 26, **42–43**
Ford, Jamie, 80
The Forging of a Black Community (Taylor), 79
"Forsaken and Forgotten" (Miyake), 224
For the Mexican Children (McCaffery), 65–66
Fort Lincoln Internment Camp, 140
Fort Missoula Internment Camp, 140
Fort Stanton Internment Camp, 140
"Fourth & Fifth Generation Japanese American Adults" (Saito), 71
Fox Drum Bebop (Oishi), 25, **26–28**
Freedman, Samuel, 156
Free to Die for Their Country (Muller), 166, 171, 173
"From Hammered-down Nail to Squeaky Cog" (Shichi), 100
From Many Lands (Adamic, ed.), 30
Fugita, Stephen, 80
Fujii, Sei: books and films about, 83; as subject of Sato's *A Rebel's Cry*, 77, 83–84
Fujii, Takuichi, illustrated diary of, 118, 121–22
Fujino, Diane C. *See Samurai Among Panthers* (Fujino)
Fujita, Fumiko Carole, 83
Fukami, Dianne, 93–94
Fukuda, Curt, 77
Fukuda, Yoshiaki, 142
Fukuhara family. *See Midnight in Broad Daylight* (Sakamoto)
Furuta family, 96–97

Furuya, Kumaki "Suikei." *See An Internment Odyssey* (Furuya)

Gamo, Yasko, 211
Ganbatte (Yoneda), 168
Garden of the World (Tsu), 77, **88–89**
Garrett, Jessie, 143
Gasa Gasa Girl Goes to Camp (Havey), 118, **122–24**
Gentlemen's Agreement, 74
Gila River detention camp: books on, 54, 67–68, 146; Hansen's research at, 67; Kikuchi's research on, 32; legal services at, 152; limited scholarship on, 145
Gilmour, Leonie, 20
Glick, Philip M., 152
Global Gender Report, Japan in, 214
Go for Broke! (1951 film), 106–7
Go for Broke (Tsuji), 13, **16**, **17–18**
Goodman, Louis, 88
The Governing of Men (Leighton), 165

Granada Relocation Center. *See* Amache Relocation Center
Grant, Glen, 72
Grant, Joe, 104
Graves, Donna, 80
The Great Unknown (Robinson), 26, **44–46**
"The Great Unknown and the Unknown Great" (Robinson), 44, 46–47
group welfare, focus on, in Japanese American culture, 25–26, 50, 72
"Growing Up Hapa in Ann Arbor" (Uttal), 100–101
Growing Up Nisei (Yoo), 185
Guterson, David, 128
Guthrie-Shimizu, Sayuri. *See Transpacific Field of Dreams* (Guthrie-Shimizu)

Ha, Hyung Hee, 113–14
Hachiya, Michihiko, 55
Hacker, David, 166, 176
Hadfield, James, 213–14
Hanada, Masako, 211
Hansen, Art: on academic book reviews, 11; admiration for NCRR, 203; "American Cultural Radicalism"

course taught by, 185–86; book reviews for *Nichi Bei Weekly*, 1, 8, 11–12; and Cal State Fullerton Asian American Studies Program, 192–93; and Chaucer's Bookstore, Santa Barbara, 217; childhood in California, 65; erroneous citation of, in Bishop's *Community Newspapers*, 146; field of expertise, 1; international *Nikkei* known by, 211–12; and Japanese American Oral History Project, 143–44; and Life Interrupted Project, 162–63; on Maeda's book reviews, 3; on Manzanar revolt, 176; and Masumoto, books by, 67–69; and Nakamura's *Nurse of Manzanar*, 59; *Nisei Naysayer* by, 226; and Redress Movement, interest in, 206; research on Heart Mountain camp, 158–59; research on *Kibei*, 168; research on Manzanar camp, 147, 166; research on sports and society, 156; and San Jose Japantown, 91–92; and Shibata's *Bend with the Wind*, 59–60, 61; and sources for Wake's *American Survivors*, 229; and *taiko* drumming, 124; as visiting professor at California Polytechnic at San Luis Obispo, 58–59; visit to Japan, 214–15; *Voices Long Silent*, 228; work for Nichi Bei Foundation, 1, 2

Hansen, Debra Gold, 93
Harada, Violet, 132
The Harvest of Hate (Robertson), 134
Hass, Kristin Ann. *See Sacrificing Soldiers on the National Mall* (Hass)
Hass, Ted, 152
Hatamiya, Leslie T., 197, 206
Havey, Lily Yuriko Nakai. *See Gasa Gasa Girl Goes to Camp* (Havey)
Hawai`i: internment camps in, 132, 136–37; U.S. annexation of, 72

Hawai`i, Japanese Americans in: books on, 63–65; internment on mainland, 138–39; migration to U.S. mainland, 72; in 19th century, 72; in 20th century, 73; volunteers for World War II service, 105; in World War II, books about, 16–18. *See also The Three-Year Swim Club* (Checkoway)
Hayakawa, Miki, 118, 119, 120
Hayashi, June, 90–91
Hayashino, Carole, 136–37
Heart Mountain (Nelson), 165–66
Heart Mountain Congress of American Citizens, 154–55
Heart Mountain Fair Play Committee, 155, 157
Heart Mountain Relocation Center: accounts of, 40–41, 145, 204; dynamic network analysis of data on, 159–60; Hansen's research on, 158–59; high school football team, 133, 156–57; legal services at, 152; postwar uses of buildings, 133, 161–62; resistance at, 159–60, 174; resistance to military service at, 106, 133, 154–56, 157–58, 165–67
Heart Mountain Sentinel newspaper, 106, 159–60
Heart Moutain Fair Play Committee, 179
Hillenbrand, Laura, 218
Hinnershitz, Stephanie. *See Japanese American Incarceration* (Hinnershitz)
Hirabayashi, Gordon, 171, 172
Hirabayashi, James A., 209
Hirabayashi, Lane Ryo: on Briones' *Jim and Jap Crow*, 30; career of, 203; on Japanese American resistance, 178, 179; on Maeda's book reviews, 3; and *NCRR* (2018 edited volume), 199, 203, 205; as *New Worlds, New Lives* editor, 209; *Nikkei in the Americas* series, 178; *A Principled Stand*, 173; Robinson on, 45. *See also Conjecturing Communities*

(Hirabayashi, ed.); *Neglected Legacies* (Hirabayashi, ed.)
Hirabayashi, PJ, 90, 92, 126
Hirabayashi, Roy, 90, 92
Hirahara, Naomi. *See Terminal Island* (Hirahara and Knatz)
Hirasaki National Resource Center at Japanese American National Museum, 179
Hirose, Halo, 219
Hiroshima: atomic bombing of, 55, 64; as immigrant city, 229; *Issei* migration from, 54. *See also* atomic bombing of Japan
Hiroshima Diary (Hachiya), 55
historians, shaping by sociocultural experiences, 232
Historical Memories of the Japanese American Internment and the Struggle for Redress (Murray), 195, 206, 226
Historic Wintersburg in Huntington Beach (Urashima), 78, **95–98**
history of Japanese Americans, preservation of: community press's role in, 44; importance for activism, 44–45; Robinson and, 45; as theme of Asian American movement of 1960s-70s, 44–45; Wintersburg, California, and, 95–98
"The History of Nikkei in Detroit" (Shimoura), 99–100
Hohri, William Minoru, 166, 196–97, 206
Hokubei Mainichi newspaper, 201
Honda, Gail. *See Family Torn Apart* (Honda)
Honda, Stan, 162
Hong, Terry, 61
Honouliuli internment camp, 136–37
The Hope of Another Spring (Johns), 118, **121–22**
Horiuchi, Edna, 201
Hoshida, George Yoshio, 138
Hoshizaki, Takashi, 166
Hosokawa, Bill, 107, 108, 109
hospital, Japanese, in Los Angeles, 84

Hotel on the Corner of Bitter and Sweet (Ford), 80
Housel, Jerry, 152
Houston, James D., 128
Houston, Jeanne Wakatsuki, 128
Howard, John, 149–50
Hunter, James Davison, 186
Huntington Beach, and historic Wintersburg, 97–98

Ichioka, Yuki, 14
Iiyama, Chizu, 202
"Imagining Communities, Imagining Selves" (Sullivan), 71
Imahara, Walter M., 133
Imamura, Anne E., 49
Immigration Act of 1924, 74, 120
Immigration Act of 1952, 142
Immigration and Naturalization Service internment camps, 141, 224
Immigration and Naturalization Service Station (Honolulu), 221
Imprisoned in Paradise (Wegars), 140

Ina, Satsuki, 4, 163
In Defense of Justice (Tamura), 167, **172–77**
Infinite Shades of Gray (2001 film), 189
Inouye, Amy, 84
Inouye, Daniel, 109
Inouye, Frank, 154
Inouye, Tatsuo Ryusei. *See Tule Lake Stockade Diary* (Inouye)
Inouye, Yuriko, 181
INRP. *See* International Nikkei Research Project
In Search of Hiroshi (Oishi), 25, 27–28
In Search of Our Frontier (Azuma), 211, **224–26**
Inside an American Concentration Camp (Hirabayashi), 178
internationalism, of public schools in Seattle, 81–82
International Nikkei Research Project (INRP), 209–10
international *Nikkei*: books on, 209–11; girls sent by Japan to U.S. in late 19th century, 210–14; Japanese Americans living in Japan, experiences of, 214–

17; number of, globally, 210
International Potlatch festivals (1934-1942), 81
internment: arrest of "dangerous persons" after Pearl Harbor, 220; Asian American Movement as response to, 183–84; books on, 16–18, 39, 40–41, 47, 62–63, 94, 101–2, 131–33, 133–36, 219–21; effect on family structure, 50; forced repatriation of some internees, 142; Hansen and Mitson's early work on, 228; of Hawai`i *Issei* on mainland, 138–39; impact on individuals, 131; impact on Japanese American communities, 74–75, 87, 131; internees' anger, 153–54; internees' inability to return to previous communities, 75; JACL role in, 104, 131; period following, 14–15; present-day echoes of, 62–63; protection of internees' property, 66–67, 77–78, 93, 94–95; protest march against (2016), 188; as social disaster, 131; tax obligations of interees, 94; and valuing of security over civil rights, 87–88; of women, 139
internment camps: coerced labor in, 149–51; of Department of Justice, 132, 138–39, 140–41; for disloyal and dangerous persons, 105, 138; dynamic network analysis of data on, 159–60; euphemistic names for, 131, 174; in Hawai`i, 132, 136–37; of Immigration and Naturalization Service, 141, 221, 224; legal services at, 151–53; local newspapers' views on, 143–46; as national monuments, 137; neighbors' views on, 132; with non-Japanese prisoners as well, 137, 141; *Something Strong Within* film on, 189; staff and families at, 133, 146–49; of War

Relocation Authority (WRA), 32, 143, 147, 174. *See also* Crystal City Internment Camp; Fort Lincoln Internment Camp; Fort Missoula Internment Camp; Fort Stanton Internment Camp; Gila River detention camp; Honouliuli internment camp; Jerome relocation camp; Kenedy Internment Camp; Kooskia Internment Camp; Manzanar War Relocation Center; Minidoka Relocation Center; Poston Relocation Center; Puyallup Assembly Center; resistance at internment camps; Rohwer internment camp; Santa Anita Assembly Center; Santa Fe Internment Camp; Seagoville Internment Center; Tanforan Assembly Center; Topaz Relocation Center; Tule Lake Relocation Center; Tule Lake Segregation Center; Tuna Canyon Detention Center

An Internment Odyssey (Furuya), 136, 138, 210, **219–22**, 220

intersectionality, and women activists, 202

Ishigaki, Eitaro, 118, 119, 120

Ishizuka, Karen: JANM documentary films by, 189; JANM exhibition curated by, 190; *Lost and Found*, 189–90. *See also Serve the People* (Ishizuka)

Issei: and American West, departure from, 224–25; Japan's view of as agents, 224

Issei: A History of Japanese Immigrants in North America (Ito), 79

Itami, David Akira, 169

Ito, Alice, 180

Ito, Kazuo, 79

Ivey, Linda L. *See Citizen Internees* (Ivey and Kaatz)

Iwakura Mission, 212–13

Iwataki, Miya, 204

Izumi, Masumi, 124–25, 182

Jackman, Norman Richard, 165
JACL. *See* Japanese American Citizens League
JANM. *See* Japanese American National Museum
Japan: girls sent to U.S. in late 19th century, 210–14; ranking in Global Gender Report, 213–14; view of *Issei* as its agents, 224
Japanese American artists: artists mentioned in Wikipedia, 117; and tension between Japanese and Western aesthetic, 117–18
Japanese American Citizens League (JACL), 59, 78; activists' opposition to agenda of, 107; books on, 15–16, 103–9; criticism of draft resisters, 106, 109; critics' demand for apology from, 108–9; decline in popularity after Civil Liberties Act of 1988, 108; deference to white Americans, 103; gathering of information on disloyal *Nikkei*, 104; and internment, 104, 105, 131; *Kibei Nisei* and, 170; Kurihara and, 174–76; and model minority stereotype, 107; postwar political agenda of, 107; postwar rise in popularity, 105, 106; and redress and reparations movement, 107–8, 195, 197, 199, 207; resentment of, by *Nikkei* majority, 104; Southern California Coordinating Committee for Defense, 104; Susan Kamei and, 134; support for Japanese American World War II military service, 104–5, 106
Japanese American identity: prewar, 25, 197–98; radicalization of *Sansei* in 1960s-70s, 198; unification around redress movement, 198–99
Japanese American Incarceration

(Hinnershitz), 133, **149–51**
Japanese American Museum of San Jose, 90, 92, 94
Japanese American National Museum (JANM): *America's Concentration Camps* exhibition (1994), 190; barracks from Heart Mountain camp exhibited at, 133, 161; *Big Drum* exhibition, 124; "Conversation on *Tule Lake Stockade Diary*," 182; Discover Nikkei project, 209–10; films by Nakamura and Ishizuka, 189; Hirasaki National Resource Center at, 179; International Nikkei Research Project (INRP), 209–10; Nakamoto's work for, 220
Japanese American Oral History Project (California State University Fullerton), 27, 143
Japanese American Resource Center, 92
Japanese Americans: future status of now-marginal groups, 113–15; image, JACL and, 78; living in Japan, experiences of, 214–17. *See also* model minority, Japanese Americans as
"Japanese Americans and the Movement for Redress" (Kitayama), 204
Japanese Americans at Heart Mountain (Kekki), **158–60**
"Japanese Americans in Redwood City" (Patel), 94
Japanese American studies, intellectualism *vs.* community support in, 113
Japanese American World War II Evacuation Oral History Project (Hansen and Jesch), 143–44
Japanese Cultural Center of Hawai'i, 136
"The Japanese Family" (Imamura), 49
Japanese Legacy (Lukes and Okihiro), 89, 90, 92
"Japanese Peruvians in California" (Tsuha), 115

Japan Oral History Association, 211–12
Jerome and Rohwer (Imahara and Meltzer, eds.), 133, **162–64**
Jerome relocation camp, 143, 145, 146, 163–64
JERS. *See* Evacuation and Resettlement Study
Jesch, Nora, 143
Jew, Victor. *See Asian Americans in Michigan* (Wilkinson and Jew, eds.)
Jewish American scholars' contributions to Japanese and Japanese American studies, 55–56
Jim and Jap Crow (Briones), 25, **28–34**
Jin, Michael R., 168. *See also Citizens, Immigrants, and the Stateless* (Jin)
Jive Bomber (Yamato), 161
Jodaiko *taiko* group, 127
Johns, Barbara. *See The Hope of Another Spring* (Johns)
Judgment without Trial (Kashima), 138

Kaatz, Kevin W. *See Citizen Internees* (Ivey and Kaatz)
Kamei, Hiroshi, 134–35
Kamei, Susan H.: family and career of, 134–35. *See also When Can We Go Back to America?* (Kamei)
Kameyama, Eri, 113–14
Kashima, Tetsuden, 138
Kashu Mainichi newspaper, 83, 84
Katabami, Reiko, 211
Katayanagi, Claudia, 176
Katsuda, Richard, 203
Katsuda, Suzy, 203
Katsutani, Fukiko, 219
Kawai, Chiaru, 211
Kawakami, Sachiko, 111–12
Kawamoto, Judy. *See Forced Out* (Kawamoto)
Keeper of Concentration Camps (Drinnon), 166, 171, 173
Kekki, Saara. *See Japanese Americans at Heart Mountain* (Kekki)
Kenedy Internment Camp, 140
Kibei Nisei: and atomic bomb, 227–28; books on, 168–70, 227–28; as

under-studied, 168, 170
Kibuchi, Yuriko Amemiya, 91–92
Kikuchi, Charles: *The Kikuchi Diary*, 33; "A Young American with a Japanese Face," 30–31. *See also Jim and Jap Crow* (Briones)
Kikuchi, Yuriko Amemiya, 33, 90
The Kikuchi Diary (Kikuchi), 33
Kikumura-Yano, Akemi, 209
Kim, Sojin, 124
The Kindness of Color (Munemitsu), 51, **65–67**
Kinoshita, Cherry, 201, 202 Kita, Sandy, 121
Kitano, Harry H. L., 197, 206
Kitayama, Glen, 204
Kiyota, Minoru, 168
Knatz, Geraldine. *See Terminal Island* (Hirahara and Knatz)
Kooskia Internment Camp, 140
Korean Americans: raised in Japan, status in Japanese American community, 78, 114; and *taiko* drumming, 126–27
Korean immigrants in San Francisco Japantown, 112
Koshiyama, Mits, 166
Krieger, Dan, 61
Kurashige, Lon, 176
Kurihara, Joseph: camps holding, as sites of strongest resistance, 173–74, 175–76; as subject of Tamura's *In Defense of Justice*, 167, 172–77; as under-studied, 173, 174–75
Kuroki, Ben, 48, 106
Kuromiya, Kiyoshi, 45
Kuromiya, Yosh, 166
Kuwabara, Kazuko, 85
Kuwabara, Masaaki, 85, 87–88

Lam, Andrew: career of, 128. *See also Repentance* (Lam)
Larson, Ronald, 83, 143
Lawyer, Jailer, Ally, Foe (Muller), 133, **151–53**
Lee, Erika, 149
Lee, Josephine, 127
Lee, Raymond, 4
Lee, Shelley Sang-Hee. *See Claiming the Oriental Gateway* (Lee)

legal services at internment camps, 151–53
Leighton, Alexander, 165
Letters to Memory (Yamashita), 51, **61–63**
Leupp Isolation Center, 174, 176
LGBTQ Japanese Americans: status in Japanese American community, 78, 114, 115; and *taiko* drumming, 126–27
Life Behind Barbed Wire (Soga), 136, 138, 220
Life Interrupted Project, 162–63
Lil Tokyo Reporter (2012 film), 83, 84
Lim, Deborah, 108
Little Tokyo Historical Society, 84
Lively, Penelope, 123
Looking After Minidoka (Nakadate), 50, **51–53**
Looking Like the Enemy (1994 film), 189
Los Angeles Rebellious Dance (Sato), 83–84
Lost and Found (Ishizuka), 189–90
loyalty oath in World War II, 32; consequences of refusing, 37–38, 101–2, 105, 180–81; problematic items in, 105; resistance to, 167
Lukes, Timothy J., 90
Lyon, Cherstin, 124, 173. *See also Prisons and Patriots* (Lyon)

MacArthur, Douglas, 174
Mackey, Mike, 178. *See also Wyoming Samurai* (Mackey)
Maeda, Brian, 176
Maeda, Daryl J. *See Chains of Babylon* (Maeda)
Maeda, Wayne: book reviews for *Nichi Bei Weekly*, 1, 3, 7, 8, 13–23; character or, 3–4; education and career of, 2–3; influence on Taguma, 6, 7; students' appreciation of, 4; Taguma's final letter to, 4–6; and Wayne Maeda Educational Fund, 2
Maki, Mitchell T., 197, 206
Manzanar Martyr (Ueno), 168
Manzanar to Mount Whitney (Umemoto), 25–26, **34–38**
Manzanar War Relocation Center: books on, 26, 35–38, 59, 143, 145;

factions at, 175–76; fictional accounts of, 129; Hansen's research on, 147; Hansen's visits to, 34; historical fiction on, 128; life after, for Matsuoka, 188; revolt at, 90, 104–5, 147, 150, 166, 173, 174, 175–76; staff and families at, 133, 146–49; Terminal Island residents in, 87

Masao (Vea), 26, **38–40**

Masaoka, Kathy, 203

Masaoka, Mike: books on, 103–10; as consultant for *Go for Broke!* film, 106–7; deference to white Americans, 103–4; and detention, 104, 105; as military service volunteer, 105; and National Japanese American Memorial in Washington, DC, 109–10; postwar rise in popularity, 105; progressives' attacks on autobiography of, 108; as spokesperson for Japanese Americans, 107; support for Japanese American World War II military service, 104–5, 106; support for U.S. patriotism, 103–4; *They Call Me Moses Masaoka*, 108

Masuda, Kasuo, 107–8

Masuda, Thomas, 152

Masumoto, David Mas: *Country Voices* (Masumoto), 67–68; *Distant Voices*, 67–68; Hansen's experience with books by, 67–69; later life of, 69; presentation to Hansen's class, 68. *See also Changing Season* (Masumoto)

Masumoto, Nikiko. *See Changing Season* (Masumoto)

Matsu, Arthur, 45

Matsuda, Gann, 203

Matsui, Doris, 4

Matsui, Robert, 109

Matsumoto, Tayzo, 157

Matsumoto, Valerie, 111

Matsunaga, Spark, 109

Matsuoka, Jim, 188, 204–5

Matsura, Frank, 118, 119, 120

Matsura and Susan Timento Pose at Studio (Matsura), 120

Mayeda, Kaz, 100

McCaffery, John, 65–66

McConahay, Mary Jo. *See The Tango War* (McConahay)
Meltzer, David E., 133
Menand, Louis, 151–53
Mendez, et al. v. Westminster (1947), 66–67
Mendez family: and desegregation of California schools, 66; ties to Munemitsu family, 66–67
Mendez vs. Westminster (2003 film), 66
Michigan. *See Asian Americans in Michigan* (Wilkinson and Jew, eds.)
"Michi Nishiura Weglyn" (Nash), 201
Midnight in Broad Daylight (Sakamoto), 50–51, **53–56**
migration of Japanese: to Hawai'i, 72; and Immigration Act of 1924, 74; to U.S., books on, 54; and U.S.-Japan Gentlemen's Agreement, 74; to U.S. mainland, 72, 73–74
Mihara, Sam. *See Blindsided* (Mihara)

military, wartime mistreatment of Japanese American soldiers, 153–54
military draft in World War II: consequences for Japanese Americans, 37–38; debate on, in Japanese American communities, 158; Japanese American resistance to, 102, 106, 154–56, 157–58, 165–66, 167, 172, 179–80; reopening to *Nisei*, 106; trial of Heart Mountain draft resisters, 155, 158
Mineta, Helen, 91
Mineta, Norman, 109, 134
Minidoka Relocation Center: books on, 52, 146; Fujii's diary on, 118, 121–22; inmates' letter on draft, 179–80; limited scholarship on, 145
Mintz, Steven, 233
Misawa, Stephen, 90
miscegenation laws, books about, 20–21
Mitson, Betty, 228
Miwa, Lawrence Fumio, 63, 64–65
Miwa family. *See Tadaima!* (Coffman)

Miya, Stephen H., 63–64
Miyagishima, Kara, 204
Miyakawa, Masuji, 45
Miyake, Lika C., 224
Miyamoto, S. Frank, 79
Miyatake, Toyo, 189
Moab Isolation Center: factions at, 176; resistance at, 174, 176
Mockett, Marie Mutsuki, 214
Modell, John, 31, 33
model minority, Japanese Americans as: activists' opposition to, 107; critics of, 102–10; as invented fiction, 103, 105–6; JACL role in, 78, 106–7; radicalization of *Sansei* in 1960s-70s and, 198; redress and reparations movement and, 196
modernism, American: Japanese American artists and, 118, 119–20; and racial exclusion, 120
Moorish, Elmer: communities' rewards for service by, 95; protection of internees' property, 77–78, 93, 94–95

Moorish Collection, 93, 94, 95
Mother's Society of Minidoka, 167, 179–80
Moving Walls (2017 documentary film), 160–61, 162
Moving Walls (traveling exhibition), 162
Moving Walls (Yamato), 133, **160–62**
Mu Daiko *taiko* group, 126–27
Muller, Eric L., 158, 166, 171, 173. *See also Lawyer, Jailer, Ally, Foe* (Muller)
multicultural democracy in U.S.: books on, 29; Kikuchi as supporter of, 29, 33–34
Munemitsu, Janice. *See The Kindness of Color* (Munemitsu)
Munemitsu family, 66–67
Munemori, Sadao, 106
Muraki, Keith, 4
Murase, Kenji, 31
Murray, Alice Yang, 105, 106, 143, 195, 206, 226
Music for Alice (Say), 60
Muslims in U.S., Asian American Movement's solidarity with, 188

"My Family's Experience of the Japanese American Internment Camps" (Sugiyama), 101–2

Nagai, Shige, 212–13
Nagareda, Jim, 90–91
Nakadate, Neil. *See Looking After Minidoka* (Nakadate)
Nakagawa, Martha, 8, 176, 182
Nakama, Keo, 219
Nakamoto, Allyson, 220, 222
Nakamoto, Helene Hideno, 41
Nakamura, Bob, 189
Nakamura, Samuel, 59
Nakamura, Toshiko Eto, 59
Nakanishi, Don, 202
Nakano, Bert, 204
Nakano, Lillian, 201, 204
Nakaoka, Susan, 201, 202
Nakayoshi Group, 112
Nash, Phillip Tajitsu, 201
Nash, Roy, 150–51
National Council for Japanese American Redress (NCJAR), 196–97
National Council for Redress/Reparations (NCRR): books on, 197; diverse membership of, 204; founding of, 196; Nikkei for Civil Rights & Redress history of, 202–6; platform of, 203–4; renaming of, 204
National Japanese American Memorial to Patriotism during World War II, 109–10
National Trust for Historic Preservation (NTHP), and historic Wintersburg, 98
Nauert, Paul, 94
NCJAR. *See* National Council for Japanese American Redress
NCRR. *See* National Council for Redress/Reparations
NCRR (Nikkei for Civil Rights & Redress), 199, **202–6**
Neglected Legacies (Hirabayashi, ed.), 199, **200–202**
Nelson, Douglas, 165–66, 204
newspapers: anti-intellectualism of, 10; local, views on internment camps, 143–46

New Worlds, New Lives (Hirabayashi, Hirabayashi and Kikumura-Yano, eds.), 209
New World Sun, 41
New York Review of Books, 233
Nichi Bei Film Showcase, 83
Nichi Bei Foundation: Hansen's work for, 1, 2; and preservation of Japanese American history, 44; Wayne Maeda Educational Fund, 2
Nichi Bei Shimbun, 111
Nichi Bei Times, Ujifusa commentary in, 201
Nichi Bei Weekly/Nichi Bei News: audience of, 11–12; book reviews, goals of publishing, 2, 10; book reviews, overview of, 10–11; Hansen's contributions to, 1; Maeda's contributions to, 1, 7; name change, 6; Robinson's column in, 14, 44, 46–47
Niiya, Brian, 35, 221, 222
Nikkei, Discover Nikkei project definition of, 209–10
Nikkei in the Americas series (Hirabayashi), 178
Nimura, Janice P.: online interview with, 214. *See also Daughters of the Samurai* (Nimura)
Nisei, departure from U.S., 227
Nisei Daughter (Sone), 79
"*Nisei* Employees *vs.* California State Personnel Board" (Ouchida), 201
Nisei Naysayer (Hansen, ed.), 226
Nisei: Quiet Americans (Hosokawa), 107
Nishi, Ernie Jane Masako, 182
Nishimoto, Richard, 178
Nishimura, Yoko, 211
Nishio, Alan, 204
Noda, Hideo, 118, 119, 120
Noguchi, Isamu, 20
Noguchi, Yone. *See Queer Compulsions* (Sueyoshi)
Nomura, Tamotsu "Babe," 156–57
No-No Boy (Okada), 79
North American Taiko Conference (2005), 125

NTHP. *See* National Trust for Historic Preservation
Nurse of Manzanar (Nakamura), 59

Obama, Barack, 137
Occupation of Japan: books on, 174; Japanese Americans' role in, 174, 177
Ochi, Kay, 203
Oda, Janice, 90–91
Oda, Lillian, 31
Odo, Franklin, 162
Ogawa, Dennis M., 72
Oishi, Gene: Agnew's racial slur incident, 26–27; "The Anxiety of Being a Japanese American," 27–28; article on racist treatment of Mexican American school children, 27; Hansen's acquaintance with, 26–27. *See also Fox Drum Bebop* (Oishi); *In Search of Hiroshi* (Oishi)
Okada, John, 79
Okamoto, Kiyoshi, 155
Okawa, Gail Y. *See Remembering Our Grandfathers' Exile* (Okawa)
Okihiro, Gary Y., 89, 90, 92, 166, 178, 221. *See also Trans-Pacific Japanese American Studies* (Takezawa and Okihiro, eds.)
Okinawan Americans: Bay Area women, 112; status in Japanese American community, 78, 114–15
"Okinawan Identity in the Diaspora" (Ueunten), 114–15
Omori, Emiko, 166, 171
Omura, James, 108
Ong, James M., 113–14, 115
Orange County, California, number of Asian Americans in, 96
Orange County Japanese American Oral History Project (OCJAOHP), 134
orientalism, books about, 21
Osaki, Paul, 3–4
The Other American Moderns (Wang), 118, **119–20**
Otsuka, Julie, 152
Ouchida, Elissa Kikuye, 201

Out of Infamy (2010 documentary film), 160
The Oxford Handbook of Asian American History (Yoo and Azuma, eds.), 185, **190–92**
Oyama, Iwao, 213
Ozaki, Otokichi Muin. *See Family Torn Apart* (Honda, ed.)

Pacific Citizen newspaper. See *Pacific Citizens* (Robinson, ed.)
Pacific Citizens (Robinson, ed.), 13, **14**, **15–16**
Pacific world perspective, 80–82
Palattella, John, 9–10
PAN-JAPAN special issues. See *Conjecturing Communities* (Hirabayashi, ed.); *Neglected Legacies* (Hirabayashi, ed.)
Patel, Jagruti, 94
Pearce, Ralph M., 77
Pearl Harbor attack: JACL and, 104; and Japanese American researchers, 31–32; protest march on 75th anniversary, 188; as turning point for Japanese Americans, 17, 36, 39, 42, 87, 139, 157, 173, 220
Pearson, Bradford. *See The Eagles of Heart Mountain* (Pearson)
Peruvian Japanese Americans: status in Japanese American community, 78, 114, 115; U.S. capture and detention of, in World War II, 223–24
picture brides, 54, 74
Plessy v. Ferguson (1896), 120
political system, U.S., oppressiveness of, 206
Pomona Assembly Center, 40
Portrait of a Negro (Hayakawa), 120
post-internment period: books on, 36, 37; internees' inability to return to previous communities, 75; and Japanese American family structure, 50. *See also* resettlement of Japanese Americans
Poston Relocation Center: internees at, 66, 133, 134; legal services at, 152; research on, 143;

resistance at, 178, 181; revolt at, 150, 165, 166, 174; strike at, 105
Potashin, Richard, 147–48
A Principle Stand (Hirabayashi), 173
Prisons and Patriots (Lyon), 167, **170–72**, 173
"Proudest of All Flowers" (Japanese American Museum of San Jose), 94
public schools in Seattle, cosmopolitanism of, 81–82
Puyallup Assembly Center: Fujii's diary on, 118, 121, 122; research on, 80

Queer Compulsions (Sueyoshi), 13, **20–21**
A Question of Loyalty (2005 anthology), 176

Rabbit in the Moon (1999 film), 166, 171
race: multiracial character of life in San Francisco, 120; and *taiko* drumming, 127
racial discrimination: American modernism and, 120; books about, 20–21; current threat of return to, 120; Jolyon Thomas's experience of, 231–32. *See also* discrimination against Japanese Americans
radicalism, Asian American: current revival of, 184, 187; global consciousness of, 184, 187–88; Maeda on, 186–87; opposition to U.S. racism and imperialism, 184, 187
radicalism, political *vs.* cultural forms of, 186
Rafu Shimpo newspaper, 86, 108, 158
Rainbow Environmental Services, 97
Reagan, Ronald W., 107–8, 199, 200
A Rebel's Cry (Sato), 77, **83–84**
Redefining Japaneseness (Yamashiro), 210, **214–17**
Redress (Tateishi), 199, **206–8**
redress and reparations movement: activists for, 135; books and articles on, 28, 52,

195, 196–99, 206; cathartic experience of government hearings on, 196; and Civil Liberties Act of 1988, 102, 107–8, 195, 197, 207; goals of, 195; government commission on, 196; Hansen's interest in, 206; history of, 195–96; importance of, 207; as most significant form of resistance, 206; opposition to U.S. racism and colonialism, 195; organizations dedicated to, 196; and radicalization of *Sansei* in 1960s-70s, 198; reparations payments to surviving detainees, 37, 102, 195, 196, 200; supporters and opponents of, 107; Tateishi's history of, 206–8; Ujifusa and, 200–201; Umemoto's refusal of reparations, 37; and unification of Japanese American generations, 198–99; women's activism and, 200–202

Redwood City, California: as Chrysanthemum Center of the World, 93–94; protection of internees' property, 77–78, 93, 94–95

"'Re-envisioning the Contours of the Japanese American Community of the Past and Present" (Ong), 115

Reflecting on WWII, Manzanar, and the WRA (Williams), 133, **146–49**

REgenerations Oral History Project (1997-2000), 90

religious freedom in occupied Japan, 230–32

Relocating Authority (Shimabukuro), 167, **177–80**

Remembering Heart Mountain (Mackey, ed.), 178

Remembering Our Grandfathers' Exile (Okawa), **138–39**

remembrance of internment, Mihara's lectures on, 40, 41

renunciation of U.S. citizenship, 102, 167, 170, 177; demonization of, 172; by Kurihara, 173–74; occupation of Japan and, 177
Repairing America (Hohri), 196–97, 206
reparations. *See* redress and reparations movement
Repentance (Lam), 119, **128–30**
resettlement of Japanese Americans: as alternative to imprisonment, 42–43; books on, 37, 41; impact on Japanese American communities, 75; Kikuchi's research on, 31–32; in Michigan, 99–100; in San Jose, 92. *See also* Evacuation and Resettlement Study (JERS)
A Resilient Spirit (Sato and Harada, eds.), 132, **136–37**
resistance: to curfews and exclusion orders on West Coast, 171; to military draft in World War II, 102, 106, 154–56, 157–58, 165–66, 167, 172, 179–80; redress and reparations movement as most significant form of, 206
Resistance (Hohri, ed.), 166
resistance at internment camps: books on, 149–51, 159–60, 165–68, 171, 173; at Heart Mountain Relocation Center, 159–60, 174; *Kibei Nisei* trouble makers and, 169–70; Kurihara's centrality to, 173–74, 175–76; Manzanar revolt, 90, 104–5, 147, 150, 166, 173, 174, 175–76; as more widespread than generally known, 179; Poston revolt, 150, 165, 166, 174; relocation of authority on, 178–79; sources for information on, 179; theoretical models of, 166; at Tucson Federal Prison Camp, 171–72; at Tule Lake camp, 85; writings demanding redress, 178–80
Righting a Wrong (Hatamiya), 197, 206

Right of Passage (2016 film), 197
Riley, Karen L., 140
Robbie, Sandra, 66
Robertson, Georgia Day, 134
Robert T. Matsui Legacy Project Website, 4
Robinson, Greg: career of, 47–48; on Kekki's *Japanese Americans at Heart Mountain*, 158; *Nichi Bei Weekly* column, 14, 44, 46–47; on Oishi's *Fox Drum Bebop*, 28; publications by, 14. *See also After Camp* (Robinson); *The Great Unknown* (Robinson); "The Great Unknown and the Unknown Great" (Robinson); *Pacific Citizens* (Robinson, ed.); *The Unsung Great* (Robinson)
Rohwer Relocation Center, 145, 163–64
Roosevelt, Franklin D.: and drafting of Japanese Americans, 167, 179–80; Executive Order 9066, 42, 104, 131, 149, 198, 228; and internment, 15

Rudd, Kevin, 194
rural Asian American experience, as understudied, 89
Russell, Andrew, 98
Russell, Jan Jarboe. *See The Train to Crystal City* (Russell)

Sacrificing Soldiers on the National Mall (Hass), 78, **102–10**
Sado, Ann, 212
Saito, Lorine Erika, 71, 72
Sakamoto, Pamela Rotner: career of, 55–56; online interview of, 55. *See also Midnight in Broad Daylight* (Sakamoto)
Sakamoto, Soichi, 218, 219
Sakauye, Eiichi, 90, 92
Sakoda, James, 31, 32
The Salvage (JERS), 32
same-sex marriage, books related to, 20
Samurai Among Panthers (Fujino), 13, **18–19**
Sand Island Internment Camp, 221, 222
San Jose Japantown (Fukuda and Pearce), 77, **90–92**
San Jose Taiko, 90, 125, 126

Santa Anita Assembly Center, 118, 123, 150
Santa Clara Valley. *See Garden of the World* (Tsu)
Santa Fe Internment Camp, 139, 140, 221, 222
Sasaki, Yasuo, 45
Sato, Claire, 132
Sato, Dale, 212
Sato, Kenichi. *See A Rebel's Cry* (Sato)
Sato, Yukiko, 211
Saving Sight (Lam), 128
Say, Allen, 60
Schools Behind Barbed Wire (Riley), 140
Scott, Otis, 4
Scottsboro Boys (Noda), 120
Seagoville Internment Center, 139, 140
Seattle: as "gateway to the Orient," 81; Japanese Americans in, books on, 79–82
Seattle Camera Club, 81
security, valuing over civil rights, 87–88
Sento at Sixth and Main (Dubrow and Graves), 80
Serve the People (Ishizuka), 44–45, 184–85, **188–90**

Shibata, Grace Eto. *See Bend with the Wind* (Shibata)
Shibata, Naomi. *See Bend with the Wind* (Shibata)
Shibata, Yoshimi, 59–61
Shibutani, Tamotsu "Tom," 31, 32
Shichi, Asai, 99, 100
Shimabukuro, Mira. *See Relocating Authority* (Shimabukuro)
Shimabukuro, Robert Sudamu, 80, 197, 206
Shimoura, Toshiko, 99–100
Shin Issei, status in Japanese American community, 78, 111, 114
Shiraishi, Iris, 127
Shojo, Honda, 121
Show Falling on Cedars (Guterson), 128
Show Me the Way to Go Home (Day), 167, **168–70**
Silicon Valley: development of Santa Clara Valley into, 88; and racial segregation, 89
Simpson, Alan K., 162
Slocum, Tokutaro "Tokie" Nishimura, 175
Smith, Bill, 219

Snivley, Samantha, 120
Social Solidarity among the Japanese in Seattle (Miyamoto), 79
Soga, Yasutaro, 138, 220
Soldiers of Conscience (Castlenuovo), 171, 173
Something Strong Within (1994 film), 189
Sone, Monica, 79
South America in World War II: struggle for dominance in, 222–23; U.S. capture and detention of Japanese, 223–24
Spickard, Paul, 105, 158
sports: as catalyst for cosmopolitanism, 82; Japanese American professional athletes, 217–18. *See also The Three-Year Swim Club* (Checkoway); *Transpacific Field of Dreams* (Shimizu)
Starkman, Naomi, 69
Stilwell, Joseph, 135–36
Stimsno, Henry, 105
Stoddard, Charles, 20
Sueyoshi, Amy, 113–14, 115. *See also Queer Compulsions* (Sueyoshi)
Sugiyama, Dylan, 101–2

Sullivan, Cheryl Lynn, 71, 76
Sumi, Pat, 186
Sumida, Alice Eto, 60
Sumida, Masuo "Mark," 60
Susman, Warren, 219
Suzuki, Kurt, 218

Tadaima! I Am Home (Coffman), 51, **63–65**
Taguma, Kenji: foreword to Robinson's *Great Unknown*, 44, 46; letter to Maeda, 4–6; Maeda's influence on, 7
taiko drumming: book on, 118–19, 125–27; demographics of drummers, 125; exhibitions of, 124–25; politics associated with, 125–26
Tajiri, Larry and Guyo: Robinson's *The Great Unknown* on, 45; as subject of Robinson's *Pacific Citizens*, 13, 15–16
Tajiri, Shinkichi, 45
Takahashi, Kyo, 101, 109–10
Takami, David, 79–80
Takei, Barbara, 176

Taken from the Paradise Isle (Hoshida), 138
Takezawa, Yasuko: *Breaking the Silence*, 79, 197–99, 206. See also *Trans-Pacific Japanese American Studies* (Takezawa and Okihiro, eds.)
Takita-Ishii, Sachiko, 176, 212
Tamai, Lily Anne Yumy Welty, 113–14
Tamaribuchi, Tiffany, 127
Tamura, Eileen, 167
Tamura, Stephen K., 134
Tanaka, Janet D., 197
Tanaka, Togo, 175
Tanforan Assembly Center, 33, 94
The Tango War (McConahay), 210–11, **222–24**
Tateishi, John. *See Redress* (Tateishi)
Tayama, Fred, 175
Taylor, Quintard, 79
Terkel, Studs, 68
Terminal Island, 85–88; ejection of Japanese Americans from, 87; stereotypical representations of, 86. See also *Terminal Island* (Hirahara and Knatz)

Terminal Island (Hirahara and Knatz), 77, **84–88**
Terry, James Hendrick, 152
They Call Me Moses Masaoka (Masaoka), 108
ThinkTech Hawai`i, 55
Third World coalitions, Japanese Americans and, 15
Thomas, Dorothy, 31, 32
Thomas, Jolyon Baraka. See *Faking Liberties* (Thomas)
Thornton, Michael, 224–25
The Three-Year Swim Club (Checkoway), 53, 210
The Three-Year Swim Club (Checkoway), **217–19**
Tomihiro, Chiye, 202
Topaz Relocation Center, 94, 145, 167, 171
The Train to Crystal City (Russell), 53, 132, **140–43**, 224
Transforming the Past (Yanagisako), 79
transnational history: Azuma's *In Search of Our Frontier* and, 225–26; Jin's *Citizens, Immigrants, and the Stateless* as, 227; turn to, 224–25

Transpacific Field of Dreams (Guthrie-Shimizu), 13
Transpacific Field of Dreams (Guthrie-Shimizu), **21–23**
Trans-Pacific Japanese American Studies (Takezawa and Okihiro, eds.), 78
Trans-Pacific Japanese American Studies (Takezawa and Okihiro, eds.), **110–12**
Truman, Harry, 155
Tsu, Cecilia M. *See Garden of the World* (Tsu)
Tsuda, Umeko, 212–13
Tsuha, Shigueru, 113–14, 115
Tsuji, Isami (Mike). *See Go for Broke* (Tsuji)
Tsuneishi, Warren, 31
Tucson Federal Prison Camp, 167, 171–72
Tule Lake Relocation Center: books on, 143, 145; conversion to segregation center, 32, 180–81; JERS research on, 32; *Kibei-Nisei* troublemakers at, 170; resistance at, 166, 167–68, 174, 176; U.S. citizenship removed from inmates, 107
Tule Lake Segregation Center: as destination for disloyal internees, 105, 180–81; internment resistance at, 85; resistance at, 167, 181–82; stockade diary of Inouye, 181–82; stockage at, 181
Tule Lake Stockade Diary (Inouye), 167–68, **180–82**
Tuna Canyon Detention Center, 87
Two Sons of China (Lam), 128
"'Typical' *Nisei*" (Nakaoka), 201, 202

Uchida, Takashi, 84
Ueda, Tei, 212–13
Ueno, Harry, 90, 168, 175, 176
Ueunten, Wesley, 111, 112, 113–15
Ujifusa, Grant, 107–8, 199, 200–201, 202, 208
Ulin, David, 85
Umemoto, Hank: friendship with Yada, 34–35; Hansen's acquaintance with, 34–35. *See also*

Manzanar to Mount Whitney (Umemoto)
Umemoto, Karen, 35
Unbroken (Hillenbrand), 218
United States v. Masaaki Kuwabara (1944), 85
Uno, Edison, 137, 142–43
The Unsung Great (Robinson), 26, **46–48**
Urashima, Mary F. *See Historic Wintersburg in Huntington Beach* (Urashima)
Uriu, Sotokichi, 213
Utsushigawa, Sumi, 141
Uttall, Lynet, 100–101
Uyeda, Clifford, 48
Uyehara, Grayce, 201, 202, 207

Valkenburg, Carol Van, 140
Vea, Sandra. *See Masao* (Vea)
Vietnam War, Asian American Movement in, 111
Villarreal, Alexander, 40
violence against Japanese Americans: chilling effect of, 101; coalescing of resistance to, 100, 101; in Michigan, 100

Voices Long Silent (Hansen and Mitson, eds.), 228

Wakayama, Ernest Kinzo, 135
Wake, Naoko: online interviews with, 230. *See also American Survivors* (Wake)
Walz, Eric, 98
Wang, Frances Kai-Hwa, 98
Wang, ShiPu. *See The Other American Moderns* (Wang)
War Relocation Authority (WRA): camps run by, 32, 143, 147, 174; JACL and, 104; and Japanese American family structure, 50; legal system within, 152
Watanabe, Tamasaku, 138–39
Wax, Rosalie [Hankey], 135
Wegars, Priscilla, 140
Weglyn, Michi Nishiura, 107, 108, 132, 160, 166, 171, 173, 176
Weir, Jennifer, 127
When Can We Go Back to America? (Kamei), 132, **133–36**

When the Akimotos Went to War (Elms), 51, **56–58**
Wilkinson, Sook. *See Asian Americans in Michigan* (Wilkinson and Jew, eds.)
Williams, Arthur L. *See Reflecting on WWII, Manzanar, and the WRA* (Williams)
Williams, Arthur L., Sr., 147
Williams, Duncan Ryûken, 112
Williams, Mary M., 147
Wintersburg, California. *See Historic Wintersburg in Huntington Beach* (Urashima)
women: activists, intersectionality and, 202; education of, girls sent by Japan to study, 210–14; international *Nikkei* known by Hansen, 211–12; internment of, 139; and redress and reparations movement, 199, 200–202; and *taiko* drumming, 126–27
Woo, Ellen D. *See The Color of Success* (Woo)
words, importance of, and Japanese American activism, 27
World War II, Japanese American experience in, 26, 38–40, 43, 47, 62
World War II military service by Japanese Americans: in Allied Translator and Interpreter Section (ATIS), 54–55; books on, 26, 38–39, 52, 54–55, 56–58, 155; draft and, 106; fictional accounts of, 129; heroism of, 105, 108; JACL publicity campaign on, 106–7; Japanese American supporters of, 104–5, 106; Japanese American units in, 38, 52, 56–58, 105, 155, 219; number of volunteers, 105; Three-Year Swim Team and, 219. *See also* military draft in World War II
WRA. *See* War Relocation Authority
Wyoming Samurai (Mackey), 133, **153–56**
Yada, Kinji, 34–35

Yamakawa, Sutematsu, 212–13
Yamamoto, Eriko, 211
Yamashiro, Jane: background of, 215–16. *See also Redefining Japaneseness* (Yamashiro)
Yamashita, Karen Tei: interview with, 61–62. *See also Letters to Memory* (Yamashita)
Yamashita, Kay, 62
Yamashita, Mariko, 211
Yamashita, Qris, 205
Yamashita family archive online, 51, 62
Yamato, Sharon: books and documentary films by, 160–61. *See also Moving Walls* (Yamato)
Yamato Garage Gang, 31
Yanagisako, Sylvia, 79
Yang, Alice. *See* Murray, Alice Yang
Yasui, Minoru, 150
Yatsushiro, Toshio, 25
Years of Infamy (Weglyn), 107, 132, 160, 166, 171, 173
"Yellow Power" (Densho organization), 183
Yen, Janice Iwanaga, 203
Yonamine, Wally, 217

Yoneda, Karl, 168, 175
Yoo, David K., 185. *See also The Oxford Handbook of Asian American History* (Yoo and Azuma, eds.)
Yoshida, Kayoko, 212
Yoshimasu, Ryo, 212–13
Yoshinaga, George "Horse," 156–58

Zamperini, Louis, 218

www.ingramcontent.com/pod-product-compliance
Lightning Source LLC
LaVergne TN
LVHW061608070526
838199LV00078B/7213